REVERSED THUNDER

REVERSED THUNDER

The Revelation of John and the Praying Imagination

Eugene H. Peterson

HarperOne
An Imprint of HarperCollinsPublishers

HarperOne

HarperCollins Web site: http://www.harpercollins.com

HarperCollins®, ♠®, and HarperOne™ are trademarks of HarperCollins Publishers.

FIRST HARPERCOLLINS PAPERBACK EDITION PUBLISHED IN 1991

Library of Congress Cataloging-in-Publication Data

Peterson, Eugene H.
    Reversed thunder : the Revelation of John and the praying
imagination / Eugene H. Peterson. — 1st HarperCollins pbk. ed
        p. cm.
    Reprint. Originally published : San Francisco : Harper & Row,
© 1988.
    Includes bibliographical references and indexes.
    ISBN 978–0–06–066503–6
    1. Bible. N.T. Revelation—Criticism, interpretation, etc.
I. Title.
[BS2825.2.P48   1990]
228'.06—dc20   90–55766

14 15 RRD(C) 40 39 38 37 36 35 34 33

For Karen
imago Dei

Contents

Introduction

The voice of the Lord is upon the waters;
    The God of glory thunders,
    the Lord, upon many waters.

PSALM 29:3

. . . the smoke of the incense rose with the prayers of the saints from the hand of the angel before God. Then the angel took the censer and filled it with fire from the altar and threw it on the earth; and there were peals of thunder, voices, flashes of lightning, and an earthquake.

REVELATION 8:4-5

Prayer [is] . . .
Reversed thunder, Christ-side-piercing speare,
The six-dayes world transposing in an houre.

GEORGE HERBERT

Every Monday I leave the routines of my daily work and hike along the streams and through the forests of Maryland. The first hours of that walk are uneventful: I am tired, sluggish, inattentive. Then birdsong begins to penetrate my senses, and the play of light on oak leaves and asters catches my interest. In the forest of trees, one sycamore forces its solid rootedness on me, and then sends my eyes arcing across trajectories upwards and outwards. I have been walking these forest trails for years, but I am ever and again finding an insect that I have never seen before startling me with its combined aspects of ferocity and fragility. How many more are there to be found? A rock formation, absolutely new, thrusts millions of years of prehistory into my present. This creation is so complex, so intricate, so profuse with life and form and color and scent! And I walk through it deaf and dumb and blind, groping my way, stupidly absorbed in putting one foot in front of the other, seeing a mere fraction of what is there. The Monday walks wake me up, a little anyway, to what I miss in my sleepy routines. The wakefulness lasts, sometimes, through Thursday, occasionally all the way to Sunday.

A friend calls these weekly rambles "Emmaus walks": "And their eyes were opened and they recognized him" (Luke 24:31).

What walking through Maryland forests does to my bodily senses, reading the Revelation does to my faith perceptions. For I am quite as dull to the marvelous word of Christ's covenant as I am to his creation. "O Lord, and shall I ever live at this poor dying rate?" Not if St. John's Revelation has its way. A few paragraphs into the Revelation, the adrenalin starts rushing through the arteries of my faith, and I am on my feet alive, tingling. It is impossible to read the Revelation and not have my imagination aroused. The Revelation both forces and enables me to look at what is spread out right before me, and to see it with fresh eyes. It forces me because, being the last book in the Bible, I cannot finish the story apart from it. It enables me because, by using the unfamiliar language of apocalyptic vision, my imagination is called into vigorous play.

In spite of these obvious benefits and necessary renewals, there are many people who stubbornly refuse to read it, or (which is just as bad) refuse to read it on its own terms. These are the same people who suppress fairy tales because they are brutal and fill children's minds with material for nightmares, and who bowdlerize Chaucer because his book is too difficult as it stands. They avoid the demands of either imagination or intellect. If they cannot read a page with a rapid skim of an eye trained under the metronome of speed reading, they abandon the effort and slump back into passivity before cartoons and commercials.

But for people who are fed up with such bland fare, the Revelation is a gift—a work of intense imagination that pulls its reader into a world of sky battles between angels and beasts, lurid punishments and glorious salvations, kaleidoscopic vision and cosmic song. It is a world in which children are instinctively at home and in which adults, by becoming as little children, recapture an elemental involvement in the basic conflicts and struggles that permeate moral existence, and then go on to discover again the soaring adoration and primal affirmations for which God made us.

The great sociologist of religion, Max Weber, placed the religious life between the poles of charisma and routine, between the spontaneous, excited outpouring of new life in the spirit and the dogged institutionalization of truth in everyday responsibilities. The mature life of faith is lived *between* the poles, not *around* either of them. What frequently happens, though, is that we flutter like butterflies around the pole of charisma, or congeal soddenly around the pole of routine. For myself, although I have occasional charismatic moments, I am mostly a creature of routine. I get up at the same time each morning and follow predictable paths through the day. The neighbors might not be able to set their watches by my passing, as Immanuel Kant's Freiburg neighbors did theirs, but neither do I give them any great surprises. God's faithfulness, new every morning, finds me heavy-lidded. I am thick-skinned to the Spirit's breeze, dull-eared to the heaven-declared glory of God. I am a solid citizen among the same people among whom Henry Adams unhappily found himself: "the feebleness of our fancy is now congenital, organic, beyond stimulant or strychnine, and we shrink like sensitive plants from the touch of a vision or spirit."[1]

Are things as bad as Adams thought? Is there no vision that can open our eyes to the abundant life of redemption in which we are immersed by Christ's covenant? Is there no trumpet that can wake us to the intricacies of grace, the profundities of peace, the repeated and unrepeatable instances of love that are under and around and over us? For me, and for many, St. John's Revelation has done it. Old dogmas are revisioned; familiar lines of scripture are revoiced; ancient moralities are subjected to intense testings from which they emerge glistening and attractive; valued but dusty beatitudes are plunged into waters from which they reappear washed, clean, and ready for fresh use.

I do not read the Revelation to get additional information about the life of faith in Christ. I have read it all before in law and prophet, in gospel and epistle. Everything in the Revelation can be found in the previous sixty-five books of the Bible. The Revelation adds nothing of substance to what we already know. The truth of the gospel is already complete, revealed in Jesus Christ. There is nothing new to say on the subject. But there is a new way to say it. I read the Revelation not to get more information but to revive my imagination. "The imagination is our way into the divine Imagination, permitting us to see wholly—as whole and holy—what we perceive as scattered, as order what we perceive as random."[2] St. John uses words the way poets do, recombining them in fresh ways so that old truth is freshly perceived. He takes truth that has been eroded to platitude by careless usage and sets it in motion before us in an "animated and impassioned dance of ideas."[3]

Maryland forests and St. John's Apocalypse show me over and over again that when I am bored it is no fault of creation or covenant. Familiarity dulls my perceptions. Hurry scatters my attention. Ambition fogs my intelligence. Selfishness restricts my range. Anxiety robs me of appetite. Envy distracts me from what is good and blessed right before me. And then Monday's unhurried pace and St. John's apocalyptic vision bring me to my senses, body and soul.

This power to wake us up is the most obvious use of the Revelation. It is also very often overlooked. Sometimes the obvious is the hardest thing of all to see. So while others have written, sometimes exceedingly well, on the obscurities in this book, I have set myself the task of not overlooking the obvious, and have written what I have seen.

But *caveat lector*: this is not a work of expository exegesis. Responsible exposition develops everything that is in the text, and only what is in the text. My concern for the contemporary is disciplined to the original text, but I have ventured something quite different. I omit much. I explain very little. Sometimes I linger, longer than I probably should, over a detail that interests me. Mostly I have enjoyed myself. I have submitted my pastoral imagination to St. John's theological poetry, meditated on what I have heard and seen, and written it down in what I think of as a kind of pastoral midrash. That St. John was a pastor, and wrote his Apocalypse as a pastor is too little taken into account by his interpreters. Two superior commentators on the Revelation, James Moffat in Scotland and Charles Brutsch in France, were convinced that pastoral work is exactly the kind of preparation one needs for effective interpretation of St. John.[4] The desk from which I write has been set in the middle of a parish for thirty years. I assume a continuity of context between

St. John as a pastor and my own pastoral work. That shared context has, more than anything else, secured my admiration for what he wrote, and stimulated me to recover his art for my own use.

My primary question before the text has not been "What does this mean?" but "How does this work in the community of believers in which I am a pastor?" I have taken the position that this book does not primarily call for decipherment, as if it were written in code, but that it evokes wonder, releasing metaphors that resonate meanings and refract insights in the praying imagination.

Still, questions of meaning have to be dealt with. There is much in St. John that is puzzling. We need intelligent and wise guides who will accompany us through the often daunting terrain of St. John's text without serious mishap. Unfortunately, while there are wise teachers available, they often get missed because there are so many more around who are simply foolish and who, like pushy guides at a tourist site, try to get us to hire them to tell us all about the "furniture of heaven and the temperature of hell,"[5] the number of the beast, and the calendar of doomsday. G. K. Chesterton once remarked that "though St. John the Evangelist saw many strange monsters in his vision, he saw no creature so wild as one of his own commentators."[6]

Among the guides whom I have found to be not at all wild, but reliable and wise, three have been especially important. Austin Farrer in *The Revelation of St. John* (London: Oxford University Press, 1964) and *A Rebirth of Images* (Westminster: Dacre Press, 1949) is demanding, but more than anyone else whom I have read, understands St. John's intent. Farrer penetrates the workings of the devout imagination with wonderful results. R. H. Charles in the International Critical Commentary's two-volume work, *Revelation* (Edinburgh: T & T Clark, 1920), gives an exhaustive grammatical, literary, and historical analysis of the text that is not ever likely to be superseded. J. Massyngberde Ford in the Anchor Bible *Revelation* (Garden City, NY: Doubleday and Co., 1975) brings everything up to date, assembling the results of the relevant scholarly discussion that has developed since the discovery of the Dead Sea scrolls. When people ask me for a commentary suitable for use in study groups, I recommend Michael Wilcock, *I Saw Heaven Opened* (Downers Grove, IL: InterVarsity Press, 1975). I have used the translation of the Revised Standard Version (RSV), except for the songs, which I have translated myself.

I have even greater outstanding debts to Hans Urs von Balthasar and Charles Williams. Balthasar, especially in his book *Prayer*,[7] has taught me to be contemplative before the Revelation, to pray the text. Williams, in his novels, poetry, and criticism showed me the workings of the imagination as a means of grace and convinced me that an *exercised* imagination is essential to a full-bodied and full-souled life in Christ. In a novel, one of his characters, Henry Lee, says, "All things are held together by correspondence, image with image, movement with movement. Without that there could be no relation and therefore no truth. It is our business—especially yours and mine—to take up the power of relation. Do you know what I mean?"[8] I think I know what he means, and I have made it my business to work at it as I have read, meditated, and prayed with St. John before me.

1. Famous Last Words

I will open my mouth in a parable;
    I will utter dark sayings from of old,
things that we have heard and known,
    that our fathers have told us.
We will not hide them from their children,
    but tell to the coming generation
the glorious deeds of the Lord, and his might,
    and the wonders which he has wrought.

PSALM 78:2–4

The revelation of Jesus Christ, which God gave him to show to his servants what must soon take place; and he made it known by sending his angel to his servant John . . .

REVELATION 1:1

The more one studies his [St. John's] book, the more convinced one feels that it was deliberately composed as a coda or finale to the whole canon.

NORTHROP FRYE

The most famous last words spoken or written are the last book of the Bible, the Revelation. No others come close in the competition. But "most famous" does not mean "most admired" or "best understood." Many, confused by the bloody dragons and dooms-day noise, are only bewildered. Others, associating them with frequently encountered vulgarities and inanities, hold them in contempt.

Still, there have always been some who stopped to look and read out of curiosity, but who stayed to understand and admire because they discovered here rich, convincingly presented truth. I am among these people. The words, for us, are famous not because they are sensationally bizarre or teasingly enigmatic. They are famous because they are so satisfyingly *true*, backed up by centuries of mature experience and tested usage. The last words of the Revelation are famous because they memorably summarize and conclude centuries of biblical insight, counsel, and experience in the persons to whom God chose to reveal himself, and who in their turn chose to live by faith in God.

The power of the Revelation to attract attention, and then, for those who attend, to make the reality of God and the life of faith coherent, develops out of a striking convergence of the ministries of theologian, poet, and pastor in the person of its author, St. John.[1] The three ministries are braided into a distinguished plait in his introductory words: "I John, your brother, who share with you in Jesus the tribulation and the kingdom and the patient endurance, was on the island called Patmos on account of the word of God and the testimony of Jesus. I was in the Spirit on the Lord's day, and I heard behind me a loud voice like a trumpet saying, 'Write what you see in a book and send it to the seven churches' . . . Then I turned to see the voice" (Rev. 1:9-12).

St. John was on Patmos, a prison island, "on account of the word of God and the testimony of Jesus." The word (*logos*) of God (*theos*) put him where he was; it also made him *who* he was. He did not identify himself by his circumstances as a prisoner but by his vocation as a theologian. He did not analyze Roman politics in order to account for his predicament, but exercised his intelligence on the word and testimony of God and Jesus: the task of the theologian.

The word and witness that shaped his life were then written down by command and under inspiration. "In the Spirit," he was commanded, "Write what you see." The result is a book that recreates in us, his readers, that which he himself experienced: it is the work of a poet.

He did this in a conscious, double companionship with the Christians and the Christ whom he knew—"your brother, who shares with you in Jesus the tribulation and the kingdom and the patient endurance." He shared everything—the difficulties, the glorious blessings, the day-by-day discipleship: this is the life of a pastor.

A theologian takes God seriously as subject and not as object, and makes it a life's work to think and talk of God in order to develop knowledge and understanding of God in his being and work. A poet takes words seriously as images that connect the visible and invisible, and becomes custodian of their skillful and accurate usage. A pastor takes actual persons seriously as children of God and faithfully listens to and speaks with them in the conviction that their life of faith in God is the centrality to which all else is peripheral. The three ministries do not always converge in a single person—when they do the results are impressive. Because St. John so thoroughly integrated the work of theologian, poet, and pastor, we have this brilliantly conceived and endlessly useful document, the Revelation.

St. John, the theologian

A fourth century scribe, set the task of copying the Revelation, wrote the title, "A Revelation of John," and then, in a moment of inspired doodling, scribbled in the margin, *tou theologou*, "the theologian." The next copyist, struck with their appropriateness, moved the two words from the margin onto the center of the page. It has been St. John the Theologian ever since (Authorized Version translation, "John the Divine").

St. John is a theologian whose entire mind is saturated with thoughts of God, his whole being staggered by a vision of God. The world-making, salvation-shaping word of God is heard and pondered and expressed. He is God-intoxicated, God-possessed, God-articulate. He insists that God is more than a blur of longing, and other than a monosyllabic curse (or blessing), but capable of *logos*, that is, of intelligent discourse. John is full of exclamations in relation to God, quite overwhelmed with the experience of God, but through it all there is *logos*: God revealed is God known. He is not so completely known that he can be predicted. He is not known so thoroughly that there is no more to be known, so that we can go on now to the next subject. Still, he is known and not unknown, rational and not irrational, orderly and not disorderly, hierarchical and not anarchic.

It is of great importance for Christian believers to have, from time to time, a reasonable, sane, mature person stand up in their midst and say "God is . . ." and go on to complete the sentence intelligently. There are tendencies within us and forces outside us that relentlessly reduce God to a checklist of explanations, or a handbook of moral precepts, or an economic arrangement, or a political expediency, or a pleasure boat. God is reduced to what can be measured, used, weighed, gathered, controlled, or felt. Insofar as we accept these reductionist explanations, our lives become bored, depressed, or mean. We live stunted like acorns in a terrarium. But oak trees need soil, sun, rain, and wind. Human life requires God. The theologian offers his mind in the service of saying "God" in such a way that God is not reduced or packaged or banalized, but known and contemplated and adored, with the consequence that our lives are not cramped into what we can explain but exalted by what we worship. The difficulties in such thinking and saying are formidable. The theologian is never able to deliver a finished product. "Systematic theology" is an oxymoron. There are always loose ends. But even the crumbs from discourse around such a table are more satisfying than full-course offerings on lesser subjects.

St. John is a theologian of a particularly attractive type: all his thinking about God took place under fire: "I was on the isle, called Patmos," a prison isle. He was a man thinking on his feet, running, or on his knees, praying, the postures characteristic of our best theologians. There have been times in history when theologians were supposed to inhabit ivory towers and devote themselves to writing impenetrable and ponderous books. But the important theologians have done their thinking and writing about God in the middle of the world, in the thick of the action: Paul urgently dictating letters from his prison cell; Athanasius *contra mundum*, five times hounded into exile by three different emperors; Augustine, pastor to people experiencing the chaotic breakup of Roman order and *civitas*; Thomas, using his mind to battle errors and heresies that, unchallenged, would have turned Europe into a spiritual and mental jungle; Calvin, tireless in developing a community of God's people out of Geneva's revolutionary rabble; Barth arbitrating labor disputes and preaching to prisoners; Bonhoeffer leading a fugitive existence in Nazi Germany; and St. John, exiled on the hard rock of Patmos prison while his friends in Christ were besieged by the terrible engines of a pagan assault.

The task of these theologians is to demonstrate a gospel order in the chaos of evil, and arrange the elements of experience and reason so that they are perceived proportionately and coherently: sin, defeat, discouragement, prayer, suffering, persecution, praise, and politics are placed in relation to the realities of God and Christ, holiness and healing, heaven and hell, victory and judgment, beginning and ending. Their achievement is that the community of persons who live by faith in Christ continue to live with a reasonable hope and in intelligent love.

The Christian community needs theologians to keep us *thinking* about God and not just making random guesses. At the deepest levels of our lives we require a God whom we can worship with our whole mind and heart and strength. The taste for eternity can never be bred out of us by a secularizing genetics. Our existence is derived from God and destined for God. St. John stands in the front ranks of the great company of theologians who convince by their disciplined and vigorous thinking that *theos* and *logos* belong together, that we live in a creation and not a madhouse.

St. John, the poet

The result of St. John's theological work is a poem, "the one great poem which the first Christian age produced."[2] If the Revelation is not read as a poem, it is simply incomprehensible. The inability (or refusal) to deal with St. John, the poet, is responsible for most of the misreading, misinterpretation, and misuse of the book.

A poet uses words not to explain something, and not to describe something, but to make something. Poet (*poētēs*) means "maker." Poetry is not the language of objective explanation but the language of imagination. It makes an image of reality in such a way as to invite our participation in it. We do not have more information after we read a poem, we have more experience. It is not "an examination of what happens but an immersion in what happens."[3] If the Revelation is written by a theologian who is also a poet, we must not read it as if it were an almanac in order to find out when things are going to occur, or a chronicle of what has occurred.

It is particularly appropriate that a poet has the last word in the Bible. By the time we get to this last book, we already have a complete revelation of God before us. Everything that has to do with our salvation, with accompanying instructions on how to live a life of faith, is here in full. There is no danger that we are inadequately informed. But there is danger that through familiarity and fatigue we will not pay attention to the splendors that surround us in Moses, Isaiah, Ezekiel, Zechariah, Mark, and Paul. St. John takes the familiar words and, by arranging them in unexpected rhythms, wakes us up so that we see "the revelation of Jesus Christ" entire, as if for the first time.

Some, when God is the subject, become extremely cautious, qualifying every statement and defining every term. They attempt to say no more than can be verified in logic. They do not want to be found guilty of talking nonsense. Others, when God is the subject, knowing how easily we drift into pious fantasies, become excessively practical. They turn every truth about God into a moral precept. But poets are extravagant and bold, scorning both the caution of the religious philosopher and the earnestness of the ethical moralist. St. John is a poet, using words to intensify our relationship with God. He is not trying to get us to think more accurately or to train us into better behavior, but to get us to believe more recklessly, behave more playfully—the faith-recklessness and hope-playfulness of children entering into the kingdom of God. He will jar us out of our lethargy, get us to live on the alert, open our eyes to the burning bush and fiery chariots, open our ears to the hard-steel promises and commands of Christ, banish boredom from the gospel, lift up our heads, enlarge our hearts.

The poet Denise Levertov wrote, "Since almost all experience goes by too fast, too superficially for our apperception, what we most need is not to re-taste it (just as superficially) but really to taste for the first time the gratuitous, the autonomous identity of its essence. My 1865 Webster's defines translation as being conveyed from one place to another; removed to heaven without dying.' We must have an art that translates, conveys us to heaven of that deepest reality which otherwise 'we may die without ever having known'; that *transmits* us there, not in the sense of bringing the information to the receiver but of putting the receiver in the place of the event—alive."[4] This is St. John's work: he takes the old, everyday things of creation and salvation, of Father, Son, and Spirit, of world and flesh and devil that we take for granted, and forces us to look at them and experience again (or maybe for the first time) their reality.

Not long before his death in 1973, W. H. Auden stated what it is we demand of a poem: "two things: firstly, it must be a well-made verbal object that does honor to the language in which it is written; secondly, it must say something significant about a reality common to us all, but perceived from a unique perspective."[5] St. John's theological poem meets both demands. It is well made: its complex structure is carefully crafted and commands the wonder and admiration of all who study it. And it takes "the reality common to us all," the gospel of Jesus Christ, and presents it in the "unique perspective" of the end, the fulfilled completion of all the details and parts of salvation.

St. John sings his songs, represents his visions, arranges the sounds and meanings of his words rhythmically and artistically. He juxtaposes images unexpectedly, and we see and hear what was there all the time if we had only really listened, really looked. He wakes up our minds, rouses our feelings, involves our senses.

St. John, the pastor

St. John's passion for thinking and talking about God, and his genius for subjecting us to the power of language so that the images are reborn in us, connecting us with a reality other and more than us, that is to say, his theology and his poetry—these are practiced in a particular context, the community of persons who live by faith in God. What he talks of and the way he talks of it take place among persons who dare to live by the great invisibles of grace, who accept forgiveness, who believe promises, who pray. These people daily and dangerously decide to live by faith and not by works, in hope and not in despair, by love and not by hate. And they are daily tempted to quit. St. John is their pastor, or, as he says, "your brother, who shares."

People who live by faith have a particularly acute sense of living "in the middle." We believe that God is at the beginning of all things, and we believe that God is at the conclusion of all life—in St. John's striking epigram: "the Alpha and the Omega" (Rev. 1:8). It is routine among us to assume that the beginning was good ("and God saw everything that he had made, and behold it was very good"). It is agreed among us that the conclusion will be good ("And I saw a new heaven and a new earth"). That would seem to guarantee that everything between the good beginning and the good ending will also be good. But it doesn't turn out that way. Or at least it doesn't in the ways we expect. That always comes as a surprise. We expect uninterrupted goodness, and it is interrupted: I am rejected by a parent, coerced by a government, divorced by a spouse, discriminated against by a society, injured by another's carelessness. All of this in a life which at its creation was very good and at its conclusion will be completed according to God's design. Between the believed but unremembered beginning and the hoped for but unimaginable ending there are disappointments, contradictions, not-to-be-explained absurdities, bewildering paradoxes—each of them a reversal of expectation.

The pastor is the person who specializes in accompanying persons of faith "in the middle," facing the ugly details, the meaningless routines, the mocking wickedness, and all the time doggedly insisting that this unaccountably unlovely middle is connected to a splendid beginning and a glorious ending. Luther's acid test of the Christian pastor was: "Does he know of death and the Devil? Or is it all sweetness and light?"[6]

When we read a novel we have an analogous experience. We begin the first chapter knowing that there is a last chapter. One of the satisfying things about just picking up a book is the sure knowledge that it will end. In the course of reading we are often puzzled, sometimes in suspense, usually wrong in our expectations, frequently mistaken in our assessment of a character. But when we don't understand or agree or feel satisfied, we don't ordinarily quit.

We assume meaning and connection and design even when we don't experience it. The last chapter, we are confident, will demonstrate the meaning that was continuous through the novel. We believe that the story will satisfyingly end, not arbitrarily stop.

It is St. John's pastoral vocation to reinforce this sense of connection in the chaotic first century. In the buzzing, booming confusion of good and evil, blessing and cursing, rest and conflict, St. John discerns pattern and design. He hears rhythms. He discovers arrangement and proportion. He communicates an overpowering "sense of an ending."[7] We are headed towards not merely a terminus but a goal, an end that is purposed and fulfilled. He spells out this sense of an ending in such a way that the people in the middle acquire an inner conviction of *meaning* something good in God.

St. John is not concerned with heaven and hell as things in themselves. He has no interest in judgment and blessing apart from the persons to whom he is pastor. He does not speculate or theorize. Every word, every number, every vision, every song is put to immediate use among these persons in the seven little congregations to which he is pastor. He is with them in their experiences of worship and apostasy, martyrdom and witness, love and vengeance, and develops the connections that maintain coherence between the beginning and the ending. These people, served by such a pastor, steadily acquire confidence that they are included in God's way and are able, therefore, to persevere meaningfully even when they cannot see the meaning.

It is generally agreed that the Revelation has to do with eschatology, that is, with "last things." What is frequently missed is that all the eschatology is put to immediate pastoral use. Eschatology is the most pastoral of all the theological perspectives, showing how the ending impinges on the present in such ways that the truth of the gospel is verified in life "in the middle." It shows us that believers are not set "at the high noon of life, but at the dawn of a new day at the point where night and day, things passing and things to come, grapple with each other."[8]

The Revelation is thick with meaning—there are layers and layers of truth here to be mined. There is a multiplicity of significance in nearly every image St. John uses. There is some of the many-sidedness of wild nature in this "great and vividly imagined poem, in which the whole world of that age's faith is bodied forth."[9] Since no one person and no single generation can expect to take possession of more than a part of its complex truth, it is important at the outset that St. John's readers cultivate courtesy among each other, lest differences in discovery develop into antagonisms of dogma. A good place to begin is to be courteous to St. John himself by honoring the fundamental concerns that we discern in his life and that come to expression in the Revelation: that his subject is God (not cryptographic esoterica), and that his context is pastoral (not alarmist entertainment). When we accept St. John as theologian, poet, and pastor, we can be wrong about specific details and still be correct in our total response to his work. Christians who honor these conditions will emphasize different aspects of the truth and uncover surprises not anticipated by previous readers, but still maintain a community of interpretation and response with all those who, in faith, read in order to run.

2. The Last Word on Scripture
Revelation 1:1–11

Blessed is the man
    who walks not in the counsel of the wicked,
nor stands in the way of sinners,
    nor sits in the seat of scoffers;
but his delight is in the law of the Lord,
    and on his law he meditates day and night.

PSALM 1:1–2

Blessed is he who reads aloud the words of the prophecy, and blessed are those who hear, and who keep what is written therein; for the time is near.

REVELATION 1:3

And from that City from which we have come on pilgrimage, letters have arrived for us: these are the Scriptures.

ST. AUGUSTINE

Only after St. John saw the word of God and the "testimony of Jesus Christ" (Rev. 1:2) did he write it (Rev. 1:3). Even then, it was not left in written form for long, but quickly returned to the sensory world: "Blessed is he who reads aloud the words of the prophecy, and blessed are those who hear" (Rev. 1:3). The Revelation begins in the experience of seeing and hearing; it ends similarly (Rev. 22:8). The written is a link between these two sensory experiences.

The Revelation makes explicit what is true of all scripture: it originates as God's word spoken and heard, or presented and seen. The Christian believes that God speaks and that, as a result of that speaking, all things are brought into being: nature and supernature, the stuff of creation and the relationships of the covenant, and, eventually, scripture. God's word brings the cosmos into existence. God's word accomplishes forgiveness. "For he spoke, and it came to be" (Ps. 33:9). God has the first word, he has the last word, and all the words in between are spoken in a vocabulary and by means of a grammar that are his gifts to us.

Jesus Christ is designated in St. John's Gospel as the "word made flesh." The gospel narrative insists and demonstrates that "word" in the first place is neither a philosophical abstraction nor ink on parchment, but an historical occurrence. St. John's letter also emphasizes the physical, sensory, and historical word of God: "which we have heard, which we have seen with our eyes, which we have looked upon and touched with our hands, concerning the word of life." (1 John: 1:1). The word of God was spoken before it was written. Jesus was seen and touched and heard, before he was written about. It is this spokenness, the living, dynamic creativity that characterizes "word of God" above everything else.

As God's word written (*scriptura*) the scriptures are a great, but mixed, blessing. They are a blessing because each new generation of Christians has access to the fact that God speaks, the manner of his speaking, the results of his speaking. The scriptures are a mixed blessing because the moment the words are written they are in danger of losing the living resonance of the spoken word and reduced to something that is looked at, studied, interpreted, but not heard personally. For from the moment that a word is written, it is separated from the voice that spoke it and is therefore depersonalized. Yet the very essence of "word" is personal. It is the means by which what is within one person is shared with another person. Words link spirits. Reduced to writing and left there, words no longer do what they are designed to do—create and maintain personal relationships of intelligence and love. When a word is spoken and heard, it joins speaker and hearer into a whole relationship; when a word is written and read, it is separated into grammatical fragments and has to be reconstituted by the imagination in order to accomplish its original work. It is possible for the reader to function apart from the senses in a way that it is not possible for the hearer or beholder. Unattended, the senses atrophy and the written word becomes increasingly abstract. Words, separated from the person who speaks them, can be beautiful just as seashells can be beautiful; they can be interesting just as skeletons can be interesting; they can be studied with profit just as fossils can be studied with profit. But apart from the act of listening and responding, they cannot function according to the intent of the speaker. For language in its origin and at its best is the means by which one person draws another person into a participating relationship. God speaks, declaring his creation and his salvation so that we might believe, that is, trustingly participate in his creation of us, his salvation of us. The intent of revelation is not to inform us about God but to involve us in God.

History is full of instances of words which, after being written, lost their voice and became nouns to be etymologized, verbs to be parsed, adjectives to be admired, adverbs to be discussed. Scripture has never been exempt from that fate. Some of Jesus' sharpest disagreements were with the scribes and Pharisees, the persons in the first century who knew the words of scripture well but heard the voice of God not at all. They had an extensive and meticulous knowledge of scripture. They revered it. They memorized it. They used it to regulate every detail of life. So why did Jesus excoriate them? Because the words were studied and not heard. For them, the scriptures had become a book to use, not a means by which to listen to God. They isolated the book from the divine act of speaking covenantal commands and gospel promises. They separated the book from the human act of hearing which would become believing, following, and loving. Printer's ink became embalming fluid.

The Revelation is the Spirit's emphatic declaration that the written word has not done its work until we hear the words in a personal act of listening. This last word on scripture is, therefore, primarily a work of the imagination — that act of mind and emotion by which letters on paper are converted to voices and visions in us. "Einstein once said that the imagination is more important than intelligence, meaning that there can be no meaningful use of intelligence unless there is imaginative perception."[1] Marks on paper, via the imagination, make pictures and sounds that involve us as living persons who hear and see and touch in our encounter with reality. The famous blessing that stands on the first page of the

Revelation (Rev. 1:3) is not for those who read for information or knowledge, but for those who read aloud and those who hear, reconstituting the words as oral and visual realities that pull us into personal encounter with the personal God. "Anything can make us look," says poet Archibald MacLeish, "only art makes us see."[2] The Revelation makes us see: "I turned to see the voice" (Rev. 1:12).

Our capacity for language is the most distinctive thing about us as humans. Words are that by which we articulate who we are. Nothing about us is more significant than the way we use words. If words are used badly, our lives are debased. The way we understand and become ourselves through the use of words has a corollary in how we understand God and his coming among us. The most distinctive feature of the Christian faith is its respect for the word: God's word first of all and secondarily our words of prayer, confession, and witness. The most-to-be feared attacks on the Christian faith go for the jugular of the word: twisting the word, denying the word, doubting the word. It is impressive how frequently the Psalmists denounced and cried out for help against lying lips and flattering tongues. Far more than they feared murderers, adulterers, usurers, and Egyptians, they feared liars. God made himself known to them by word, and it was by words that they shaped their response to him. When words are ruined, we are damaged at the core of our being.

The subtlest and most common attack in the satanic assault on God's ways among us is a subversion of the word. This subversion unobtrusively disengages our imagination from God's word and gets us to think of it as something wonderful in print, at the same time that it dulls any awareness that it is spoken by a living God. It has been an enormously successful strategy: millions of people use the Bible in which they devoutly believe to condemn people they do not approve of; millions more read the word of God daily and within ten minutes are speaking words to spouses, neighbors, children, and colleagues that are contemptuous, irritable, manipulative, and misleading. How does this happen? How is it possible for people who give so much attention to the word of God, to remain so unaffected by it? Not, surely, through unbelief, but through lack of imagination: the Enemy subverted the spoken word into an ink word. The moment that happens, the imagination atrophies and living words flatten into book words. No matter that the words are believed to be true, they are not voiced words – Spirit-voiced and faith-heard – and so are not answered. They go through the minds of the readers like water through a pipe.

Three groups of people are called forth in the Christian community to meet these attacks on the word of God: teachers to instruct us in the truth of God's word so that it will not be misunderstood; apologists to answer the arguments of critics so that the word of God will not be discredited; and masters of the imagination, to keep us awake and aware before the living God who speaks to us in these scriptures and to remind us that we are living beings who are being spoken to. St. John is preeminent among these masters. In the Revelation he exercises all five senses, plus his mind and emotions, prodding the imagination to experience afresh, personally and wholly, what is in danger of being only acknowledged intellectually.

Of the five senses, hearing is central to the Revelation: underneath the message to be heard is the experience of hearing. "He who has ears to hear let him hear!" Hear what? Never mind what, let him *hear*. Resonance is set up. God's voice and human ears are connected. Hearing is then joined to seeing. The testimony in the first chapter, "I turned to see the voice" (Rev. 1:12) puts them at work in tandem. Ears and eyes are put to interactive and complementary use. Sounds of voices, thunders, and songs fill the air. Silence is significant. Sights of colorful, outrageously constructed beasts, a magnificent, statuary Christ, visually composite women, and precious gems are rich fare for the eyes. A documentation of the sensory material that demands participation of eye and ear would repeat nearly every line of the book.

The appeal to touch comes in the use of numbers: the series of sevens, the combinations of fours and threes, the cryptic sixes, the myriads, the multitudes. Number is an extension of tactility. From counting on one's fingers (digits), number becomes a way of extending the sense of touch. "Baudelaire had the true intuition of number as a tactile hand or nervous system for interrelating separate units. . . . Number, that is to say, is not only auditory or resonant, like the spoken word, but originates in the sense of touch, of which it is an extension."[3]

Number directs the imagination towards an apprehension of totality. After we have numbered what is there to be numbered, after we have counted it out, it is then accounted for. The very act of numbering develops a realization of context, or order. When that which is before us is numbered it can then be added up to give a total. Johannes Pederson, in his magisterial work on the Hebrew mind, showed that the biblical language was always working towards what he called "totality-formation."[4] The Hebrews did not analyze reality into discrete units, but were always gathering it into integrated wholes. They did this by arranging and repeating, and with every rearrangement and repetition intensifying the sense of totality. St. John, the most Hebrew of all the New Testament writers, uses numbers this way: forming wholes around centers. He constantly feels the idea of totality working through the details, and involves us in that feeling through the language of number.

So these numbers exert a powerful effect on us even when we don't understand their symbolic references, or when we misunderstand them. For numbers arouse the tactile, "feeling," imagination. The mass numbers in Revelation 7 are an instance. The incursion of violent evil is inaugurated by the breaking of the seals in Revelation 6. This terrifying assault is countered, not by argument but by the *feel* of righteous, victorious magnitude, by means of the squared and multiplied number, 144,000, and the "multitude which no man can number" (Rev. 7). The numbers in Revelation 7 awaken the sense of touch, extending the *feeling* of God's protection and victory in the face of pressing evil. They convey the experience of developing wholeness in the midst of fragmentation.

The sense of smell is associated with prayer. The bowls of incense, representing the prayers of the church, can be both seen and smelled (Rev. 8:3–4). The sense of smell is not only the most subtle and delicate of human senses, it is also the most iconic, in that it involves the entire human sensorium more fully than any other sense. The sense of smell is the sensory analogue to prayer. Prayer cannot be practiced in detachment. Invisible and involving, prayer penetrates and permeates.

The sense of taste is featured in the message to the seventh church, the tepid Laodicean congregation, which must be spewed out of the mouth because of its tastelessness (Rev. 3:16). It is also represented in the little scroll which was sweet in the mouth but bitter in the belly (Rev. 10:10), the potent mixed drink of judgment drunk by the whore of Babylon (Rev. 18:6), and the Lamb's marriage supper at which the faithful will feast (Rev. 19:9).

These observations do not minimize the place of the rational understanding in reading the Revelation, or the scriptures in general. There are two very famous appeals to reason within the book itself: "let him who has understanding reckon the number of the beast" (Rev. 13:18); "this calls for a mind with wisdom" (Rev. 17:9). But the place of the sensory imagination is prominent. And even though the Revelation has been used by many as a field in which to exercise literary ingenuity, its major impact through the centuries has been to nurture synthesizing imagination and not analytic reason. Christians have not gotten new ideas out of the Revelation; they have had their imaginations aroused and become responsive to God's word in tone and nuance.[5] The sensory imagination is sacramental; it makes connections between what is sensed and what is believed. Susan Sontag's advice in respect to reading literature in general is exactly what the Revelation provides in reading the word of God written: "What is important now is to recover our senses. We must learn to see more, hear more, feel more."[6] For the senses engage the total person, not just the intellect, in response to what God says to us: "Blessed is he who reads aloud the words of the prophecy, and blessed are those who hear." And not merely hear, but "who hear, and who keep what is written therein." Scripture is read and heard—and touched and smelled and tasted—in order to be practiced. It is not for entertainment. It is not for diversion. It is not for culture. It is not a key for unlocking secrets to the future. It is not a riddle to intrigue the pious dilettante.

The word *keep* (*tēreo*) does not mean "keep safe" by putting it in a strong box. It means to keep at it, to keep it in use, to keep it active in everyday life. The intent of scripture is always to enlist participation, body and soul. Erich Auerbach, contrasting scripture with other ancient literature, wrote: "the scripture stories do not, like Homer's, court our favor, they do not flatter us that they may please and enchant us—they seek to subject us, and if we refuse to be subjected we are rebels."[7] It is tragically ironic that the very book in the Bible that says this most emphatically, which underlines and puts exclamation points around it, has been treated by so many as a crossword puzzle.

If the Revelation is masterful in getting us involved in a living response to scripture, it is also unavoidable in its claim that scripture is God's word to us, not human words about God. Reading scripture as if it were the writings of various persons throughout history giving their ideas or experiences of God, is perhaps the commonest mistake that is made in reading scripture. And the deadliest.

Any person carelessly or ignorantly reading scripture, supposing himself or herself to be reading the thoughts of inspired poets and the deeds of brave saints, gets a jolt from the Revelation. St. John makes it impossible to persist in such carelessness or ignorance. The first sentence announces, "The revelation of Jesus Christ, which God gave him to show to his servants . . . and he made it known by sending his angel to his servant John." What is announced here is claimed for all of scripture: It originates in God ("which God gave"), it is about God ("revelation of Jesus Christ"), and God provides the means for our reception ("by sending his angel"). Origin, content, and means are all in God. Scripture is that which comes from God to the human. God tells us his mind, revealing to us his creation, showing his salvation. It is *God's* word.

St. John only writes after he hears or sees what God speaks or shows: "Write what you see in a book" (Rev. 1:11). The divine origin, content, and meaning continue to the conclusion: "I Jesus have sent my angel to you with this testimony for the churches" (Rev. 22:16).

It is no part of St. John's task to say how this happens. The way the inspiration takes place—the process by which various human languages written in sometimes faulty grammar are used by God the Spirit to speak God's word personally to us—is a mystery that defeats complete understanding. What is indisputable, though, is that persons of faith believe it to happen and claim to experience its effects. Others may choose not to believe such testimony. They may conclude that such writers and readers of scripture are superstitious fools or unscrupulous mountebanks. If they do so conclude, and if they value their time and intelligence, they will not waste either time or intelligence on the reading of scripture. Reading the Bible as literature has never amounted to much. Austin Farrer observed that "the prevalent doctrine about Scriptural inspiration largely determines the use men make of the Scriptures. When verbal inspiration was held, men nourished their souls on the Scriptures, and knew that they were fed. Liberal enlightenment claims to have opened the scriptural casket, but there appears now to be nothing inside—nothing, anyhow, which ordinary people feel moved to seek through the forbidding discipline of spiritual reading."[8]

St. John's word for what he writes is *revelation*, in Greek, *apokalupsis*. The word becomes both title to his book and a description of all scripture. "Apocalypse means the revelation of what took place in the Incarnation hidden in a humble form."[9] The word means, literally, "to uncover." Imagine a pot of stew on a stove. A person enters the house and becomes aware of rich aromas coming from the kitchen. The smells are inviting. He guesses at some of the ingredients. He asks others in the house what is in the pot and gets different opinions. The cook doesn't seem to be anywhere around. Finally, everyone troops into the kitchen. One of the company takes the lid from the pot; they all crowd close and peer into it. Uncovered, the stew with all its ingredients is exposed to the eye: Apocalypse! What was guessed at is now known in detail and becomes food for a hearty meal.

All scripture is, in one way or another, apocalypse, or revelation. Apart from scripture there are guessed-at relationships between God and his creatures, surmised anticipations of God's intent, conjectures and speculations on God's nature and ways of working.

But in the pages of scripture we see the acts of salvation, of providence, of blessing. God's word brings creation into being, brings people into existence. We see God bridging the abyss of sin and establishing peace. We see God disciplining and nurturing rebellious and recalcitrant people to the end that love can be experienced and developed to maturity. We see God entering our history in the form of a servant so that we can freely participate in the redemption that God is working in us. The history of Israel, the person of Jesus Christ, the pentecostal community of faith are ingredients revealed to our understanding and available for our use as persons who want to believe and live by faith in God.

In parallel with the word *revelation* is the word *prophecy*. The revelation announced in verse 1 is described as prophecy in verse 3. The two words are parallel, but there is a nuance of difference. The emphasis in revelation is on seeing something, in prophecy on hearing something. God acts among us and we see what he does (revelation); God speaks to us and we hear what he says (prophecy).

A common way to misunderstand prophecy, and especially the prophecy of the Revelation, is to suppose that it means prediction. But that is not the biblical use of the word. Prophets are not fortune tellers. The prophet is the person who declares, "Thus says the Lord." He speaks what God is speaking. He brings God's word into the immediate world of the present, insisting that it be heard here and now. The prophet says that God is speaking now, not yesterday; God is speaking now, not tomorrow. It is not a past word that can be analyzed and then walked away from. It is not a future word that can be fantasized into escapist diversion. It is personal address now: "for the time is near" (Rev. 1:3, 22:10). "Near" means "at hand." Not far off in the future but immediately before us; only our unbelief, or ignorance, or timid hesitancy separate us from it. Jesus also announced the immediacy of the prophetic word when he preached "the kingdom of God is at hand" (Mark 1:15). St. John's "near" and Jesus' "at hand" are the same root word (*eggus/eggizein*).[10] The prophetic word eliminates the distance between God's speaking and our hearing. If we make the prophetic word a predictive word we are procrastinating, putting distance between ourselves and the application of the word, putting off dealing with it until some future date. The revelation of "what must soon take place" (Rev. 1:1) means precisely, *soon*—as soon as hearts are responsive and ears receptive and eyes perceptive. It is all there before us: God's salvation is complete, ready to be received. "Behold, I stand at the door and knock; if any one hears my voice and opens the door, I will come in to him and eat with him, and he with me" (Rev. 3:20). The one who stands at the door is he who gathers past and future into an eternal, immediate now, "he who is and who was and who is to come" (Rev. 1:4, 8).

There are, to be sure, references to the past and implications for the future, but the predominate emphasis of the prophetic word is on the now. There are predictive elements in some prophecy (and some in the Revelation), but they are always in service to a present message. The Bible warns against a neurotic interest in the future and escapist fantasy into the future.[11] It forbids trafficking with persons who make predictions (Deut. 18:14–15). All that is very clear and well known, yet there are persons who persist in making an exception to the last book of the Bible and read it as if it were all prediction. The Revelation, though, is not an exception to the biblical rule but an emphasis of it: God speaks to us, now. God makes his will known to us, now. In the Revelation we are immersed not in prediction, but eschatology: an awareness that the future is breaking in upon us. Eschatology involves the belief that the resurrection appearances of Christ are not complete. This belief permeating the Revelation makes life good, for when we are expecting a resurrection appearance we can accept our whole present and find joy not only in its joy but also in its sorrow, happiness not only in its happiness but also in its pain. We travel on through either happiness or pain because in the promises of God we see possibilities for the transient, the dying, and the dead. "By means of this eschatological dimension we look to the future not as mere repetition and confirmation of the present, but as the goal of the events that are now taking place. This gives meaning to the journey and its distresses; and today's decision to trust in the call of God is a decision pregnant with future."[12]

In such ways, with such words, we are forcefully reminded that scripture is God's word to us and not a collection of human words about God. And we are reminded that it is God's word to us now, in this living present, not a word about yesterday or tomorrow. St. John shows us how to read scripture with awe, ready to hear and believe, rather than curiosity seekers looking for fine thoughts from saintly ancestors that may, perchance, hint at ways in which we may improve ourselves or adorn our culture.

The Revelation is the last word *on* scripture, the voice-vision that insists that it is God's word we are hearing, not a human word about God. The Revelation activates our imaginations so that what is written becomes heard and seen personally. It is also the last word *of* scripture. Scripture, the Bible, consists of sixty-six books written over a millennium, in three languages, by numerous authors, both named and anonymous. The variety of style and content is enormous. It is not unlikely, presented with such vast and diverse fare, that the reader will end up with a mass of impressions, but no picture; with thousands of vivid details, but no plot; with dazzling items of truth, but no wisdom. The Revelation is written the way it is and placed where it is as a defense against such a final randomness and incoherence. Scripture does not merely stop. There is an emotionally and mentally satisfying finish, a *telos*.

In the first chapter of the Revelation God identifies himself with the sentence, "I am the Alpha and the Omega" (Rev. 1:8). In the final vision this is expanded to "I am the Alpha and Omega, the first and the last, the beginning and the end" (Rev. 22:13). Alpha is the first letter in the Greek alphabet; Omega is the last. Alpha and Omega include between them all the letters. Anything written must use the letters of the alphabet. God is all the letters of the alphabet. All that is written comes from who God is. A revealing God who is complete in himself has given us a revelation of himself which is now complete. The beginning has a conclusion. First and last are before us. The revelation is entire. The last word of scripture has the effect, then, of all well-made conclusions: it gives clarity and sense to the beginning and middle. What was unknown at the beginning, and unfinished in the middle, is now known and clear.

The Revelation has 404 verses. In those 404 verses, there are 518 references to earlier scripture. If we are not familiar with the preceding writings, quite obviously we are not going to understand the Revelation. St. John has his favorite books of scripture: Ezekiel, Daniel, Zephaniah, Zechariah, Isaiah, Exodus. But there is probably not a single canonical Old Testament book to which he doesn't make at least some allusion. The same cannot be said of his use of New Testament writings, but the data for the writing—the life, death, and resurrection of Jesus Christ, and the community of Christians living by faith in Christ—are all assumed, and worked into the fabric of his poem.

The statistics post a warning: no one has any business reading the last book who has not read the previous sixty-five. It makes no more sense to read the last book of the Bible apart from the entire scriptures than it does to read the last chapter of any novel, skipping everything before it. Much mischief has been done by reading the Revelation in isolation from its canonical context. Conversely, the Revelation does some of its best work when it sends its readers back to Genesis and Exodus, to Isaiah and Ezekiel, to Daniel and the Psalms, to the Gospels and Paul. St. John did not make up his visions of dragons, beasts, harlots, plagues, and horsemen out of his own imagination; the Spirit gave him the images out of the scriptures that he knew so well; then he saw their significance in a fresh way. Every line of the Revelation is mined out of rich strata of scripture laid down in the earlier ages.

This thorough immersion in the scriptures which the Revelation demonstrates has an interesting corollary. In these 518 references to earlier scripture there is not a single direct quotation.[13] That means that though St. John is immersed in scripture and submits himself to it, he does not merely repeat it—it is recreated in him. He does not quote scripture in order to prove something; rather, he assimilates scripture so that he becomes someone. By this interlacing one with another, the images and ideas of the Bible become as "living fibres in a living body. Separation is death, the mind may distinguish between facts, but in life nothing is isolated."[14]

The Revelation, extending St. John's experience ("I fell at his feet") puts a stop to all bookish approaches to the scriptures that merely study them out of pious duty or for intellectual curiosity. The scriptures are not a textbook on God; they are access to the living word of God that speaks a new world into being in us. If we start with Genesis and read to the last sentence in Jude, it is all there before us. But the unity is audible rather than visible. What is required is not that we read more but that we listen carefully; not study more but see believingly. Too many people put off the hearing and seeing for yet another day, perversely using the Revelation as a convenient excuse to ask more questions. But—"If they do not hear Moses and the prophets, neither will they be convinced if someone should rise from the dead" (Luke 16:31) or, *mirabile dictu*, have the Revelation explained to you! The intent of the Revelation is to put us on our knees before God in worship and to set the salvation-shaping words of God in motion in our lives. We are always trying to use scripture for our purposes: scripture uses us. God's gracious purpose in giving us his word in written form is not to turn us into Bible students, but to provide a means by which we can hear him speak and be turned into *Christians*—awed worshipers, sacrificing sufferers, devout followers.

This last book of the Bible takes the entire biblical revelation and re-images it in a compelling, persuading, evangelistic vision which has brought perseverance, stamina, joy, and discipline to Christians for centuries, and continues to do so. Not everything about everything is in the scriptures, but all that God intends for us to know of his love for us and his salvation for us and our responses to him is here. The law and the prophets and the writings are set under the incarnation of God in Jesus Christ and made to work for our salvation. The incarnation works retroactively on all other scripture and reshapes it in this final vision. The Revelation does not add to what is already there, but shows how all of scripture is put to work in the church and the world. The Revelation is not, as some have assumed, a change of strategy on God's part after the original plan of salvation turned out not to work; it is the original plan itself, working powerfully, gloriously, and triumphantly.

This is reinforced by words of warning in the conclusion: "I warn everyone who hears the words of the prophecy of this book: if any one adds to them, God will add to him the plagues described in this book, and if any one takes away from the words of the book of this prophecy, God will take away his share in the tree of life and in the holy city, which are described in this book" (Rev. 22:18–19). Scripture is complete. We cannot add to it; we must not subtract from it.

Interestingly, this warning is a quotation (or near quotation, since St. John never quotes verbatim) from the book of Deuteronomy. Deuteronomy is the last book of the Torah (the first five books of the Bible). To the Hebrew, the Torah was complete scripture, to which everything else (the prophets and the writings) was commentary. In Deuteronomy 4:2, the people are warned: "You shall not add to the word which I command you, nor take from it; that you may keep the commandments of the Lord your God which I command you." And in Deuteronomy 12:32, a similar warning: "Everything that I command you you shall be careful to do; you shall not add to it or take from it." Neither Jews nor Christians interpreted that to mean that nothing more should be written—otherwise our Bibles would consist only of Genesis through Deuteronomy. It has been interpreted to mean that what God has revealed is sufficient. We have a complete revelation. Dilution is not permitted; additions are forbidden. Scripture is not to be toyed with. It is not to be twisted and squeezed into our needs and wishes. We are to submit to scripture and let it develop in our lives. As Heidegger puts it, we must "listen to the voice of Being." Scripture is God's word in its totality, intended to make a total humanity in us.

Long and pious association with scripture can blunt its sharp edges. Familiarity with scripture can dull our perception of its uniqueness. If that should happen, the Revelation pulls us out of our complacent doze and puts us on our feet, erect before the reality of all scripture, "a strange new world, a world of God. There are no transitions, intermixings or intermediate stages. There is only crisis, finality, new insight."[15]

3. The Last Word on Christ
Revelation 1:12-20

> . . . let thy hand be upon the man of thy right hand,
>   the son of man whom thou hast made strong for thyself!
> Then we will never turn back from thee:
>   give us life, and we will call on thy name!
>
> Restore us, O Lord God of hosts!
>   let thy face shine, that we may be saved!
>
> PSALM 80:17-19

> Then I turned to see the voice that was speaking to me, and on turning I
> saw seven golden lampstands, and in the midst of the lampstands one like
> a son of man
>
> REVELATION 1:12-13

> Is the Christ of the Gospels, imagined and loved within the dimensions
> of a Mediterranean world, capable of still embracing and still forming the
> centre of our prodigiously expanded universe? Is the world not in the
> process of becoming more vast, more close, more dazzling than Jehovah?
> Will it not burst our religions asunder? Eclipse our God?
>
> TEILHARD DE CHARDIN

In the opening words of the Apocalypse, "the revelation of Jesus
Christ," the preposition "of" carries a double meaning: the revelation is *about* Jesus Christ; the revelation comes *by means of* Jesus
Christ. Jesus Christ is both the *content* of the revelation and the
agent of the revelation. Jesus Christ is the way in which God
reveals himself to us; Jesus Christ is also God himself being revealed to us.

It follows then that the Revelation is, in the first place, not information about the bad world that we live in, or a report on the first
century church under persecution. First of all, it is a proclamation
by and about Jesus Christ. Items regarding future and past are
introduced insofar as they are useful in providing material that is

expositional of Jesus Christ. The Revelation is nothing if not focused on Jesus Christ.

It is difficult to sustain this focus. There are so many fascinating symbols to pursue and so many intriguing subjects to take up that only a highly disciplined imagination holds everything in subordination to Jesus Christ. But it is the only way the Revelation can be read sanely. It is the only way any scripture can be read rightly. Everywhere and always we have to do with the "gospel of Jesus Christ." Without this controlling center, the Bible is a mere encyclopedia of religion with no more plot than a telephone directory. People who do not take these opening words at their full value will very likely end up using the Revelation as a Rorschach test rather than a religious text, reading more into the ink than they read out of it.[1]

A conscientious reader of the Bible is always in danger of ending up with a mind full of unsorted and unevaluated sayings and incidents: a talking snake, a floating ax head, a curiously repeated law not to boil a kid in its mother's milk, carefully compiled but dubiously important genealogies ("the name of Abishur's wife was Abhigail, and she bore him Ahban and Molid"), thundering prophetic oracles introduced by the awesome "Thus saith the Lord," pungent aphorisms ("you are the salt of the earth . . . the light of the world"), unforgettable paradoxes ("I have been crucified with Christ; it is no longer I who live, but Christ who lives in me"), and stirring perorations ("I have fought the good fight, I have finished the race, I have kept the faith"). By the time we get to Jude, it is entirely possible to be reduced to puzzling over the significance of the archangel Michael contesting the devil over the body of Moses. What are we to make of this grand but bewildering mass of material? Is there plot, order, development, or theme? There has been so much action and so much said, such a diversity of style and content, that the devout mind is liable to confusion. If the field of study is expanded to religion through history and across cultures, the bewilderment deepens.

Then we turn the page and find, after a few introductory sentences, a magnificent Christ described in such a way that everything, absolutely everything, is imaginatively subordinated to him. This Christ has been suggested, anticipated, prayed for, and promised in the Hebrew scriptures. He has been taught and preached in the Epistles. He has been presented in the Gospels. Careful reading and sustained attention would have maintained an awareness throughout of Christ. But we do not always read carefully. Our attention wanders. We patter off into arguments about predestination; we wool-gather in the third heaven; we digress into conjectures on the atonement; we divert ourselves by counting miracles or collecting grammatical oddities. And then St. John's vision interrupts us. We are startled out of our woolgathering digressions, our tangential arguments, our inattentive diversions. Our imaginations are kindled with a vision – of Christ. We are roused, attentive, alert. Everything is suddenly in proportion. *Christ* is the last word. This last word controls all the preceding words, much as the existence of a mountain peak determines the preparations and pace and path of climbers headed for it, even when they don't see it. This is the goal towards which everything was aimed. The ten thousand details now find their place in the whole. Oddities and puzzles and curiosities, dull places and favorite places, all arrange themselves quite effortlessly now around the Christ.

The Revelation gives us the last word on Christ, and the word is that Christ is center and at the center. We can understand nothing if we do not have a center. If this "centre cannot hold/ Mere anarchy is loosed upon the world."[2] One of the gifts of the Revelation is to present Christ in such a way that our imaginations are enlisted by the vision (as the mind of the early church was) in tirelessly christologizing the scriptures. That did not mean clumsily imposing Christ on the scriptures, but soberly discerning the lines that led to Christ.

The task of keeping Christ as center is continuingly difficult. Other things elbow their way to the front: the golden rule, the doctrine of atonement, the ten commandments, Paul's teaching on justification, diagrams of the trinity, denunciations of the wicked. There is not much chance of losing Christ altogether – too much has been said, too much preached, too much written for anyone to forget that he is one to be reckoned with. But it is very easy to remove him from the center and give him an honored place in a religious hall of fame along with Zoroaster, Buddha, Moses, and Mohammed. But the Revelation gets the last word, and this last word is a skilled and convincing assertion that Christ is the center.

How will Christ be presented so that we will recognize and hold on to this centrality? A shepherd Christ tending his flock on the Palestinian hills? A benevolent Christ holding little children in his arms? A tragic Christ nailed to the cross? A compassionate Christ touching the leper? A Socratic Christ in sharp-edged dialogue with Nicodemus? Given the rich details provided by prophetic promises and gospel stories, the possibilities are numerous.

It is the will of our Lord the Spirit to provide something quite different. St. John is commanded by the trumpet voice to begin his writing by describing a vision of Christ "like a son of man." The phrase "son of man" originates in the vision of Daniel:

> I saw in the night visions,
>   and behold, with the clouds of heaven
> there came one like a son of man,
>   and he came to the Ancient of Days
> and was presented before him.
>   And to him was given dominion
> and glory and kingdom,
>   that all peoples, nations, and languages
> should serve him;
>   His dominion is an everlasting dominion,
> which shall not pass away,
>   and his kingdom one
> that shall not be destroyed.
>
> (DAN. 7:13–14)

"Son of Man" is a commanding, redeeming, glorious figure.[3] He is not, as Tom Howard once put it, "a pale Galilean, but a towering and furious figure who will not be managed."[4] The phrase was meditated and elaborated during the period between Old Testament Daniel and New Testament Revelation by many, but most especially by an anonymous apocalyptic seer who wrote a book entitled *Enoch,* in which he painted verbal pictures of the Son of Man that filled the cosmos with re-creating light and energy. The Son of Man was the one who would reclaim all the splendor of Adam and in the process reclaim all his descendants to their glorious original identities in the image of God.

When Jesus designated himself Son of Man, which he did frequently, it could only have evoked puzzled consternation: this apparently ordinary, itinerant rabbi, the *Son of Man*? Where are the lightning flashes and the flowing robes? His use of the title aroused expectations of redemption; his refusal to call down legions of angels to establish his power dashed the expectations. Yet he continued to insist on the title.

It is difficult to recapture by an act of imagination the incongruity of a person self-designated as the Son of Man, hanging pierced and bleeding on a cross. The incongruity is less dramatic but even more offensive when this Son of Man has dinner with a prostitute, stops off for lunch with a tax-collector, wastes time blessing children when there were Roman legions to be chased from the land, heals unimportant losers and ignores high-achieving Pharisees and influential Sadducees. Jesus juxtaposed the most glorious title available to him with the most menial of life-styles in the culture. He talked like a king and acted like a slave. He preached with high authority and lived like a vagabond.

Jesus was systematic in this double affirmation: he was, in fact, Son of Man "given dominion and glory and kingdom"; he was, in fact, completely at home in the ordinary, the everyday, the common. He did not give an inch in either direction: he was very God, very man.

The task of faith, for those who agreed to be his disciples, was to accept the literal truth of the title Son of Man under such conditions, to immerse themselves in cross-bearing, self-denial, suffering, and death at the same time that they believed that everything they did and spoke was part of the victorious rule of God's kingdom. When they met Jesus their minds were filled with visions of end time rescues by angelic hosts. They were waiting to be rescued from history by a *deus ex machina*. Slowly, painfully, gradually, they gave up their illusory dreams of an Enochian Son of Man and became disciples of *this* Son of Man.

The task was accomplished by the disciples with Jesus on the roads of Palestine in the fourth decade of the first century. The Gospels and the Acts tell the story. The same task was accomplished again in the last decade of the same century. That story can be read between the lines of the Revelation. But the tasks, while the same, were also different. The first generation of disciples had the task of accepting the glorious apocalyptic title, Son of Man, as the truth about the very human Jesus of Nazareth who spoke in the vernacular of their language, ate matzos and shish kebab with them, got tired and went to sleep before their eyes. The Danielic Son of Man was assimilated into the observed dailiness of Jesus of Nazareth. Eternal glories were channeled into the ordinary. The everyday was made splendid with grace, healing, peace, and blessing.

For Christians of the second and third generations (St. John's congregations), the struggle was in the opposite direction. They were thoroughly conversant with the historicity of Jesus. They had sat under the teaching and preaching of eye witnesses. They knew those who had seen and heard and touched the Son of Man (1 John 1:1-4). The danger now was not that the heavenly image would be out of touch with the way God actually chose to work in history, but that the immediate data of experienced history would smother the heavenly vision. They were plunged, inescapably, into suffering and tribulation and day-by-day decision making in matters of faith and morals. There was no getting around the fact that belief in the Son of Man involved confronting and living through all matters ranging from domestic love to political allegiance, from the liturgical significance of each detail in common worship to the spiritual significance of every war and famine and death. It was an intense time of crisis: there was no alternative to living out their faith historically. Salvation had to be worked out in the midst of hate and suffering, or not at all. The adolescent fantasies of heaven-hurled thunderbolts annihilating the wicked enemy had long ago been purged from the devout imagination; decades of persecution, tribulation, and bloodshed had accomplished that task. The chastening of the church had been thoroughgoing. Now the danger was in the other direction, as it has been ever since—the reduction of the gospel to stoicism, to getting by, to grim morality and a tough, sinewy, joyless virtue.

It was time to reintroduce the apocalyptic splendor of Daniel's (and Enoch's) Son of Man. It is appropriate that this be the last word. For while there is always the danger in the life of faith of escapist dreaming and fanatical irresponsibility, the long-range danger has more often been of a meager, diminished hope. Disraeli said, "Life is too short to be small." The great danger is that the largeness and mystery of Christ may be lost and religion become flat and insipid. Berdyaev's verdict on his generation was, "Historical Christianity has grown cold and intolerably prosaic; its activity consists mainly in adapting itself to the commonplace, to the bourgeois patterns and habits of life. But Christ came to send heavenly fire on earth."[5]

And so the last word on Christ is the glorious, Danielic vision of the Son of Man. Daniel's vision has passed through the refining fires of Jesus' passion and the early church's tribulation; it is now recast in such a way that all the original splendor is evident— "kingdom of daylight's dauphin . . . Brute beauty and valour and act."[6] Elements of the earthly are used to insist on the heavenly. The familiar, instead of holding us down and limiting us, is a springboard allowing us to leap to the unfamiliar and so live in graceful freedom. The details of the vision combine the celestial and the mundane. Fading echoes and memories from messianic promises and Jesus' life are caught, clarified, and amplified. St. John's mixed metaphor of seeing and hearing, "I turned to see the voice," fixes our attention.

The Son of Man vision is presented in a familiar context: "I saw seven golden lampstands, and in the midst of the lampstands one like a son of man." The lampstands are identified a few lines later (Rev. 1:20) as churches.

It is impossible among people familiar with ancient Israel and early church to glamorize communities of faith. Churches are characteristically poor, often sordid, frequently faithless. It is precisely in this environment that God chooses to show the Christ in the splendid form of Son of Man. But this procedure should be no surprise by now: the site of his birth was a manger, and the palace of his coronation was a cross. God deliberately set Jesus among the common and the flawed—the historical situation just as it was. Jesus is never known in any other context. The revelation of Christ is not embarrassed or compromised by association with the church; quite the contrary, it insists on this context.

So it is no use looking for him in purer surroundings (although he is not anywhere absent) for it is his will to identify himself in revelation in the community of faith. It is understandable that there are many who resent having to deal with the church, when they are only interested in Christ. The church is so full of ambiguity, so marred with cruelty and cowardice, so tarnished with hypocrisies and sophistries, that they are disgusted with it. The whole business of religion is so susceptible to superstition and fraud that it is no wonder that many refuse to be associated with it and seek Christ in other ways or in other places—in gnostic systems, for instance, or in mystical flights. But there is no biblical evidence that such seeking will prosper. Christ is known (by faith) to be preexistent with the Father. He is believed to be glorious in the heavens. But he is *received* in the everyday environs of the church in the company of persons who gather to worship and witness.

The vision of Christ begins with a description of his clothing: "a long robe with a golden girdle round his breast." Before we know what the Son of Man looks like, we know what he does. Clothing defines role: he vests with the garment (*podēre*) prescribed for Aaron in his priestly work (Exod. 29:5). The Son of Man is a priest. Just as a police officer's uniform creates a set of expectations in the person who meets him (quite apart from his size or appearance), so this priestly dress shapes the responses that develop throughout the unfolding details of the vision. The expectations have to do with getting out of what is insufficient or oppressive and getting into what is whole and free. A priest is a bridge (*pontifex*).

A priest presents God to us; he also presents us to God. He brings together the divine and the human. Priests do not protect God's holiness from human sinfulness by setting up barriers to access.

Nor do priests protect human weakness from divine judgment by arranging ritual defense systems. The priest opens up routes closed by fear or guilt or ignorance or superstition so that there is access. A priest mediates. He is just as much on God's side as on our side. He is just as much on our side as on God's side.

If we aspire after more than we are, a priest promises help. If we regret the mess we are in, a priest promises help. If the Son of Man does the work of priest, there is much to be in awe of but nothing to be afraid of: mediation results in loving union. If the Son of Man does the work of priest, there is much to be repented of but nothing of which to despair: mediation results in gracious forgiveness.

After the clothing, the head and eyes are the first things we look at in a person. If the clothes present a role, the head and eyes declare character. Are the role and the person congruent? Does the person fit the uniform? The head and eyes of the Son of Man show him to be the forgiven and forgiving person. This mediator both does and is his work. This priest who gives evidence that all is pure between us and that God is himself pure and purifying.

He is pure: "his head and his hair were white wool, white as snow." We remember the prophet's promise, "Your sins are like scarlet, they shall be as white as snow . . . they shall become like wool." We remember the psalmist's prayer, "Purge me with hyssop, and I shall be clean; wash me, and I shall be whiter than snow." It happened. Christ is fulfilled promise and answered prayer— clean, holy.

And he is purifying: "his eyes were like a flame of fire." A host of biblical images accumulate in the fire-flaming eyes of the Son of Man: pillar of fire, burning bush, altar fires, fiery furnace, fiery chariots. Fire penetrates and transforms. Holiness gets inside us and when it gets inside us it changes us. Christ's gaze penetrates and purifies. He doesn't look at us, he looks *into* us. We are not a spectacle to Christ, we are invaded by him. "He is a consuming fire, that only that which cannot be consumed may stand forth eternal. It is the nature of God, so terribly pure that it destroys all that is not pure as fire . . . He will have purity. It is not that the fire will burn us if we do not worship thus; but that the fire will burn us until we worship thus; yea, will go on burning within us after all that is foreign to it has yielded to its force, no longer with pain and consuming, but as the highest consciousness of life, the presence of God."[7]

"His feet were like burnished bronze, refined as in a furnace." Already alert to Daniel through the evocation of the Son of Man, we can hardly fail to recognize a contrast between St. John's vision of the Son of Man and the "great image" that Nebuchadnezzar dreamed and Daniel interpreted (Dan. 2:31–45). That image had a head of fine gold, a torso of silver, belly and thighs of bronze, and legs of iron, but feet that were a mixture of iron and clay. The iron and clay did not make a good bond. The image itself was magnificent, constructed of precious and strong metals, but it was set on a base that was flawed. When struck by a rolling rock, it fell apart. No matter how wonderful the image, its inadequate base doomed it to destruction. It "became like the chaff of the summer threshing floors; and the wind carried them away, so that not a trace of them could be found" (Dan. 2:35).

Later Daniel is addressed by the "man clothed in linen" and "having the appearance of a man" (Dan. 10–11). He also has a body of precious and magnificent construction, but is supported by legs of "burnished bronze" like St. John's Son of Man. The historical succession of kingdoms, each doomed to judgment (Nebuchadnezzar's dream image), is given its interpretation by one who survives and triumphs. The context of interpretation is larger than the text to be interpreted.

The Son of Man, the Christ, is seen in St. John's vision in contrast to the flawed feet of Nebuchadnezzar's dream and in continuity with the bronze underpinnings of the strengthening angel who was seen by Daniel in the "likeness of the sons of men" (Dan. 10:16). The succession of kingdoms of this earth, no matter how impressive and powerful, is set on a base that is flawed. Christ's kingdom is set on a base that is as strong as its superstructure is magnificent. The bronze base is firm. Bronze is a combination of iron and copper. Iron is strong but it rusts. Copper won't rust but is pliable. Combine the two in bronze and the best quality of each is preserved, the strength of the iron and the endurance of the copper. The rule of Christ is set on this base: the foundation of his power has been tested by fire.

St. John in his Gospel describes the Christ as the Word. More than any other Gospel writer, he presents us with the Christ *speaking*. Biblical faith is not guesswork in a moral-spiritual fog; it is response to an exact word spoken in Jesus Christ. The Bible begins with God speaking, speaking into existence first creation and then redemption. The speaking develops into conversation as people respond (pray), using their precious gift of speech. The word God speaks is important; the word we speak is important. Both words are uttered in the speech of Jesus Christ.

There is more to the meaning of these words than can be discovered in a dictionary. Dimensions of meaning resonate through one's manner of speaking and tone of voice. How something is said matters as much as what is said. So much is conveyed by tone and timbre: we know at once whether the speaker is timid and hesitant, bored and frivolous, impulsive and angry, matter-of-fact and detached. We interpret all words through a screen of sound. The meaning of the word receives its nuance by the sound of the voice which prepares us for an appropriate act of response to what we understand with our minds. And so before we are told what the Son of Man says, we are introduced to his way of speaking: "and his voice was like the sound of many waters." The metaphor says nothing about the meaning of the words; it describes the sound of the voice. Christ's voice is commensurate with his appearance, awesome and commanding. Our response, even before we comprehend the meaning of the message, is being shaped into forms of robust worship and hearty song. A gossiping, mincing response to "the sound of many waters" is unthinkable.

So far the vision has elaborated aspects of his being; now it tells his function: "in his right hand he held seven stars." The "seven stars" would be the planets, the unfixed stars, of which seven were known in the first century. The movements of these planets among the constellations and in relation to sun and moon was the fundamental stuff of astrology. The influence of astrology permeated all popular religion in the ancient world. The shifting locations of the planets in the twelve constellations of the zodiac were believed to determine destiny. Both public and private affairs were controlled by the seven planets. Studying and interpreting them was skilled and valued work. The astrologist was a person of prestige in the ancient world.

And Christ holds the seven stars in his right hand! "Right hand" means ready for use. A soldier with a sword in his right hand is ready to fight; a shepherd with a staff in the right hand is at work; a hammer in the right hand is ready to pound a sixpenny nail into a loose floorboard. What is in my right hand is what I am capable of doing and what, in fact, I am ready to do. What does Christ do? He runs the cosmos. It is that simple. The planets do not control us; Christ controls the planets. Later in the vision (Rev. 1:20), the stars will be identified as "the angels of the seven churches." What pagans thought were gods and goddesses, impersonal, remote, and controlling, are ministering angels, God's messengers bringing his word and glory into the midst of the Christians as they worship and sing and pray.

The writer to the Hebrews told us that the "word of God is living and active, sharper than any two-edged sword, piercing to the division of soul and spirit, of joints and marrow, and discerning the thoughts and intentions of the heart" (Heb. 4:12). In a similar way St. John uses the metaphor of the sword to demonstrate what takes place when Christ speaks.

Any beleaguered community, terrorized by the brandished sword, is tempted to meet force with force, sword with sword. But while scripture is full of military action, gradually, and in Jesus finally, military force becomes a metaphor for the word of God. Christ does not come with the sword (he ordered Peter to put his sword away for good), but with the word, which is like a sword. God's will is articulated sharply and penetratingly out of Christ's mouth. These words conquer. Christ's words are not limp. They cut through willful resistance, divide good from evil, overcome rebellion, and establish righteousness. The power that the world acknowledges comes out of the mouth of a gun; the power that the person of faith respects comes from the mouth of Christ.

When Moses returned from the mountain of revelation, his face was shining so brightly that the people could not look on it. The Aaronic benediction prays, "The Lord make his face to shine upon you, and be gracious to you" (Num. 6:25). In Christ the blessing of God is made personal in the shining face: "And his face was like the sun shining in full strength." God in Christ is warmth and sunlight.

Much of life is spent in darkness, whether literal or metaphorical. No one seems completely at home in the dark, even though most of us learn to accustom ourselves to it. We invent devices to make the dark less threatening—a candle, a fire, a flashlight, a lamp. In the darkness we are liable to lose perspective and proportion: nightmares terrorize us, fears paralyze us. In the darkness our imaginations fashion spectres. Sounds are ominous. Movements are ghostly. A light that shines in the darkness shows us that the terror and the chaos have no objective reality to them. "The light shines in the darkness, and the darkness has not overcome it" (John 1:5). Light reveals order and beauty. Or, if there is something to be feared, the light shows the evil in proportionate relationship to all that is not to be feared.

We do not live in darkness, but in light. We are not cursed; we are blessed. Light, not darkness, is the fundamental reality in which we live. And God is light. Biblical writers, pondering the qualities of light, found in their meditations truth upon truth about God. It is Christ's most comprehensive work to reveal it.

St. John has used seven items to describe the Son of Man. The items are arranged symmetrically. The first and last items, the white head and shining face, are most important: forgiveness and blessing are the first and final impressions. The second and sixth items, eyes and mouth, are the organs of relationship, sight and sound being the chief means of communication: Christ shows God to be in relationship with us. The third and fifth items, feet and right hand, are the paired members of the body that represent capability: feet give solid underpinning and mobility; the right hand is the instrument of the executive will: God is capable and active on our behalf. The fourth item in the series of seven is the voice. It is at the center. All prophetic and apostolic words converge in this voice that thunders sounds of passionate love and urgent mercy.

One other thing: the vision is both heard and seen. The elements seen (head and hair, eyes, feet, right hand, face) and those heard (the thundering voice, the sword-like speech) are, throughout scripture, the means of revelation. St. Luke's words parallel St. John's vision: "all that Jesus began to do [what was seen] and teach [what was heard]" (Acts 1:1). We have neither invisible words apart from the visible forms that they bring into being, nor visible actions apart from the accurate articulation of words. The invisible and visible, the interior and exterior, the fact and the meaning, are a unity in Christ.

This is the most elaborate, but not the only vision of Christ in the Revelation. There is also a vision of the Lamb standing, "as though it had been slain" (Rev. 5:6-7), showing the action of redemption accomplished in crucifixion; the vision of the birth of Jesus thrown on a cosmic screen (Rev. 12:1-6); the vision of the Lamb surrounded by the 144,000 (Rev. 14:1); the Son of Man crowned and armed for judgment (Rev. 14:14); and the vision of Christ mounted and leading the armies of heaven, "King of kings and Lord of lords" (Rev. 19:16). Finally, there is the Christ of the second coming (Rev. 22:12-17). In all, seven Christ visions are distributed through the pages of the Apocalypse.

The believing imagination is fecund in creating pictures by which Christ can be understood as first, last, and center. Always the images are minted out of scriptural metal and then shaped to express whatever is required at the moment and in the context to focus faith in and through Christ. The visions make our imaginations supple and alert, so that we may realize that Christ centers our lives in every time, under any condition, as we seek the means of obedient response in the church community and in current events.

St. John's visions show a mind conversant with the messianic expectations that the Spirit had set moving through the life of Israel, and grounded in the details of the incarnation furnished by the

Gospel writers. But it also shows that his mind was open to freshly discovered and perceived realizations of the Christ that come when a stormy passage plunges us into the "suffering and sovereignty and endurance" (Rev. 1:9).

Our imaginations are constricted. We see Christ walking around Palestine with some rather dense fishermen, helping people, and saying verses suitable for memorizing in Sunday school or placing on a decorative plaque—and we suppose we have it all. St. John's vision trains us to re-see Christ in whatever terms are necessary to affirm his centrality in *this* time and place, among *these* people.

The vision is not just vision. Intelligence and will are also addressed. On seeing Christ in this vision, St. John falls in a dead faint. He is lifted to his feet by the reassuring words, "Fear not," the same words by which Peter's sea-storm terror was changed to trust, and Mary Magdalene's empty-tomb panic was changed into excited witness. Then, "Write what you see." The vision initiates a task. St. John has work to do, carrying out his pastoral work of telling "the mystery" among the communities of worshiping, working, suffering Christians in Asia. This mystery is not a puzzle that baffles; it is an infinity to explore. Christ's words and presence illuminate what we know familiarly so that we see it extraordinarily. This is in contrast to the information so often purveyed by experts that reduce everyday things to a lowest common denominator so that we are diminished in our esteem and despised in our activities. How differently this vision works: "The seven stars are the seven churches," the very communities of faith in which St. John has been living his life are correlated with the movements in the heavens which gloriously "are telling the glory of God [and . . . proclaim] his handiwork" (Ps. 19:1). This is not reduction, but expansion. Visions do that.

Prior to the vision, St. John is on the prison island in isolated exile. He is cut off from his churches by a decree out of unholy Rome. Rome is the ascendant power. The gospel has been proved a weak and ineffective sally against unstoppable evil. Two generations after the euphoria of Pentecost it is thoroughly discredited. Everything St. John has believed and preached is, to all evidence, a disaster.

And then, without a single thing having happened in Rome or in Asia—no earthquake to change the face of the earth, no revolution to change the government in Rome—St. John is on his feet. He has a message. He has a job. He has a means for bringing God home to the people and the gospel to the world. The difference between St. John the prisoner and St. John the pastor is Christ, in vision and in reality.

St. John, away from his churches, fretting from lack of intimate knowledge of his people, sees the penetrating, attentive eyes of his Savior. St. John, weak from confinement, sees the strong, burnished feet of his Lord. St. John, used to speaking with authority to his apt-to-stray sheep but now without voice, hears the authoritative voice of the Ruler of church and world. St. John, homesick for his congregations, sees them held in the right hand of the Shepherd of Israel. St. John at the mercy of the political sword of Rome, sees the word of God proceeding swordlike and not returning void. St. John, nearing the end of his days, the energy of his countenance in eclipse, sees the presence of a radiating Christ throwing blessing on all.

By virtue of the vision, the crushed exile becomes a vigorous prophet. In time of crisis, like ruined Samson in the temple of Dagon, he receives a fresh visitation from God which delivers the people from oppression. Visions, if they are truly visions and not wish-fulfillment dreams, make things happen.

St. John exiled is now St. John empowered. The vision did it. From rocky Patmos he is lifted to the realm of the Spirit and given the Christic vision. He is returned to earth and made a pastor again, but this time a pastor with power. Rome shut St. John away so his churches could neither see nor hear him. The Spirit filled his eyes with sights and his mouth with speech that have given sight and direction to Christians ever since. The banishing decree of Rome was itself banished. Anybody can dream up a happy ending to a story, but it is a poor joke for the oppressed and persecuted, for exiles and strangers. A vision, though, sees what is actually there, not what frustration would wish were there. "In dreams begins responsibility."[8] In visions are born realities.

4. The Last Word on the Church
Revelation 2 and 3

Your people will offer themselves freely
  on the day you lead your host
    upon the holy mountains.
From the womb of the morning
  like dew your youth will come to you.

PSALM 110:3

As for the mystery of the seven stars which you saw in my right hand, and the seven golden lampstands, the seven stars are the angels of the seven churches and the seven lampstands are the seven churches.

REVELATION 1:20

All your dissatisfactions with the Church seem to me to come from an incomplete understanding of sin . . . What you seem to demand is that the Church put the kingdom of heaven on earth right now and here—that the Holy Ghost be translated at once into all flesh. The Holy Spirit rarely shows Himself on the surface of anything. To have the Church be what you want it to be would require the continuous miraculous meddling of God in human affairs, whereas it is to retain our dignity that God has chose to operate in another manner. We can't reject that without rejecting life . . . Christianity makes a difference; but it cannot kill the age.

FLANNERY O'CONNOR

The gospel is never for individuals but always for a people. Sin fragments us, separates us, and sentences us to solitary confinement. Gospel restores us, unites us, and sets us in community. The life of faith revealed and nurtured in the biblical narratives is highly personal but never merely individual: always there is a family, a tribe, a nation—*church*. God's love and salvation are revealed and experienced in the congregation of the people "who know the festal shout" (Ps. 89:15), not in "the garden, alone."

So it comes as no surprise to find that St. John's vision is not a private ecstasy given to compensate him for his rockbound exile;

it is "for the seven churches that are in Asia" (Rev. 1:4). All revelation is. The gospel pulls us into community. One of the immediate changes that the gospel makes is grammatical: we instead of I; our instead of my; us instead of me.

Sin, both our own and that of others, drives us into customized selfishness. Separation from God becomes separation from neighbor. The same salvation that restores our relation with God reinstates us in the community of persons who live by faith. Every tendency to privatism and individualism distorts and falsifies the gospel. The Bible knows nothing of the soul who is, in Plotinus's words, "alone with the Alone."

In the Revelation the opening lines call down a blessing on him "who reads and those who listen and keep." It is assumed that the Revelation will be read and heard in church. That individuals would take the scroll and go off to read it in the privacy of their own rooms is not for a moment imagined. Attention to the Gospel message is always an act of community, never an exercise in private. A believing community is the context for the life of faith.

Love cannot exist in isolation: away from others, love bloats into pride. Grace cannot be received privately: cut off from others it is perverted into greed. Hope cannot develop in solitude: separated from the community, it goes to seed in the form of fantasies. No gift, no virtue can develop and remain healthy apart from the community of faith. "Outside the church there is no salvation" is not ecclesiastical arrogance but spiritual common sense, confirmed in everyday experience. Whenever persons attempt to live in defiance of it they are attenuated and impoverished. Submitting to it they are generously rewarded. "The sacrifice of selfish privacy which is daily demanded of us is daily repaid a hundredfold in the true growth of personality which the life of the body encourages. Those who are members of one another become as diverse as the hand and the ear. That is why worldlings are so monotonously alike compared with the almost fantastic variety of the saints. Obedience is the road to freedom, humility the road to pleasure, unity the road to personality."[1]

Notwithstanding this chorus of accumulated wisdom, there are always times in the life of faith when it seems far better to go it alone. In St. John's day it was politically dangerous to assemble together; a private faith would have been safer and more convenient. Sometimes it is a bore to be with others; faith in Christ does not in itself make a person an interesting conversationalist or stimulating companion. A secret, individualized faith does not have to endure tedious relationships with unimaginative pilgrims. But the biblical witness consistently challenges our privatism and individualism: "It is not good for a man to be alone;" "I will make your seed as the sand of the sea;" "forsake not the assembling of ourselves together;" "when you pray, say, *Our Father;*" "Love your neighbor as yourself;" "Bear one another's burdens." The life of faith is developed under the image of the Trinity in the context of community.

When St. John turned towards the trumpet voice that commanded his attention, the first thing he saw was seven gold lampstands, "which are the seven churches" to which he was pastor. Then, in their midst, he saw the one "like a Son of Man" who was Jesus, the Christ. Christ is not seen apart from the gathered, listening, praying, believing, worshiping people to whom he is Lord and Savior. It is not possible to have Christ apart from the church. We try. We would very much like to have Christ apart from the contradictions and distractions of the other persons who believe in him, or say that they do. We want a Christ who is pure goodness, beauty, and truth. We prefer to worship him under the caress of a stunning sunset, or with the inspiring tonalities of a soaring symphony, or by means of a penetrating poetry. We would like to put as much distance as possible between our worship of Christ and the indifferent hymn singing and fussy moralism which somehow always get into the church. We are ardent after God but cool towards the church. It is .not irreligion or indifference that keeps many away from the church, but just the opposite: the church is perceived and experienced as a carcinogenic pollutant in the pure air of religion. Many people, wanting to nurture faith in God, instead of entering a company of saints who still look and act a lot more like sinners, take a long walk on an ocean beach, or hike a high mountain, or immerse themselves in Dostoevsky or Stravinsky or Georgia O'Keeffe.

But to all this aspiring aestheticism the gospel says No: "Write to the seven churches." We would prefer to go directly from the awesome vision of Christ (Rev. 1) to the glorious ecstasies of heaven (Rev. 4, 5), and then on to the grand, victorious battles against dragon wickedness (Rev. 12–14). But we can't do it. The church has to be negotiated first. The only way from Christ to heaven and the battles against sin is through the church. And not just one church, but seven!

Baron von Hugel's niece, Gwendolyne Greene, tried to get out of going to church because "only the best" was attractive to her. Every church she knew, she complained, was so muddling, dull, and repulsive. How is it possible to be lifted on wings of adoration to God while surrounded by ugly architecture, off-key hymns, stupid sermonizing, and dozing hypocrites? But the good old Baron wouldn't let her off. He wrote:

The touching, entrancing beauty of Christianity depends upon a subtle something which all this fastidiousness ignores. Its greatness, its special genius, consists, as much as anything else, in that it is without this fastidiousness. A soul that is, I do not say tempted, but dominated, by such fastidiousness, is as yet only hovering around the precincts of Christianity. But it has not entered its sanctuary, where heroism is always homely, where the best always acts as stimulus towards helping towards being (in a true sense) but one of the semi-articulate, bovine, childish, repulsively second-, third-, fourth-rate crowd. . . . The heathen Philosophies, one and all, failed to get beyond your fastidiousness; only Christianity got beyond it; only Christianity—but I mean, a deeply *costingly* realized Christianity—got beyond it. It is really, a very hideous thing; the full, truly free, beauty of Christ alone completely liberates us from this miserable bondage.[2]

A cursory reading of the seven messages to the seven churches makes it clear that "church" is not a spiritual aristocracy, but simply a geographically identified assembly of ordinary believers. These churches are not referred to in terms of their character or piety or heroism, but simply by location: Ephesus, Smyrna, Pergamum, Thyatira, Sardis, Philadelphia, Laodicea. The seven cities are located along a Roman postal circuit in what is now modern Turkey. Each can be found on a map. Each has been excavated by archaeologists.

But while the churches are located geographically, they are defined theologically. A church is composed of persons who live in a particular town, eat food bought in the local markets, work at jobs provided by the economy, and speak a language in common with others in the region. But it is comprised of something quite apart from the conditions of piety, culture, and politics, namely, the person of Jesus Christ. God makes the church. The Holy Spirit breathes on the chaotic and random population, "without form and void," and makes a people of God, a church, Each of the seven churches, and every church since, is defined by the living Christ. A church only has being in relation to Christ. Apart from Christ, these churches would have location but no identity.

The Ephesian church acquires identity from "him who holds the seven stars in his right hand and walks among the seven gold lampstands"; the Smyrnan church from "the first and the last, who was dead and lives"; the Pergamene from "him who holds the sharp, two-edged sword"; the Thyatiran from him who has "eyes like flames of fire, and whose feet are like bronze"; the Sardinian from him who "has the seven spirits of God and the seven stars"; the Philadelphian from "the holy and the true, who has the key of David and who opens and no one can shut, who shuts and none can open"; the Laodicean from "the Amen, the faithful and true witness, the beginning of God's creation." There is no church apart from Christ. Elements from the Christ vision in Revelation 1 define the church communities in Revelation 2 and 3.

It is impossible to discover the nature of the church through the disciplines of sociology. Not by analyzing the piety of a people do we fix the church's identity. The church is formed by Christ's word and sustained by his being. No objective institutional analysis will show this. No subjective spiritual introspection will discover this. It is a revelation of Christ. Sociological analyses of the church, so dear to the hearts of reformers, are virtually worthless. Hand-wringing laments on the church, so dear to the hearts of moralists, are worse. What is unique and characteristic of the church is the identity conferred by Christ and the common life brought into being by the Spirit.

The second century Muratorian canon observed that both St. Paul and St. John wrote letters to seven churches. Seven churches summarize all churches. Every church is located in a specific place; all churches exist under the conditions of geography, politics, and economics; each church is visible. At the same time, every church gets its identity from Christ and what he does; churches exist only in derivation from Christ; the church is invisible to all who unbelievingly close their eyes to the one "like the Son of Man." Apart from the Christ, shown to us in the vision, we are nothing but a society of pious, or not so pious, souls. Also, while all churches get their identity from Christ, each congregational identity is partial: each church is defined by only a piece of the vision. No single congregation exhibits the wholeness of Christ. It is not possible to look at any one instance of the church and find an entire representation of Christ, although we very certainly can be led to that wholeness as we listen to what "the Spirit says to the church" and respond in worship.

One phrase is repeated without variation in the messages to the seven churches: "He who has an ear, let him hear what the Spirit says to the churches."[3] Whatever differences there are between the churches, two things are constant: the Spirit speaks, the people listen. The church assembles persons to whom Jesus keeps his promises: "I will send him [the Counselor] to you. And when he comes, he will convince the world concerning sin and righteousness and judgment: concerning sin, because they do not believe me; concerning righteousness, because I go to the Father, and you will see me no more; concerning judgment, because the ruler of this world is judged. . . . When the Spirit of truth comes, he will guide you into all the truth; for he will not speak on his own authority, but whatever he hears he will speak, and he will declare to you the things that are to come" (John 16:7–11, 13). For that promise to be completed there must be listening ears attentive to the Spirit-spoken words. Listening is the common task of the church. Churches are listening posts.

Listening is a spiritual act far more than an acoustical function. Expensive and sophisticated amplification equipment does not improve listening, it only makes hearing possible. Because listening so frequently decays into mere hearing, and because there can be no church apart from listening, the last word spoken to every church is "He who has an ear, let him hear what the Spirit says to the churches." From Genesis ("And God said, Let there be . . .") to Jesus ("and the word became flesh and dwelt among us") the personal word is central, and therefore the personal act of listening is essential. Mouths speak in order that ears may hear. The hearing that begins as a physical function becomes a spiritual response. When it does not, the problem is diagnosed as "heavy ears" (Isa. 6:10). A vivid Hebrew idiom speaks of uncovering the ears so that God's word can get in (1 Sam. 20:2).

"Morning by morning he wakens, he wakens my ear to hear as those who are taught. The Lord God has opened my ear, and I was not rebellious, I turned not backward" (Isa. 50:4–5). It was promised that when the Messianic age dawned, the ears of the deaf would hear (Isa. 35:5). When the Messianic age did dawn, one of the conspicuous things that took place was the opening of ears by Jesus (Mark 7:33). Professor Horst thinks that it was significant that in the saying about hewing off hand or foot or plucking out the eye (Mark 9:43–47) there is nothing about maiming the ear. "The ear is indispensible because of preaching."[4]

St. Matthew, St. Mark, and St. Luke agree in placing Jesus' parable about hearing, with its staccato conclusion, "He who has ears to hear, let him hear," as the first of the parables. If the divine word is primary, then human hearing is essential: *that* we hear is required; the *way* we hear is significant. The parable, with its metaphor of soil for ears, provides an ingenious tool for a self-administered hearing test: What is the quality of my hearing? Are my ears thick with callouses, impenetrable like a heavily trafficked path? Are my ears only superficially attentive like rocky ground in which everything germinates but nothing takes root? Are my ears like an indiscriminate weed patch in which the noisy and repetitive take up all the space without regard for truth, quality, beauty, or fruitfulness? Or are my ears good soil which readily receives God's word, well-tilled to welcome deep roots, to discriminately choose God's word and reject the lies of the world, to accept high responsibility for protecting and practicing the gift of hearing in silence, reverence, and attentiveness so that God's word will be heard, understood, and believed?

The parable has been immensely important to Christians: it has emphasized the primacy of hearing, it has exposed the several ways in which we can appear to hear but, in fact, not hear, and it has insisted on the responsibility of each of us to listen: "He who has ears to hear, let him hear." All this is now brought to an impressive conclusion at the very place that it needs to be taken seriously and lived obediently, in the church, the one place in the world where persons deliberately come together and uncover their ears so that the sounds of God's word will be heard, accurately and believingly.

Marshall McLuhan made the arresting observation that nature has not equipped mankind with earlids. But we compensate for nature's oversight by developing selective listening. We are conveniently deaf to sounds that challenge our pride, or command our obedience, or interrupt our fantasies, or call attention to our lapses. "Heavy ears" make it possible to pursue wrongful pleasures, indulge empty dreams, and escape onerous tasks with only minimal discomfort of conscience. But the convenience is purchased at an exorbitantly high price: we sacrifice great chunks of reality for these brief, superficial, and mostly doggish comforts. A few people become aware that they are missing too much, that there are vast symphonies of sound reverberating down the corridors of history, and that they are hearing only the rusty squeaking of a few hinges; that there are trumpet voices of ecstasy sounding heights and depths of glory, and all they are hearing are assorted grunts and groans from overfed, insentient neighbors. They come to Christ to have their deafness cured. He puts his fingers in their ears and commands, *"Ephphatha"*: the old Isaianic prophecy is fulfilled again and again and again. With ears that hear, these persons are gathered into churches to practice their newly-acquired ability to listen. They hear God speak words that create and command, that comfort and direct, that save—words that make all things new: "let him who has an ear hear what the Spirit says to the churches."

Between the opening Christological identification and the concluding evangelical call to listen, there is an individualized message to each of the seven churches. Each message is different in content but has a common outline that serves a common purpose: to provide spiritual direction to a people who are called to live by faith in Christ "in but not of the world." The spiritual direction begins with an affirmation, is followed by a correction, and concludes with a promise. There is, first, a positive affirmation; second, a corrective discipline; and third, a motivating promise. In two of the churches (Sardis and Laodicea) the word of affirmation is omitted; in one (Smyrna) the course of discipline is absent. Otherwise, the three-part spiritual direction is identical in each of the churches.

The most prominent impression from the Son of Man vision in Revelation 1 is of a great effusion of light, a dazzling incandescence. Light cascades from that image in great force and quantity, and floods the churches. It is the first-day light of Genesis, and the light that enlightens every person who comes into the world.[5] The light does two things: it shows what is good and therefore to be celebrated in the light; it exposes what is sinful to the healing warmth of the light. The light reveals and heals.

The first element in spiritual direction is accurate affirmation. Each of the messages begins with the Lord saying, "I know . . ." (*oida*). J. M. Ford translates this as "I discern . . .",[6] a primary verb in all spiritual direction. The message that follows demonstrates an accurate knowledge of everything that is going on in that particular congregation. The message develops in relation to what is going on in the city and church economically, culturally, and politically. The social situation outside and the religious situation inside are comprehended in the formulation of the message. His is not external knowledge such as might be gathered by an industrious journalist; it is a precise knowledge of what it means *there* to live as *God's* people—an appreciative knowledge of what it means for them to live in the name of Jesus.

The churches are affirmed for untiring, unflagging, and vigilant work (Ephesus); for brave suffering (Smyrna); for courageous witness (Pergamum); for growing and developing discipleship (Thyatira); and for brave steadfastness (Philadelphia). We are not measured by our contribution to society, or evaluated according to our potential. The church is a community where who we are and what we do is recognized and celebrated quite apart from the fads and fashions of the world. As such the church is a glorious place: quiet, unnoticed, courageous lives develop out of the affirmations that take place in these communities. Quite apart from the incentives that society supposes are necessary to sustain motivation and enterprise, these people exercise a steadfastness.

But the church is also a distressing place. It is shaped and sustained by the living truth of Christ that is essential for a complete humanity. It is marked by symbols that affirm the security of God's love. But there are always some (and often many) who live as parasites on these vigorous truths and fatten on the red blood of redemption. Outsiders often see nothing but these parasite persons and suppose that they are characteristic of the church. They are not, any more than barnacles are the hull of a ship. No church ever existed in a pure state. The church is made up of sinners. The fleas come with the dog.

In addition to the sins that people bring into the community of faith when they enter, there are sins that develop out of the life of faith itself. The worst sins are not even possible to persons who do not live a life of faith. So correction is essential in spiritual direction: "I have this against you. . . ." The church attracts to itself persons who like to live in the atmosphere of the holy but have little interest in being holy themselves. They find delight in working on committees and find security in ordering their lives within the reassuring traditions of the fathers. They are faithful in showing up in church on Sundays and are fortified by listening to the moral instruction of their leaders. But they have no appetite for holiness, or joy, or love. They are wholly conventional and entirely dull. The church is sought out as a sanctuary for living in pious sloth. These people ignore anything to do with Christ that cannot be capsuled as a bromide. Therefore the church needs to be continuously in reformation: "I have this against you. . . ."

Five of the seven churches (Smyrna and Philadelphia are the exceptions) require reformation in one way or another. Typically, what is evident is that they contained the forms of religion after losing the Spirit. They are corrected for abandoning their first zestful love of Christ (Ephesus); being indifferent to heretical teaching (Pergamum); being tolerant of immorality (Thyatira); being apathetic (Sardis); letting luxurious riches substitute for life in the Spirit (Laodicea). "There is not another institution," wrote Charles Williams, "which suffers from time so much as religion. At the moment when it is remotely possible that a whole generation might have learned something both of theory and practice, the learners and their learning are removed by death, and the church is confronted with the necessity of beginning all over again. The whole labor of regenerating mankind has to begin again every thirty years or so."[7] None of these churches had been in existence for more than half a century and yet already degeneration was in process. They were going through religious motions after Spirit-motives were gone. Their sluggish lives were propped up by termite-riddled timbers of a once vigorous religion.

The third element of spiritual direction is promise. The motivating promise, eternal life, is the same for each church, but is presented under a variety of images: tree of life (Ephesus), crown of life (Smyrna), white stone (Pergamum), morning star (Thyatira), white garments (Sardis), a pillar in the temple (Philadelphia), and eating and ruling with Christ (Laodicea). No affirmation can be sustained and no discipline carried through without adequate motivation. The promise of eternal life, not as reward but as the destiny which completes life begun in faith, is the adequate motivation for "him who conquers."[8]

This outline is a summary of the spiritual direction that takes place in the church. The church is the place where we come to find out what we are doing that is right; it is a place of affirmation. The church is the place where we come to find out what we are doing that is wrong; it is a place for correction. The church is the place where we come to hear the promises; it is a place of motivation. No Christian community can do without any part of this message. We need affirmation, we need correction, we need motivation.

In the church we are always in process of being affirmed. We find those parts of our lives that are working well, and discovering them gives zest, confidence, and assurance. We are always in process of being corrected. We find those parts of our lives that aren't working well. There is a relentless quality to the word of God that insists that we face up to our sloth, our pride, our avarice—all the things that separate us from God's complete victory in us, every part that is diseased or immature, that defeats our joy or interferes with another's salvation. And we are in process of being motivated. For none of what we do in faith is short term; it is all long-range. The motivation to live strenuously for a lifetime must be adequate to sustain us through every shadowed valley and every parched wilderness. The promise of eternal life, and only the promise of eternal life, is sufficient to provide such motivation.

This three-part spiritual direction trains God's people to live a life of confident faith in Christ in a hostile environment. The process of affirmation, correction, and promise is what the Greeks called *paidea*, the complex process whereby the community passes on its passion and its excellence.[9] "Those whom I love, I reprove and chasten [*paideuo*]" (Rev. 3:19). The training takes place in seven areas: we are trained to love (Ephesus), to suffer (Smyrna), to tell the truth (Pergamum), to be holy (Thyatira), to be authentic (Sardis), to be in mission (Philadelphia), and to worship, using things to praise God, receiving gifts to serve God (Laodicea). The church is the community of people who explicitly and consciously submit themselves to the direction and training of our Lord the Spirit, so that excellence is pursued in these seven areas. Strengths are recognized and developed; weaknesses are exposed and corrected. We get encouragement (no one is all bad); we get correction (no one is all right); we become motivated, acquiring the inner energy to persevere through the pain of growth to the satisfactions of wholeness and completion.

St. John neither complains of nor glorifies his churches. He accepts them as facts. They are God's means for calling persons together so that they can realize who their Lord is, and who they are, and develop the relationships that are coherent with those identities. For persons and congregations who have been bombarded with tedious, footnoted, complaining analyses of the church for these many years, the seven succinct letters of St. John are a relief. Numb from the overkill exposés of the secular preachers, we respond to St. John's mercifully brief missives with gratitude. One thing the church does not need is long-winded analysis. If the Revelation is to be trusted (and it *has* been impressively successful in enabling churches to flourish through difficult times), what is necessary is vision, hope, and encouragement, plus some quietly straightforward, no-nonsense guidance.

The churches of the Revelation show us that churches are not Victorian parlors where everything is always picked up and ready for guests. They are messy family rooms. Entering a person's house unexpectedly, we are sometimes met with a barrage of apologies. St. John does not apologize. Things are out of order, to be sure, but that is what happens to churches that are lived in. They are not show rooms. They are living rooms, and if the persons living in them are sinners, there are going to be clothes scattered about, handprints on the woodwork, and mud on the carpet. For as long as Jesus insists on calling sinners and not the righteous to repentance—and there is no indication as yet that he has changed his policy in that regard—churches are going to be an embarrassment to the fastidious and an affront to the upright. St. John sees them simply as *lampstands*: they are places, locations, where the light of Christ is shown. They are not themselves the light. There is nothing particularly glamorous about churches, nor, on the other hand, is there anything particularly shameful about them. They simply are.

The church is to the gospel what the body is to the person: under the conditions of our creation necessary, but not the thing itself. The body can be abused by overeating or by overwork. It can be maimed by accident or by disease. Still, it is necessary. Persons do fine things in abused and neglected and inadequate bodies. The body can also be pampered and perfumed apart from any intention to work or to love, and still be a means for work and love. Thus also the church. A corrupt church still functions as the church. Dirty lampstands do not extinguish Christ's light. A prettified church, still, despite itself, functions as a church: polished gold does not outshine Christ's light. Of course, it is better that it be neither of these things, neither tarnished out of neglect or polished in vanity. It is better that it simply be there, unselfconsciously and inconspicuously receiving and sharing the light of Christ.

Much anger towards the church and most disappointments in the church are because of failed expectations. We expect a disciplined army of committed men and women who courageously lay siege to the worldly powers; instead we find some people who are more concerned with getting rid of the crabgrass in their lawns. We expect a community of saints who are mature in the virtues of love and mercy, and find ourselves working on a church supper where there is more gossip than there are casseroles. We expect to meet minds that are informed and shaped by the great truths and rhythms of scripture, and find persons whose intellectual energy is barely sufficient to get them from the comics to the sports page. At such times it is more important to examine and change our expectations than to change the church, for the church is not what we organize but what God gives, not the people we want to be with but the people God gives us to be with – a community created by the descent of the Holy Spirit in which we submit ourselves to the Spirit's affirmation, reformation, and motivation. There must be no idealization of the church. And lamentation ought to be restrained. Eulogy and anguish are alike misplaced. Churches are not little Jerusalems, either old or new.

It is God's will that we have a church. The life of faith always and necessarily takes place in a community of persons who are located somewhere in time and place. Geography is as important in the Christian way as Christology. Ur, Nazareth, Damascus, Patmos, and Thyatira are as essential as the fire-blazing eyes of the one like the Son of Man whose voice is like many waters. There is no evidence in the annals of ancient Israel or in the pages of the New Testament that churches were ever much better or much worse than they are today. A random selection of seven churches in any century, including our own, would turn up something very much like the seven churches to which St. John was pastor.

5. The Last Word on Worship
Revelation 4 and 5

Let the heavens praise thy wonders, O Lord,
    thy faithfulness in the assembly of the holy ones!
For who in the skies can be compared to the Lord?
    Who among the heavenly beings is like the Lord,
a God feared in the council of the holy ones,
    great and terrible above all that are round about him?

Blessed are the people who know the festal shout,
    who walk, O Lord, in the light of thy countenance.

PSALM 89:5-7, 15

And the four living creatures said, "Amen!"
and the elders fell down and worshiped.

REVELATION 5:14

Bracketed between the first
tentative prayers, a silence fills
this place, a shadowed listening
as our separateness seeks out
the Spirit's focus for this hour
and gathers strength enough
to peer and soar
into small, shining arcs of praise
held at their lower ends
by the old hymns. Christ
in this crowd of rest and rising
humbles himself again to our
humanity; and like the sheep
(trembling in the shearer's hands)
surrenders to us once more
in quietness.

LUCI SHAW

The last word to the Laodicean church was an invitation to worship: "Behold, I stand at the door and knock; if any one hears my voice and opens the door, I will come in to him and eat with him, and he with me. He who conquers, I will grant him to sit with me on my throne, as I myself conquered and sat down with my Father on his throne" (Rev. 3:20–21). At the Lord's table, hymns were sung, the word read and preached, prayers offered, offerings made, the life of Christ received under the forms of bread and wine. The Lord's table, to which the Laodiceans were invited, was the place of worship.

Had the Laodiceans neglected, perhaps even scorned, worship? They are portayed as rich and self-sufficient. There was no sense of need to drive them to their knees in supplication. There was no poverty to draw them into the community of friends where all things are held in common and shared in love. There was no hunger and thirst after righteousness to impel them to the banquet table laden with the blessings of redemption: "For you say, I am rich, I have prospered, and I need nothing" (Rev. 3:17).

St. John's message to the rich Christians is severe and indicting. Contrary to their well-fed appearance, he sees them as "wretched, pitiable, poor, blind, and naked" (Rev. 3:17). He calls them to repentance and to ardor. His concluding word is a metaphor: there is a closed door which needs to be opened so that they can eat the sacramental meal to which Christ comes as host, sharing his life with them. A door, only a door, separates these "wretched, pitiable" Christians from the bounty of the eucharistic table. Christ himself knocks at the door. Persistently, patiently, week after week, the invitation sounds: "Let us worship God." Open the door. Come to the feast. Will they do it?

The Laodiceans had just heard one of the most powerful (and briefest!) sermons in the history of Christian preaching. The preacher gave the invitation, "I stand at the door and knock", and then he "looked, and lo, in heaven an open door!" (Rev. 4:1). They did respond. Through the door he sees his Laodiceans gathered in Lord's Day worship as had been their custom from the beginning. St. John's vision now shows them the glorious significance of what they do in their Sunday worship.

St. John's first Lord's Day vision showed the complete reality of Christ (Rev. 1:12–20). The prophecies, memories, and experiences of hundreds of years were put together in that vision so that we will live in the light of the entire revelation, not just bits and pieces of it. This second Lord's Day vision shows the entire reality of worship, our response to the revelation of Christ. The hymns, sermons, insights, prayers, and offerings experienced in various degrees of wakefulness, and with more or less understanding, are put together in a single coherent vision so that we see our response to the living reality of God in its totality, and not just subjective segments of it. St. John, again "in the Spirit" (Rev. 4:2), as he was on the day he received the vision of Christ and the messages to the seven churches (Rev. 1:10), again hears the trumpet voice (Rev. 1:10, 4:10) and sees what takes place when Christians worship.

Christians worship with a conviction that they are in the presence of God. Worship is an act of attention to the living God who rules, speaks and reveals, creates and redeems, orders and blesses. Outsiders, observing these acts of worship, see nothing like that. They see a few people singing unpopular songs, sometimes off-key, someone reading from an old book and making remarks that may or may not interest the listeners, and then eating and drinking small portions of bread and wine that are supposed to give nourishment to their eternal souls in the same way that beef and potatoes sustain their mortal flesh. Who is right? Is worship an actual meeting called to order at God's initiative in which persons of faith are blessed by his presence and respond to his salvation? Or is it a pathetic, and sometimes desperate, charade in which people attempt to get God to pay attention to them and do something for them (1 Kings 18)?

Jesus stands at the door and knocks. What happens when we open the door? Revelation 4 and 5 answers the question and gives the last word on worship in five parts: worship centers, gathers, reveals, sings, and affirms. First in the vision is a throne: "A throne stood in heaven." This throne was promised in the Laodicean message —"I will grant him to sit with me on my throne"— and now, in worship, here it is. A throne centers authority. Worship is centering. The word *throne* appears in nearly every chapter of the Revelation (the exceptions are Rev. 9, 10, 15, 17, 18). Twice it is used to refer to false centers of authority, Satan's throne (Rev. 2:13) and the beast's throne (Rev. 16:10).

In worship God gathers his people to himself as center: "The Lord reigns" (Ps. 93:1). Worship is a meeting at the center so that our lives are centered in God and not lived eccentrically. We worship so that we live in response to and from this center, the living God. Failure to worship consigns us to a life of spasms and jerks, at the mercy of every advertisement, every seduction, every siren. Without worship we live manipulated and manipulating lives. We move in either frightened panic or deluded lethargy as we are, in turn, alarmed by spectres and soothed by placebos. If there is no center, there is no circumference. People who do not worship are swept into a vast restlessness, epidemic in the world, with no steady direction and no sustaining purpose.

Israel was plagued for centuries by Baal worship—portable centers for worship set up on every hill and under every green tree. But they were not true centers; they were arbitrary locations, similar to the sites for emperor worship in the Roman first century. In Israel, Jeremiah called for a return to the center; some of the people listened and responded. "Behold, we come to thee; for thou art the Lord our God. Truly the hills are a delusion, the orgies on the mountains. Truly in the Lord our God is the salvation of Israel" (Jer. 3:22-23). The hills *are* a delusion, and so is every casual or pompous way station at which people seek easy and instant centering. People who do not worship live in a vast shopping mall where they go from shop to shop, expending enormous sums of energy and making endless trips to meet first this need and then that appetite, this whim and that fancy. Life lurches from one partial satisfaction to another, interrupted by ditches of disappointment. Motion is fueled by the successive illusions that purchasing this wardrobe, driving that car, eating this meal, drinking that beverage will center life and give it coherence.

Over against these false places of worship, Jeremiah declares "a glorious throne, set on high from the beginning is the place of our sanctuary" (Jer. 17:12). This is the throne that St. John sees in his vision. "The throne of God—the fact of the throne, and the fact of

God enthroned—is the revelation of the Bible. The throne is the supreme revelation of scripture. In early Bible history the throne is unnamed, but is ever present. All the pictures of the early times are pictures of men setting their lives into relationship with the throne of God and thus finding peace, or rebelling against the government of God and thus perishing. In the failure of the chosen people to recognize the abiding fact of the throne of God lay the establishment of the monarch in Israel, that wholly evil thing. "'They have not rejected thee,' said God to Samuel, 'they have rejected me'; and out of that rejection began all their trouble."[1]

The effect of the centering is a vast gathering. The vision first comprehends the God-center of reality; it then names that which is gathered to the center: "Round the throne were twenty-four thrones, and seated on the thrones were twenty-four elders clad in white garments, with golden crowns on their heads." The twenty-four elders are a double twelve, the twelve Hebrew tribes and the twelve Christian apostles, the old Israel and the new Church.

The throne assembles around itself that which has been directed Godward through centuries of living by faith: the sacrifice and obedience, the preaching and praising, the repenting and offering of the people of Israel named after Jacob's sons, and along with them the twelve apostles sent forth by Jesus in acts of healing and blessing, feeding and helping, delivering and preaching. All are gathered around their center. The two twelves include the old and the new, prophecy and fulfillment, and everything in between: shy, hesitant looks upward to an undefined deity, along with confident and articulated praise to the God who revealed himself in Jesus Christ. Every acquired strength is looking for a place to work, every impulse to love is looking for a person to meet. Every firm commitment to deny self, every clear decision to follow Christ, along with every failed resolve and blind groping are gathered around this centering throne.

Can this gathering be done without erasing anything significant in any person's experience, without canceling any truth however badly or partially held, without squelching any voice however faltering or weak? Can the gathering be a true gathering, and not just a sorting out? Are the centering energies of that throne so over-whelming that the gathered are simply absorbed, losing identity? The double twelves maintain discrete identities, at the same time that they arrange convergent harmonies.

In addition to the representative persons around the throne, there are representative animals: "on each side of the throne, are four living creatures" (Rev. 4:6). The four creatures are all aspects of creation, just as the twenty-four elders are all the facets of faith. The noblest (lion), the strongest (ox), the wisest (human), and the swiftest (eagle) are centered in God.

Life as we encounter it is chaotic. The raw material served up by the day is disordered and turbulent. Nature is clamorous and many-headed. We ourselves are many-hearted and conflicted. How can we master such a mob? Is there any hope for harmony in such a chaos? The act of worship gathers into its centering rituals and harmonizing rhythms every aspect of creation. Worship does not divide the spiritual from the natural, it coordinates them. Nature and supernature, creation and covenant, elders and animals are all gathered. Worship that scorns creation is impoverished. The rabble of creation "red in tooth and claw" comes to order before the throne and finds itself more itself: each creature is alert (full of eyes) and soaring (six wings). In George Herbert's words, "All creatures of my God and king, lift up your voice and sing!"

In worship every sign of life and every impulse to holiness, every bit of beauty and every spark of vitality—Hebrew patriarchs, Christian apostles, wild animals, domesticated livestock, human beings, soaring birds—are arranged around this throne center that pulses light, showing each at its best, picking up all the colors of the spectrum in order to show off the glories. For the one seated on the throne "appeared like jasper and carnelian, and round the throne was a rainbow that looked like an emerald." Light with the colors of precious stones (jasper, carnelian, emerald) bathes everyone gathered in worship. Lives that have been defaced by sin into blurred charcoal outlines are now seen in their true colors. Every faded tint and wavering line are restored to original sharpness and hue. Precious stones are precious because they collect and intensify light. Light is full of color, all colors, but our dull eyes are unperceptive. A stone, selecting certain colors out of the air and intensifying them, shows us the deep glory of the color that was in the light all the time. The ancient world valued stones not for decoration, but for their capacity to reveal and deepen the colors of light. In the first chapter of Genesis, the command, "Let there be light," was spoken from this color-laden throne. "God is light and in him is no darkness at all." Worship is precious stones that reveal all the colors of light in and around us and dazzle us. Light is reflected off ugly billboards, debased in neon signs, and filtered through polluted air, smudging the world into oatmeal gray. Then a precious stone shows us a real red or green or blue; we are shaken and awake in wonder again.

In front of the throne that gathers and illuminates all persons and creatures is "a sea of glass, like crystal." The glass sea is before the throne. In order for worshipers to get to the throne it is necessary to get through or past this "sea." The crystal sea is a baptismal font. In Solomon's temple there was a great brass sea, that is, a large basin, set for purposes of cleansing at the entrance to the place of worship. In the early Christian centuries, the usual places of worship were homes. In the Roman style of home-building, there was always a place for washing, a *pluvinium*, at the entrance, and Christians as they worshiped in these homes used the washbasin as a baptistry. Baptism was (and is) entrance into the worshiping community of Christians. The world is comprehensively but not indiscriminately gathered around the throne of God—it is first cleansed in baptism and then presented. The waters of baptism, like the Red Sea and the Jordan River with which they are often identified, are waters through which we pass, leaving an old way of life and entering a new one, miraculously alive and cleansed. The baptismal "sea" will recur in the vision (Rev. 15:2). Later in St. John's vision we will see an altar in the place of worship.[2] The throne, the sea, and the altar are the glorious originals of the pulpit, font, and table in the house churches where St. John's congregations gathered week by week in their Lord's Day worship.

In the midst of this glory, St. John becomes aware that there is a sealed scroll and that "no one in heaven or on earth or under the earth was able to open the scroll or to look into it, and I wept much that no one was found worthy to open the scroll or to look into it" (Rev. 5:3–4). In the midst of the splendor, surrounded with this vitality, immersed in the act of worship that centered life and gathered all things before God, St. John was not satisfied: "I wept much."

"Scroll" to a first-century Christian would mean scripture. The scrolls they were most familiar with were the great scrolls of scripture in the synagogues. Scrolls were respected and valued. God's people believe that God speaks, that he tells us who he is and what he does. He is not a *deus absconditus* but a *deus revelatus*. His words are spoken to his people so that they will know his action for them, his will in them. And these words were written in scrolls. It is to be expected in the act of worship that a scroll will appear.

But the scroll is sealed. The text of the scrolls had been carefully, reverently, and meticulously preserved, but its meaning was sealed under centuries of argument and unbelief. It was an old problem. Seven hundred years earlier Isaiah had lamented that the vision was sealed up and no one was qualified to unseal it (Isa. 29:11–12). It was discussed but not believed; it was copied but not obeyed. One of the great excitements and glories of Christian worship was that the preaching of Christ unsealed the scrolls of scripture. Jesus in the Nazareth synagogue set the pattern: "And he stood up to read; and there was given to him the book of the prophet Isaiah. He opened the book . . . And he closed the book . . . And he began to say to them, 'Today this scripture has been fulfilled in your hearing'" (Luke 4:16–21). Jesus unsealed the scroll by revealing its present meaning, his inaugurating leadership in the kingdom of God, the good news.

St. Luke reports a repetition of the pattern a few years later. Philip met an Ethiopian reading the Isaiah scroll while traveling through Gaza. They conversed: "'Do you understand what you are reading?' . . . 'How can I unless someone guides me?'" (Acts 8:30–31). Then Philip taught him how to read in the way that he himself had been taught to read. He preached Christ to him, and Christ unsealed the scroll. The Ethiopian had been reading Isaiah 53. Philip identified Isaiah's "lamb" with "the good news of Jesus." Jesus Christ, the Lamb, unsealed the scroll, revealing the word of God so that it was understood personally and immediately. The perplexed traveler was no longer perplexed: he heard, believed, and was baptized. The Ethiopian took his place before the throne in worship and then "went on his way rejoicing" (Acts 8:39).

In the vision, the moment the Lamb takes the scroll, St. John's tears cease. The next sound is not weeping but a great redemption hymn, confident in worldwide salvation: "by thy blood didst ransom men for God" (Rev. 5:9). Scripture read and preached discovers that Christ (the Lamb) reveals the meaning of *my* life and fulfills my destiny. Without preaching, no matter how splendid the throne and how numerous the elders and creatures, there is no assurance that *I* am included and so the consequence is despair, enough to make a person weep. It is not enough to see the glorious throne, hear the wondrous songs, and realize the vast inclusions. If I do not discover that they include me, I will not praise but weep. If I cannot see myself among those who throw their crowns in reckless joy, shouting, I can only hang my head and weep.

St. John weeping is the emotional pivot in the act of worship. What about me? What about this world in which I live? How does this very inadequate sinner living in this very wicked world fit into all this? It does little good to know that God is holy if I am excluded from the holiness. Personal existence is called into question before the majesty and holiness of God; preaching answers the question. Preaching addresses the new-felt impoverishment of the person overwhelmed by signs of holy splendor. Preaching presents the personal word that invites participation in the adoration. Preaching rescues the word from its captivity in the sealed scroll and leads it out, proclaiming the "acceptable year of the Lord" (Luke 4:19). It makes plain that the great act of redemption includes *each* person in the glory: "Weep not; lo, the Lion of the tribe of Judah, the Root of David, has conquered, so that he can open the scroll and its seven seals." Worship is preaching; opening the scroll, reading out the gospel, inviting the sinner, demonstrating the personal dimensions of the eternal and glorious will of God. The Acts of the Apostles and the Letters of Paul are full of this preaching: the news of God had arrived – and it was good!

During the act of worship something has been happening to the worshipers: minds are cleared; perceptions come into focus; spirits are renewed. As this takes place, ordinary speech, impatient of pedestrian prose, dances – is condensed into poetry and then raised into tune. Worship sings. Singing is speech intensified and expanded. Song takes the natural rhythms and timbre of speech and develops its accents and intonations into music.

There are songs everywhere in scripture. The people of God sing. They express exuberance in realizing the majesty of God and the mercy of Christ, the wholeness of reality and their new-found ability to participate in it. Songs proliferate. Hymns gather the voices of men, women, and children into century-tiered choirs. Moses sings. Miriam sings. Deborah sings. David sings. Mary sings. Angels sing. Jesus and his disciples sing. Paul and Silas sing. When persons of faith become aware of who God is and what he does, they sing. The songs are irrepressible.

Five songs are sung in the act of worship described in Revelation 4 and 5, but song is not confined to those chapters. How could it be? Singing cannot be "kept in its place." Songs break out through the Revelation.[3] When the great judgment is visited on Babylon, the place of antiworship, song is silenced: "the sound of harpers and minstrels, of flute players and trumpeters, shall be heard in thee no more" (Rev. 18:22). The first five songs set the pattern for worship. The first two are hymns to God the Creator, the next two are hymns to Christ the Redeemer, the fifth is a hymn to Creator and Redeemer together, combining the themes that, like artesian waters, push through the surface into song whenever Christians worship.

The first song is adoration of the being of God. The three-lined hymn, each line consisting of three words or phrases, limns the wholeness of the godhead. All being is included in God. All reality is here. At the center everything is pure and powerful, personal and majestic, eternal and timely. The living creatures form a quartet to sing it:

> Holy, holy, holy
> Is Lord God Almighty
> The is, the was, the cometh

The second song connects our adoring responses with God's creating goodness. Who God is and what he does are related to how we are made and who we are. The representative elders who have experienced in Israel and in church the delight of being created, blessed, and led by such a God are the choir.

> Worthy! O Lord, Yes!
> Our God: take the glory!
> the honor! the power!
> You created all.
> All that exists is created.

The third song is to Christ, the Lamb of God. Praise now connects our adoring response with God's redeeming mercy. The opening line is the same as in the second song, but the theme shifts to redemption and our participation in it. The singers are the same choir of twenty-four elders who having praised a good creation now realize a miraculous redemption.

> Worthy! Take the book,
> open its seals.
> Slain, paying in blood, you
> purchased for God persons
> From each family and language and
> culture and race.
> Then you made them
> kingdom-priests for our God
> Priest-kings,
> They'll rule the earth.

The fourth song begins like the third but uses the ascription of the second and is sung by an uncountable company of angels. The new detail is that it is addressed to the redeeming Lamb. Redemption takes its place alongside creation.

> The slain lamb is worthy! Take the power,
> the wealth, the wisdom, the strength,
> the honor, the power, the blessing!

The fifth song, repeating "blessing and honor," joins the twin glories of creation (King) and redemption (Lamb) and lifts them in praise, enlisting the voices of all creatures plus the angels in the choir.

> For the King! for the Lamb!
> The blessing, the honor, the glory, the strength
> For age after age after age.

Persons who worship, sing. In the church's life hymnbooks are prayer books. Worship stirs deep responses of adoration which are formed into rhythms and melodies of gratitude, and enlists the voices of creatures from every corner and century, putting them tunefully to work in praise.

The last word in worship is amen: "and the four living creatures said, Amen! and the elders fell down and worshiped" (Rev. 5:14). Amen means "yes." It is the worshiping affirmation to the God who affirms us. God says yes to us. We respond to his yes by saying yes, amen. Worship is affirming.

The end result of the act of worship is that our lives are turned around. We come to God with a history of nay-saying, of rejecting and being rejected. At the throne of God we are immersed in God's yes, a yes that silences all our noes and calls forth an answering yes in us. God, not the ego, is the center. God is not someone around whom we make calculating qualifications, a little yes here, a little no there. In worship we "listen to the voice of Being" and become answers to it. The self is no longer the hub of reality, as sin seduces us into supposing. We are trained from infancy to relate to the world in an exploratory, exploitive way, refusing and grabbing, pushing and pulling, fretting and inveigling. As knower and user the ego is a predator. But in worship we cease being predators who by stealth approach everyone as prey that we can pull into our center; we respond to *the* center. We are privileged listeners and respondents who *offer* ourselves to God, who creates and redeems. Amen! Amen is recurrent and emphatic among God's people. It is robust and exuberant. There is nothing cowering, cautious, or timid in it. It is an answering word, purged of all negatives.

Justin Martyr in his description of Christian worship in the middle of the second century (c. 150 A.D.), tells us that prayers always concluded with a vigorous amen by the congregation. Justin uses a colorful and enthusiastic word to describe their amen — *epeuphēmei*, "shout in applause."[4] The word expressed the conviction that not only would prayers be fulfilled by God in the future, but that the fulfillment was already present in Christ. "All the promises of God," St. Paul had written, "find their Yes in [Christ]. That is why we utter the Amen through him to the glory of God" (2 Cor. 1:20).

Isaiah had given God the title "amen" (Isa. 65:16), and St. John gave Jesus the same title (Rev. 3:14). When the four living creatures shout their amen, they are making their own what has been made a reality for them by God.[5] Amen was often on our Lord's lips: "Amen, Amen, I say unto you" occurs no less than sixty-three times in the gospels. The German scholar Schlier concludes his study on the word *amen* by saying, "In the 'Amen' of Jesus the whole of Christology is contained in a nutshell."[6] When we Christians say or sing or shout, "amen," God hears our unequivocating assent to his irrevocable Yes to us, the Yes of our redeemer Lamb, the Yes of our creator King.

A second generation of gentile Christians tried for a time to translate the Hebrew *amen* into Greek. But the word *aleuthinos* lacked the affirmative robustness — literally it means "that which is not false" — and so they gave it up. They also abandoned the Septuagint *genoito*, which had been used to translate *amen* into Greek in the Old Testament. Its wistful tone, "would that it were so," missed the confident firmness of a present fulfillment. In a surprisingly short time there was consensus. Soon all were using Hebrew *amen* which Jesus himself had used.[7] Christians ever since have continued to use it to express a worshiping response to the deepest affirmations of their lives, echoing the amens of St. John's lion, ox, human and eagle.

The act of worship rehearses in the present the end that lies ahead.[8] Heaven is introduced into the present. It also, of course, conserves the past and so acts as a stabilizing force, but its dynamic function is anticipation: a community planning its future in the light of its charter. St. John's vision shows his congregations that what they are presently doing in worship corresponds to what presently takes place at the very heart of things, heaven.

The church at worship is centered and gathered at God's throne, receiving the revelation of the preached and preaching Christ, singing the great hymns, affirming and being affirmed. Details from this vision will be reintroduced as St. John's vision develops. This is the reality in which we participate in every act of worship, which shapes both our lives and our history.[9]

One common way to deflect St. John's vision from a revisioning in the present day believer is by feeling sorry for our first-century brothers and sisters in Christ. Politically and economically they had it rough; it is quite natural to feel sorry for them. But, natural or not, feeling sorry for them is the last thing we should do. It is fatal to the imagination. The exercise of pity, especially from a distance, engenders smugness: "Isn't it a shame that you are suffering so (but aren't I lucky to have escaped!)" Pity is almost always a condescending emotion, for it puts us in a superior position to the persons we are feeling sorry for at the very moment that they are most likely to be *our* superiors—when they are in a position to give us what we most need.

Nothing could be farther from the truth than to imagine the Christians in those seven Asian congregations as huddling wretches, holding on to the faith by their fingernails, with St. John, their pastor, reaching frantically for a desperate means (apocalypse!) to secure their endurance through the worst of times. These men and women from the moment of their baptism in the name of the Trinity, knew their lives as miracles of resurrection. The people who gathered each Lord's Day to sing their Lord's praises and receive his life were the most robust in the Roman empire. They were immersed in splendors. They brimmed with life. Even when their zeal cooled, as it sometimes did, and their taut loyalties went a little slack, as sometimes happened, there was far more going on in their lives than in the Babylon-seduced lives of their contemporaries. And they knew it. When they forgot, St. John reminded them. We must never forget that the pictures of wildly celebrative praise in heaven and catastrophic woes wreaked on earth, the exposure of evil in its hideous blasphemies and the revelation of goodness in its glorious adorations—that all this was made out of the stuff of their daily traffic in scripture, baptism, and eucharist. In this heaven-penetrated, hell-threatened environment they lived their daily lives. Nothing outside of faith or defiant of faith could equal it for depth of meaning and drama of incident. There cannot have been many dull moments in those lives, nor need there be in ours. When dull moments did come, they were recognized as the work of the devil and were chased by the apocalypse-informed imagination at worship.

"Many a congregation when it assembles in church must look to the angels like a muddy puddly shore at low tide; littered with every kind of rubbish and odds and ends—a distressing sort of spectacle. And then the tide of worship comes in, and it's all gone: the dead sea urchins and jellyfish, the paper and the empty cans and the nameless bits of rubbish. The cleansing sea flows over the whole lot. So we are released from a narrow selfish outlook on the universe by a common act of worship."[10]

6. The Last Word on Evil
Revelation 6 and 7

We do not see our signs;
   there is no longer any prophet,
   and there is none among us who knows how long.
How long, O God, is the foe to scoff?
   Is the enemy to revile thy name for ever?
Why dost thou hold back thy hand,
   Why dost thou keep thy right hand in thy bosom?

PSALM 74:9–11

Then one of the elders addressed me, saying, 'Who are these, clothed in
white robes, and whence have they come?' I said to him, 'Sir, you know.'
And he said to me, 'These are they who have come out of the great tribulation; they have washed their robes and made them white in the blood of
the lamb.

REVELATION 7:13–14

I find it most true, that the greatest temptation out of hell is to live without
temptations. If my waters should stand, they would rot. Faith is the better
of the free air, and of the sharp winter storm in its face. Grace withereth
without adversity. The devil is but God's master fencer, to teach us to handle our weapons.

SAMUEL RUTHERFORD

The puzzling ascendancy of evil must have occupied many Christian minds at the time of St. John's exile. If the kingdom of God has
been inaugurated by Christ, why are Roman armies so much in evidence? The gospel declared God's love for the world; Roman
decrees put the people who believed it in prisons and on crosses.
Christ lived, suffered, died, and rose again – and the world was getting worse, not better. Annie Dillard asks the question that presses
for an answer in this kind of world – she ranks it as the chief theological question of all time – "What in the Sam Hill is going on here
anyway?"[1]

St. John takes up the question, but he won't be stampeded into a response. The question of evil clamors for an answer, but it is not the first question. When we experience evil in any form it is felt as total. It blots out everything else. A toothache eliminates awareness of health in every other part of the body. A sore toe makes it impossible to appreciate the wonderful fact that my elbow bends effortlessly.

No response is ventured to the question of ascendant evil until there is firm rooting in a far more comprehensive reality. St. John doesn't broach the business until he has presented first the vision of the victorious Christ (Rev. 1), then the triumphant worship (Rev. 4-5), and linked them with the everyday exigencies of the church messages (Rev. 2-3). Is it not clear that the magnificent ruling Christ towers over everything? Is it not also clear that Christ not only towers *over* but sees *into* the detailed conditions of the faith communities, is completely conversant with their virtues and failures, and cares for them? And is it not now indisputably clear that through worship there is an immersion in the centering reality of God's rule and redemption? Christ is the person in whom God's will is victoriously accomplished. The church is the community in which we know and are known by God. Worship is the action by which we practice and enjoy the presence of the creating and redeeming God. St. John takes his time. Twenty percent of the Revelation is written before he turns to the question of evil in history—the pain and wickedness that are everywhere and so distressingly evident politically, socially, and personally.

In the midst of the great act of worship, St. John had wept because there was no one to unseal the scroll and proclaim God's word personally to him (Rev. 5:4). Then Jesus Christ, in the form of the Lamb, came forward to unseal the scroll, that is, to preach to him. Immediately his weeping ceased: God reveals his word as Christ preaches to us. Is there meaning in the evil chaos of history? We hope there is a clue tucked away in the rubble. The unsealing of the scroll—the revelation of Jesus Christ whereby God's will is known among us—is a proclamation of this good news in the midst of history. There is a correspondence between what is going on in the midst of worship and what is going on in the midst of history, and Jesus Christ, unsealing the scroll, provides it. We do not have to wait for a future revelation to find the meaning. We do not have to unravel a puzzle to figure out the meaning. It is *presented* to us. And Christ is the one who presents it.

History tumbles out a mass of data—wars, famines, murders, and accidents—along with sunrises and still waters, lilies of the field and green pastures. God's people have been convinced that it is possible in prayer and praise, in listening and believing, to discern meaning in this apparent chaos and therefore to read good news in the daily life of history. The means by which this is done is through the proclamation of Jesus Christ, the Lamb slain from the foundation of the world. "We do not need Christ to tell us that the world is full of trouble. But we do need his explanation of history if its troubles are not to be meaningless."[2] In his life, death, and resurrection history comes to focus.

St. John's vision presents Jesus proclaiming God's meaning in a seven point sermon. As each seal, in turn, is broken, another aspect of God's meaning is presented so that, item by item, the materials of history are ordered and arranged and good news is comprehended. The first four unsealings show, in sequence, four horses. The horse is the animal for battle: oxen for farming, donkeys for transportation, horses for battle. The basic nature of history is warfare. Persons who live by faith live in conflict. History is a long sequence of battles—the forces of good and evil in pitched conflict. Sensitive persons know this. Artists know this. Students of history lay bare the documenting sources. People of prayer are in the middle of it even when the guns are silent. The battle rages within the soul; it is fought out in family circles; it is contested between nations. War is the human condition. To be human is to be at war.

If there is no preaching, this history which is warfare is sheer evil. God may be in heaven but the devil runs history. Nice guys finish last. Ivan, the atheist brother in Dostoevsky's Karamazov family, kept a notebook in which he entered every horrible atrocity he learned of or heard of: the notebook was his laboratory for proving the nonexistence of God.[3] Ivan's notebook is a perennial bestseller. The question every person of faith must face is, Do God's love and redemption *work* in this history in which I live? Or do they only function on a transcendental plane apart from my daily life so that I must develop another plane of consciousness to reach into them, but then return to the ordinary things of life and make do with them as best I can? Or is God's love and redemption something that is ahead and will be accomplished in the future, while I must put up with things as they are and use whatever survival techniques I can acquire to keep myself alive and in faith until the time comes? Or is it all working right now? Are war and famine and sickness the supreme realities? Or are peace and bounty and health at the heart of things? These are the questions that preaching answers. Jesus' sermon comprehends all sermons in its seven seal outline.

The first element in the war which is history is Christ: "And I saw, and behold, a white horse, and its rider had a bow; and a crown was given to him, and he went out conquering and to conquer." Christ is in history ruling and conquering. The only way to understand history is to begin, openly and firmly, with Christ. Christ is the first word. Whatever the subject, we begin with Christ. He is the Alpha in the alphabet of historical discourse. He is not an afterthought brought in as a rescue operation after sin has done its worst.

The favorite psalm in the early Christian community was the Psalm 110: "The Lord sends forth from Zion your mighty scepter. Rule in the midst of your foes! . . . The Lord is at your right hand; he will shatter kings on the day of his wrath." Biblical Christians do not sentimentalize Christ. There is fierceness and militancy here. The world is in conflict; our Christ is the first on the field of battle. High issues are decided every day. Christ is not only worshiped each Sunday, he is triumphant each week day. That, of course, is not the way the newspapers report it; that is not the way our own emotions respond to it; but that is what the preached revelation proclaims.

The rider on the white horse reappears in Revelation 19, verse 11: "Then I saw heaven opened, and behold, a white horse! He who sat upon it is called Faithful and True, and in righteousness he judges and makes war." Throughout the Revelation, which is to say, throughout history, this Christ is leading the hosts of salvation across daily fields of battle "conquering and to conquer."

It is quite true that this white horse is a product of the believing visionary imagination, and not an observed historical item. Neither Gibbon nor Toynbee gave so much as a single line to it. The forms under which the Christ conquers are the Palm Sunday donkey, the slain Paschal Lamb, and the failed messiah, mocked and crucified. But it is precisely these forms that are realized in faith as conquering. Christ has not changed his way of working. The white horse is not a signal that Christ has given up on donkeys and lambs and crosses and is now taking up with horses and spears and scepters. Rather it is a validation that the means Christ has chosen to accomplish his will and work out his salvation are, in fact, and against appearances, victorious.

The preaching continues by assembling before Christ all that opposes Christ. A vision of Christ is not sufficient to sustain a life of faith if there is no accounting of how the vision fares in the rough and tumble of the world. In preaching, Christ moves from the place of worship into the arena of history where lions and gladiators defy and deny God. Everywhere there are persons and groups bent on destroying a good creation: killing and mutilating living beings, exploiting a bountiful earth, crippling and weakening precious bodies. The world as we observe it is shot through with evil. The evil is summarized in the three horsemen of war (red horse), famine (black horse), and sickness unto death (pale horse). War is social evil; famine is ecological evil; sickness is biological evil. War attacks the goodness of community; famine violates and ravages God's bounty; sickness destroys and wastes God-given bodies: sins against society, sins against the land, sins against the body.

Each of these evils is common, but each is also disguised so that we culturally accept its presence as something normal, even good. War is disguised as patriotism and a glorious struggle for freedom. Famine is disguised as a higher standard of living. Sickness is disguised by technology. Evil introduces, by turns, conflict, greed, and deceit into social and personal existence and undoes creation, subverting its purpose and contradicting its design of redemption. These evils present such a benign appearance in their disguises that the world unthinkingly accepts them as the forces of history, to which Christ is a lovely but essentially ineffective minority protest.

War is dressed up in the Sunday best of "competition." We are trained from an early age to get what we want not in cooperation with others but in competition against them. The means are essentially violent, whether physical or psychological, weapons or propaganda. I want what my brother has, I covet what my sister owns, I envy who my neighbor is. I set out to satisfy myself by whatever means are present to my hand. Not for long does that other person (or nation) retain a name or identity. Each is labeled as an obstacle, an obstruction, or alien force to be overcome. "What causes wars, and what causes fightings among you? Is it not your passions that are at war in your members? You desire and do not have; so you kill. And you covet and cannot obtain; so you fight and wage war" (James 4:1-2). An accumulation of these actions, from time to time, achieves critical mass and the world goes to war. For a time, writ large in the headlines, war is perceived as an evil, and there are prayers for peace. But not for long, for it is quickly glamorized as patriotic or rationalized as just. But war is a red horse, bloody and cruel, making life miserable and horrid. It is the action of power-hungry persons; it is the delusion of insane pride; it is an expression of greed gone crazy. But nothing evil has the staying power of goodness. The energy of evil cannot sustain itself for long: it loses momentum, totters, stops. Peace treaties are signed, or labor contracts ratified, or divorce settlements arbitrated. There are handshakes all around. Overt war slips into the background of everyday affairs where it continues a less energetic but still killing work under the admired forms of competition and acquisition, and undercover builds up momentum for its next outbreak.

The perennial ruse is to glorify war so that we accept it as a proper means of achieving goals. But it is evil. It is opposed by Christ. Christ does not sit on the red horse, ever. When Jesus said that he came to bring not peace but a sword he was talking of the peace that allows persons to vegetate in sins and the sword that separates us from them. No—war is hell. War is evil. In a world where persons refuse God's lordship and reject Christ's salvation, war is the route to achieve mastery and discover glory. But always and everywhere Christ is in battle against it. And the white horse will conquer the red horse.

Famine insinuates itself among us under all forms of achieving a higher standard of living. Famine is nature out of balance. The necessities are scarce while the luxuries are mockingly in abundance. The rider of the black horse carries a balance in his hand. A voice is heard: "A quart of wheat for a denarius and three quarts of barley for a denarius, but do not harm the oil and wine!" A quart of wheat is starvation rations for a family and a denarius is a day's wage. What is necessary for minimal living is unavailable while the luxuries of life, oil and wine, are abundant. Greed does it. People exploit the earth, leaving it depleted and poor, in order to get rich. The greed is glorified under the sacrosanct phrase "higher standard of living" and used to excuse everyday insanity. We put millions of people to work at idiot jobs to make machines that pollute the air we breathe, so that we can move rapidly from one place to another in projectiles at lethal speeds (killing and maiming other millions—more than have died in all the wars ever fought on the earth) so that we have more time to sit before outrageously priced electronic devices that flicker with forms of flesh fantasies that attempt to convince us (usually successfully) that we must have oil and wine luxuries for which we must go back to the idiot jobs to make the lethal machines.

Famine is the condition in which we have most of what we don't need and almost nothing of what we do need. Paul Goodman clarifies the evil: "What do we need? We don't need constant stimulation, poisoned food, carcinogenic air, useless work for which we are highly paid."[4] Who believes that there is a famine in the land? Not many, but there is. At certain places on the globe, the imbalance and greed conspire so that the famine is obvious to all—the malnutrition and starvation can be photographed. But the bloated bellies and spindly limbs that are literal fact for some are a gruesome parody of the lives of most others.

The rider on the black horse does his work. But the rider on the white horse also does his. The Lord who teaches us to pray, "Give us this day our daily bread" is at work restoring the earth and the people in it to balanced sanity. He brings his people to a weekly eucharistic meal that trains them to live by grace and not by greed.

Sickness is disguised by technology. This evil insinuates itself into our lives in the widespread glorification of technology with its corollary depreciation of human health. The machine is more important than the body. We atrophy our legs by immobilizing them in an automobile for several hours a week. We drug our minds and nerves by dosing them with narcotics and stimulants in appalling quantities. And then we think we have access to health because we can go to a modern hospital when we hurt or malfunction. The gigantic medical facilities that are the new cathedrals of our society are not signs of health, but of sickness— only an unprecedentedly sick society would provide a market for such complexes.

Our bodies are systematically abused so that they no longer function easily and naturally as temples of the Holy Spirit. The anxiety and tension that are accepted as the necessary price for living in a technological world diminish our capacity to live at the same time that they produce incentives for living. We accept the myth that the most important thing to do with our bodies is to put them to work to make money or achieve reputations. Sickness increases. The rider on the pale horse represents pestilence— epidemic disease, the sickness unto death. The incidence of disease and sickness rises exponentially while, mockingly, the size of our hospitals increases and medical technology becomes more and more refined. The modern nations with the greatest access to medical technique are the sickest.[5]

Sickness is the condition in which our bodies are weakened or impaired so that they no longer are effective as temples of holiness shaping rituals of love and witness. One of the most conspicuous features in Christ's conquering ministry was healing: the body is holy, even as the land is holy, and the community is holy. The healings continue. The pestilential pale horse makes his mark in history, but healings have the last word. The final healing is resurrection.

The four horsemen are brought out on the field of history by the imperative "Come!" commanded from the throne: in acts of worship the battle is joined. The preached and conquering Christ rips the respectable disguises off the three evil horsemen and forces them to show their true colors: the red horse of war butchering the community of love and trust; the black horse of famine draining the color out of life; the pale horse of sickness emptying vitality from humanity. "Come!" Be in contest with the white-horsed Christ who will do battle and conquer, overcoming strife, restoring the land, healing our bodies. The evil in people and lands and bodies is unmasked for what it is, faced and fought. It is three against one, an unfair fight it would seem. By our calculations there is little chance for victory.

There is more. There is both a narrower and a wider dimension of evil to take into account. The narrower dimension is the evil of religious persecution, shown in the fifth unsealing (Rev. 6:9–11); the wider is the evil of natural catastrophe shown in the sixth (Rev. 6:12–17). Persecution is narrower because it is suffered only by the minority who live by faith. It is the affliction that comes because of, and only because of, identity as God's people. Catastrophe is wider in the sense that nature is more inclusive than history, including animals as well as people, primitive tribes as well as sophisticated civilizations, the innocent along with the guilty. A pogrom is selective, an earthquake promiscuous. Persecution is focused, catastrophe indiscriminate.

Suffering the evil of persecution, the meek of the earth cry out "How long?" These little ones (see Matt. 18:10–14) are promised that in a short time God will judge and avenge their persecutors. Caught in the evil of catastrophe, the mighty of the earth cry out "No longer!" These great ones learn that power and status provide no exemption from the common lot and that in judgment there is no delay.

The believing imagination has now been provided with images that account for every aspect of evil: social strife, ecological disaster, sickness unto death, religious persecution, natural catastrophe. Nothing that we experience as evil is unnoticed or unacknowledged. It is all out in the open, included in the preached meaning of history. Christians do not shut their eyes to the world's cruelty in themselves or others. St. John has trained us to be especially attentive to it, to name it with honesty—no euphemisms, no evasions—and deal with it courageously. Despite the numerous caricatures of pious people who stubbornly shut their eyes to the cruelties all around them lest they be disturbed in their heavenly meditations, and despite the uncontested innocence of some who seem to remain naively happy in their belief that the world is a mighty fine place after all, my own conviction is that Christians, for the most part, are the very persons in our society who can be counted on to have no illusions about the depth of depravity in themselves or in the world at large. No other community of people has insisted so consistently through the centuries on calling evil by its right name. No other community has so mercilessly exposed its rationalizations, nor so courageously confessed its own complicity. With admitted exceptions, the faith community knows more about what is wrong with the world than any other, and is, at the same time, less cynical or despairing about it.

Revelation 6 ends with a question that must be answered, although we do not really expect an answer. The question is rhetorical and assumes a negative response: "Who can stand?" Why, of course, no one. The end of the world has come. History is falling apart at the seams. Everything that was supposed to be fixed is loose. The once solid earth is treacherous with fissures and crevasses. The mathematically precise movements of sun, moon, and stars are in chaos. Everything by which humanity gets its bearings is gone. There is no one capable of standing upright under such conditions: no king, no general, no athlete. Who can stand? Not one. "If the foundations are destroyed, what can the righteous do?" (Ps. 11:3).

The question does not expect an answer. We already know the answer. But it gets an answer—and the answer is a surprise. The giving of the answer is so urgent and of such moment that the seventh unsealing is delayed until the answer is given in full. Who can stand? The angels can. The angels are God's messengers who carry out his commands and deliver his counsel. *They* stand. They are not intimidated by the evil horsemen on the fields of history or undone by the plaintive cries from under the altar, or confused by the anarchy in the skies of the cosmos. Evil does not dismay them. Evil does not enervate them. The whole machinery of providence and redemption remains intact. Evil—devastating as it appears—causes no flutter of fear or stumbling hesitation among the angels. They stand their ground (Rev. 7:1, 11).

And a "multitude which no man could number" stands (Rev. 7:9). The identifying signs (Rev. 7:9–10) show them to be Christians. This is the big surprise. Christians appear to be a sorry minority. What with war, famine, pestilence, persecution, and catastrophe, with attendant defections, the ranks get pretty well decimated. There are moments of pageantry, to be sure. There are times when everyone agrees for a day or so to sing and celebrate. Then there is the return to what, by some linguistic trick of the devil, we have agreed to call the "real world"—the world of pride and persecution, disease and disaster. The intricately filigreed life of faith is set aside in exchange for a makeshift affair cobbled together by the devil out of power, status, guns, and self-help. But that is not the real world. That world is doomed and dying. It is a world in which the last despairing word is "Who can stand?" St. John sees and hears another reality, less visible but more solid, that is already in existence and into which no evil can penetrate. It is the Christian reality, the life of faith.

Revelation 6 and 7 are connected by question and answer. Who can stand in this world of evil? The Christian can stand. The chapters are connected in another way, by the word *seal*. In Revelation 6 the seals are opened by Christ, and the unsealings show the contents of history. The contents are frightful, exceeding the private experience of any single person. In Revelation 7, the unsealings are more than matched by sealings that protect persons of faith from the eternal consequences of historical evil. For no evil was permitted until "we have sealed the servants of our God upon their foreheads" (Rev. 7:3). The sealing is inclusive: every person from every tribe. The number, 144,000 is, as most numbers are in the Revelation, symbolic, and what it symbolizes is a vast, thorough-going completeness. The millions who believingly prayed, "no evil shall befall you, no scourge come near your tent" (Ps. 91:10) are in the number. Other millions who trustingly sang "The Lord will keep you from all evil; he will keep your life" (Ps. 121:7) are also in the number.

These are not the first sealings in scripture. Old Testament Ezekiel (Ezek. 9) and Intertestamental Enoch (En. 66) give sealings against grievous judgments let loose in the world. More significant for Christians is St. Paul's "In him you also, who have heard the word of truth, the gospel of your salvation, and have believed in him, were sealed with the promised Holy Spirit, which is the guarantee of our inheritance until we acquire possession of it, to the praise of his glory" (Eph. 1:13–14, 4:30).

St. Paul combines the two symbols, stand and sealed, in his letter to the Corinthians: "He who makes firm our *standing* in the Anointed, and who has anointed us, is God; who has *sealed* us also, and set the earnest of the Spirit in our hearts" (2 Cor. 1:21–22, Austin Farrer's translation). In the light of this background, familiar to biblically literate readers, the impact of Revelation 7 is felt in the *present* experience of believers. It is in the midst of experienced historical evil that we are protected (sealed). Many read this as a description of heavenly bliss. I find that highly unlikely. St. John's vision enlarges the imagination to comprehend what Ezekiel and Enoch and St. Paul witnessed: we are protected from the God-separating effects of evil even as we experience the suffering caused by evil.

There are parallel visions in Revelation 7, the 144,000 (Rev. 7:4–8) and the "multitude which no man could number" (Rev. 7:9). They are the same people. Rhymed repetition is a favorite device among poets to achieve emphasis. The art of rhyme is to nearly but not quite duplicate sound. The near-identity of sound provides emphasis; the slight difference in sound heightens awareness of meaning. The rhyming of sounds is a commonplace in poetry. Hebrew poets (who are the ones St. John grew up with) rhymed not sounds but meanings. They put alongside one another not attention-getting sounds but awareness-evoking meanings. The sentence in Psalm 34:3 is typical: "O magnify the Lord with me,/and let us exalt his name together!" There are three rhymed meanings: exalt/magnify, the Lord/his name, with me/together. St. John does this too, but he rhymes visions, as, for instance, in Revelation 7: two parallel pictures, like enough to provide emphasis by repetition, different enough to tease the mind into active participation. He is providing us a picture of what happens to persons who live by faith in a world noisy with evil.

St. John *hears* the number of the sealed as 144,000. When he looks, he *sees* a multitude that no man can number. Sound is "rhymed" with sight. People who live by faith in Jesus Christ are protectively sealed against evil by the Spirit. St. John hears God's declaration of the total number—absolutely complete, not a single one missing, the all-inclusive 144,000 (12 squared, then multiplied). When he himself looks, he sees that this definite total known to God is a numberless multitude beyond calculation from any human point of view. Similarly, these people are all Israel, that is, God's people from his standpoint; from our standpoint, they come from "every nation under heaven."

These people are not only secure, they are exuberant. This is a curious, but wholly biblical, phenomenon: the most frightening representations of evil (Rev. 6) are set alongside extravagant praise (Rev. 7). Christians sing. They sing in the desert, they sing in the night, they sing in prison, they sing in the storm. How they sing! (Rev. 7:10, 12, 15–17). The songs of the vision are the response to the statistics of evil. Any evil, no matter how fearsome, is exposed as weak and pedantic before such songs. "At Assisi once, when a theologian attacked Fra Egidio by the usual formal arrangement of syllogisms, the brother waited until the conclusions were laid down, and then, taking out a flute from the folds of his robe, he played his answer in rustic melodies."[6]

One more detail: in any enumeration of a series, the first and last numbers are most important. In the seven seals which, as a whole, show the evil that is experienced in history, the first seal is a revelation of Christ triumphant over evil, and the seventh is a revelation of the attentive silence in heaven in which the prayers of every believer are carefully heard and answered (Rev. 8:1–4). All evil takes place between that beginning and ending. Evil is contained.

Evil is not minimized, but it is put in its place, bracketed between Christ and prayer. There is a detailed listing of evil and a courageous facing of evil, but no explanation of it. Nowhere in the Bible is there any attempt to answer the question, "Why does a good God permit evil?" Evil is a fact. The Bible spends a good deal of space insisting that certain facts are evil, and not minor blemishes on the surface of existence. But the Bible does not provide an explanation of evil—rather, it defines a context: all evil takes place in an historical arena bounded by Christ and prayer. Evil is not explained but surrounded. The Revelation summarizes the context: admit evil and do not fear it—for "he who is in you is greater than he who is in the world" (I John 4:4); endure evil, for you are already triumphant over it— "I saw Satan fall like lightning from heaven" (Luke 10:18). The Revelation expands the apostolic and dominical words into visions. By putting evil in its place and enumerating it accurately in the precise part of the story where it belongs, it is seen as finite episode and not a total triumph.

I was teaching this passage to a small group of people a number of years ago, and one of the members of the group, suddenly realizing its relevance, asked if she could tell her story. Years previously, she told us, she had had a nervous breakdown. Her whole life was in chaos. Nothing fit together. She could see no meaning in anything. She felt overwhelmed by evil, and guilt, and sheer bad luck. She went to a counselor and was guided by him to take a good look at each detail that she had lumped into a large pile and called "evil." Item by item the feelings and events and actions were examined. Not one of them, she said, became any less horrible or less palatable as she did that. But something else happened while she was doing it. She began to discover other items in her life that had been obscured by the great lump of piled-up wrongs: relationships that were delightful, songs that were ravishing, sights that were heart-stopping. She began to experience the wonder of her own body and how much of it was working well. She began to trust the integrity of her own feelings and how valuable they were. She began to realize the preciousness of other lives and ways she could appreciate them. Later she came to know God, and the entire world that she now recognized in Revelation 7, came into focus for her. None of the evil was abolished, but it was all in a defined perspective. The nameless evils had names. The numberless wrongs were numbered. She was hardly aware of the point at which the proportions shifted, but now it was the good that seemed endless, and the glories that were beyond counting. Nothing in her life had changed; everything in her life was changed. She wondered if something similar might not happen under the influence of St. John's guiding imagination.

7. The Last Word on Prayer
Revelation 8 and 9

I call upon thee, O Lord; make haste to me!
  Give ear to my voice, when I call to thee!
Let my prayer be counted as incense before thee,
  and the lifting up of my hands as an evening sacrifice!

PSALM 141:1-2

And another angel came and stood at the altar with a golden censer; and he was given much incense to mingle with the prayers of all the saints upon the golden altar before the throne; and the smoke of the incense rose with the prayers of the saints from the hand of the angel before God.

REVELATION 8:3-4

The real power of prayer in history is not a fusillade of praying units of whom Christ is the chief, but it is the corporate action of a Saviour-Intercessor and His community, a volume and energy of prayer organized in a Holy Spirit and in the Church the Spirit creates. The saints shall thus judge the world and control life. Neither for the individual nor for the Church is true prayer an enclave in life's larger and more actual course. It is not a sacred enclosure, a lodge in some vast wilderness. That is the weak side of pietism.

P. T. FORSYTH

The Apocalypse is a fusion of vision and prayer. When the seventh seal is opened, there is silence in heaven for about half an hour. A climax has been reached. The silence prepares the imagination to receive an incredible truth. While conflicts raged between good and evil, prayers went up from devout bands of first century Christians all over the Roman empire. Massive engines of persecution and scorn were ranged against them. They had neither weapons nor votes. They had little money and no prestige. Why didn't they have mental breakdowns? Why didn't they cut and run? They prayed.

It was in order to hear those prayers that there was silence in heaven. Out of the silence, action developed: an angel came before the altar of God with a censer. He mixed the prayers of the Christians with incense (which cleansed them from impurities) and combined them with fire (God's spirit) from the altar. Then he put it all in the censer and threw it over heaven's ramparts. The censer, plummeting through the air, landed on earth. On impact there were "peals of thunder, voices, flashes of lightning, and an earthquake" (Rev. 8:5). The prayers which had ascended, unremarked by the journalists of the day, returned with immense force—in George Herbert's phrase, as "reversed thunder."[1] Prayer reenters history with incalculable effects. Our earth is shaken daily by it.

The vision convinces the Christian of the potencies of prayer. Prayer is access to an environment in which God is the pivotal center of action. All other persons, events, or circumstances are third parties. Existence is illuminated in direct relationship to God himself. Neither bane nor blessing distracts from this center. Persons who pray are not misled by demons of size, influence, importance, or power. They turn their backs on the gaudy pantheons of Canaan and Assyria, Greece and Rome, and give themselves to the personal intensities that become awe before God and in intimacy with God. And they change the world.

St. John describes himself at the opening of the Revelation under two conditions: "on the island called Patmos" and "in the Spirit on the Lord's Day." "On the island called Patmos" St. John was exiled. He was isolated. He was removed from help and solace. He was prisoner. A faceless bureaucracy to which he had no access spoke the determining words and carried out the orders that defined his environment and the conditions of his life. His freedom disappeared at the stroke of a magistrate's pen. He was no longer permitted to do the work in which he was passionately involved. No more conversations with dear brothers and sisters over an Isaiah parchment; no more shared eucharistic celebrations in the homes of his courageous companions in faith; no more visits to the sick and dying to comfort them with the words of their Lord; no more ladeling out cups of cold water to thirsty travelers in faith's way. Exile.

Exile is the experience of powerlessness, *in extremis*. Everything is determined by another. We are removed from where we want to be and whom we want to be with. We are isolated from place and persons. We are victims. The worst punishment possible in ancient Israel was banishment. To be separated from family and country, from community worship and family faith—that was the cruelist decree. The severest judgment that the nation experienced was exile to Babylonia. A person created for personal relationships of love cannot live adequately without them. Exile dehumanizes. It sentences us to death by bread alone. "On the island called Patmos" Rome showed St. John who was in charge. Every lonely hour on the barren rock was proof that Rome determined St. John's destiny, that Rome's word was the final word on his life, that Rome's decree set the limits within which he was permitted to exist. St. John was alone, powerless, and bereft.

"In the Spirit of the Lord's Day" meant something quite different. "In the Spirit" meant that St. John knew himself to be in touch and participant with all the energy of the Godhead. At the very time that he was *on* Patmos he was *in* the Spirit. "I came to be in spirit" is a more literal rendering (*egenomen en pneumati*).[2] The man was praying. St. John was no longer, if in fact he ever was, thinking about God, or talking about God; he was attending *to* God. He "came to be in spirit." He was now in that condition in which God's word was a personal address to him, in which God's vision was a personal revelation to him. Praying is that act in the life of faith which consciously and deliberately enters into a speaking/listening attentiveness before God—his relationship with his creation and creatures and their relationship with him. Whenever we concentrate, focus, and attend, we pray. Prayer is the coming into awareness, the practicing of attention, the nurturing and development of personal intensity before God.

Throughout the Revelation (throughout the Bible!) God takes the initiative. He speaks. He shows. He commands. He blesses. If there is to be a completion to the process of communication, there must be someone to see and hear what God presents and speaks. There must be, in other words, a person who prays. St. John did not see and hear what he wrote in the Revelation by sitting around on a

Sunday without anything to do, waiting for something interesting to show up. He was *praying*. He was in a prepared posture of receptivity before God.

Prayer is language used to address God, not explain him or report on him. It is answering speech. The task of the gospel is to move us away from talking about God to talking to him. In this concluding installment of scripture the movement is accomplished: St. John is on his knees. In this position he is responsive in a quite different way to a much different word than the one that put him on Patmos: "I saw . . . I heard."

Prayer combines the experiences of being "on Patmos" and being "in the Spirit." It is the realization of personal powerlessness and, at the same moment, participation in God's power: I can do nothing, God can do anything. Until we come to the place of exile we are not minded to undergo the disciplined quietness and passionate waiting that bring us to the point of hearing, seeing, and receiving God's fullness. The seeing and hearing that go into the Revelation only come to the person who prays. True knowledge of God is never knowledge about God; it is always relation with God. When the Revelation concludes, St. John is still praying: "Amen. Come, Lord Jesus!" (Rev. 22:20).

"Lord's Day" provides a center for prayer. The word, for St. John, means Sunday, the day of resurrection and the Christian's bright "first day." But most people in the first-century Roman empire would have understood the word to refer to the emperor's feast.[3] It was not the first time, nor would it be the last, that Christians appropriated a pagan word and transformed its meaning.

A new center was necessary. Jerusalem, the millennium-old center for worship, had been destroyed by pagan arrogance. The vaunted laws of the Roman empire had decreed the Christian to be a criminal. The *pax Romana* had become, for persons of faith, persecution to the death. Conditions in some parts of the empire were nightmarish. The extravagant beast-images of the Revelation do not exaggerate. The world was topsy-turvy. Many a Christian would pray Psalm 55: "My heart is in anguish within me, the terrors of death have fallen upon me. Fear and trembling come upon

me, and horror overwhelms me. And I say, 'O that I had wings like
a dove! I would fly away and be at rest; yea, I would wander afar,
I would lodge in the wilderness, I would haste to find me a shelter
from the raging wind and tempest.' "

"Lord's Day," the day of the emperor's feast when the rule of Rome
was praised for holding the world together in peace and justice,
was a joke for the Christian. But did that mean that peace and justice were a joke? As Christians prayed, "Lord's Day" acquired a new
meaning: the first day of the week, the day of resurrection, a day
to begin a new cycle of prayer in which God's first words in the Genesis week, "Let there be light," imposed order on the old chaos.

All of us are subject to jarring inconsistencies and dislocating contradictions. We are disoriented and stagger dizzily under the impact
of accidents and disappointments. If that is all we are conscious of
we go crazy and live in bedlam. We maintain sanity by living in
response to that which keeps us alive: food and trust, love and shelter, clothing and forgiveness, work and leisure. The exteriors and
interiors of life cohere. The clamoring needs within and the
imposed necessities without find their place in a hierarchy of providence. Prayer discovers the coordination of all needs under the mastery of the one who supplies all needs. Prayer is a focus upon God
whereby all things come into focus. By centering attention on God
the center, all things become centered. Life is not indiscriminate
bits and pieces, mingled treasure and rubble. It is coherent.

The literary art of the Revelation is itself a triumph of coherence
over chaos. The least attentive reader is aware that terrifying violence and bewildered questions have been arranged by St. John in
intricate patterns of awesome beauty and surging energy. The
arrangement is no more complex than the material requires, but
the material is, in fact, endlessly complex. History is not simple.
It cannot be subsumed under a slogan. There is diversity and
mystery.

The everyday data of a typical week are assembled on the pages
of the Revelation: political terrors and liturgical mysteries, painful
separations and unanswered prayers, glorious hymns and
unfulfilled prophecies, felt glories and brutal cruelties, heartrend-

ing deaths and unquenchable hopes. All this is the experience of persons who decide to live by faith in Christ. St. John's Revelation choreographs all this in a ballet of images. The repeated use of the number seven, a number that communicated a sense of wholeness to the ancient and biblical mind, sets up cadences of wholeness in the imagination. "Lord's Day" is the first day of resurrection in which the fallen creation enters a new week of redemption.

The pagan world assigned each day of the week to the care of a god or goddess. Each divinity made its own capricious demands and dispensed good or ill arbitrarily. The pagan deities were at odds with each other, bickering and quarreling. The week was a hodgepodge of scheming and intrigue. The Christian, in contrast, discovered all time under the lordship of Christ. Time is redeemed. God shapes creation; Christ redeems creation. The first day is the headwaters of the ever rolling stream of time. The Lord's Day is the source for the succeeding days. All the events and experiences of the week flow out of the archetypal patterns of creation and redemption.

Attempting to find meaning in a week of days, each of which is ruled by different and quarreling divinities, is like attempting to write a letter on a typewriter and discovering that there are 26 typewriters, each with a single key, distributed throughout a city. To write my letter, I have to go to one office to get the "a" typed, to another for the "r" and to a third for the "t." One day I show up at the office of the "r" typewriter and find the owner on vacation for two weeks. Another time I go to the place of the "o" typewriter and discover that the secretary has raised her fee and that I am without sufficient funds.

To make a rational petition or formulate an adequate thanksgiving apart from a single God of creation and redemption is like that. Lord's Day, the day of the clear and coherent revelation of the God who makes and saves, was set by St. John in deliberate contrast to the emperor's day with its bazaar of deities, each promising or demanding one thing or another from the people. In prayer we address a personal, intelligent center. We direct all our words and gestures, our feelings and needs, to God. We are not dismembered but assembled. We are not scattered but gathered. We are not diluted but concentrated. We experience coherence.

Then, silence in heaven "for about half an hour" (Rev. 8:1). We live in a noisy world. We are yelled at, promoted, called. Everyone has an urgent message for us. We are surrounded with noise: telephone, radio, television, stereo. Messages are amplified deafeningly. The world is a mob in which everyone is talking at once and no one is willing or able to listen. But God listens. He not only speaks to us, he listens to us. His listening to us is an even greater marvel than his speaking to us. It is rare to find anyone who listens carefully and thoroughly. It is rare to find our stammering understood, our clumsy speech deciphered, our garbled syntax unravelled, sorted out and heard—every syllable attended to, every nuance comprehended. Our minds are taken seriously. Our feelings are taken seriously. When it happens we know that what we say and feel are immensely important. We acquire dignity. We never know how well we think or speak until we find someone who listens to us.

Persons in love often describe the distinguishing feature of their new relationship in some such words as, "for the first time in my life I can say everything I feel and think." This is not because they have added new words to their vocabulary or because they have taken speech lessons. It is because they have met someone who listens. True speaking is made possible when there is true listening. What good are words without a listener?

Silence in heaven for about half an hour: God listens. Everything we say, every groan, every murmur, every stammering attempt at prayer: all this is listened to. All heaven quiets down. The loud angel voices, the piercing trumpet messages, the thundering throne songs are stilled while God listens. "Hush, hush, whisper who dares? Christopher Robin is saying his prayers." The prayers of the faithful must be heard: the spontaneous hallelujahs, the solemn amens, the desperate "Why hast thou forsaken me?" the agonized "Take this cup from me," the tempered "Nevertheless not my will but your will," the faithfully spoken "Our Father who art in heaven," the joyful "Worthy art thou, our Lord and God, to receive glory and honor and power, for thou didst create all things, and by thy will they existed and were created." All the psalms, said and sung for centuries in voices boisterous, subdued, angry, and serene are now heard—heard personally, carefully, accurately. God silences the elders and the angels. Not one of our words is lost in a wind tunnel of gossip or drowned in a cataract of the world's noise. "The distinctive feature of early Christian prayer is the certainty of being heard."[4] We are listened to. We realize dignity. Dramatic changes take place in these moments of silence. The world rights itself. We perceive reality from the vantage point of God's saving work and not from the morass of desperate muddle. We acquire hope.

After the early citation of St. John "in the spirit," the next explicit reference to prayer is at the opening of the fifth seal, when St. John saw "under the altar the souls of those who had been slain for the word of God and for the witness they had borne; they cried out with a loud voice, 'O sovereign Lord, holy and true, how long before thou wilt judge and avenge our blood on those who dwell upon the earth?' Then they were each given a white robe and told to rest a little longer, until the number of their fellow servants and their brethren should be complete, who were to be killed as they themselves had been" (Rev. 6:9–11).

It is on this same altar that the prayers of those under the altar are mixed with the Spirit's fire and used in God's action answer. Their prayer was "How long?" The impatient question has a long history.[5] The answer is now in view. God is completing his work. The events in which we are presently involved are part of the design that is bringing the story of salvation to completion.

The answer is sufficient. When we know that delay is not procrastination, that our waiting is not because of someone's indifference, that we have not been forgotten, then the waiting is not intolerable. Important things are being done while we wait. The action on earth, seen from the heavenly place is a drama of victorious redemption. The first unsealing, in which the conquering Christ rode into history mounted on a white horse, is connected with the fifth unsealing, as the martyrs, robed in white, are assured that Christ is conquering on their behalf.

Prayer orients us to God's design. That which seems like sheer muddle in the helter-skelter of the day, in the oscillation between throne and altar, assumes lineaments of design. If there is design there is also hope. Our vertigo is cured. We discern direction, plot, and purpose.

Out of the silence of heaven, actions are prepared. The prayers are not simply stored on the altar, they are mixed with the fire of God's spirit and returned to the earth. Prayer is as much outer as inner. It is the most practical thing anyone can do. It is not mystical escape, it is historical engagement. Prayer participates in God's action. God gathers our cries and our praises, our petitions and intercessions, and uses them. The prayers that ascended to God now descend to earth. God uses our prayers in his work, "Prayer," wrote Pascal, "is God's way of providing man with the dignity of causality."[6]

The trumpet is the metaphor St. John uses to show how certainly and powerfully God is at work with our prayers. As our prayers return to earth in the censer, seven angels get ready to blow their trumpets. As the unsealings were signs of revelation, so the trumpetings signal proclamation. The Christian imagination associates the prayer-signalled trumpets first of all with the conquest of Jericho. Israel, promised the new land, arrived at its threshold after long trials and tribulations, only to find it blocked by the fortress city of Jericho. The Hebrews had lived for years on promises and vision. Their lives had been fed on wilderness fare and a long discipleship. Now, at the boundary to the new land, ready to enjoy what had been long promised and hoped for, they were met by an impregnable walled city. Archaeologists have excavated walls at Jericho that were fourteen feet thick. The walls were not that thick when Joshua arrived, but the reputation was: there was no getting past that city. No weapons they had would faze that fort. But prayer did it.

Now Jericho was shut up from within and from without because of the people of Israel; none went out, and none came in. And the Lord said to Joshua, "See, I have given into your hand Jericho, with its king and mighty men of valor. You shall march around the city, all the men of war going around the city once. Thus shall you do for six days. And seven priests shall bear seven trumpets of rams' horns before the ark; and on the seventh day you shall march around the city seven times, the priests blowing the trumpets. And when they make a long blast with the ram's horn, as soon as you hear the sound of the trumpet, then all the people shall shout with a great shout; and the wall of the city will fall down flat, and the people shall go up every man straight before him." (Josh. 6:1-5)

The accumulation of sevens—seven priests, seven rams' horns, seventh day, seven times—set in relation to Christian praying, is a forceful message: when we pray, we participate in doing God's will "on earth as it is in heaven." Jericho is the most vivid memory evoked by the trumpets, but there are many others. Praying Christians remember that the Lord said to Moses, "Make two silver trumpets; of hammered work you shall make them; and you shall use them for summoning the congregation, and for breaking camp" (Num. 10:1-2). The trumpets are to be used again to call the people to war "that you may be remembered before the Lord your God, and you shall be saved from your enemies" (Num. 10:9). The trumpets are to be blown on days of gladness "at your appointed feasts, and at the beginnings of your months" to signal "remembrance before your God" (Num. 10:10). The most prominent of the trumpet-announced feasts was New Year's Day (Rosh Hashanah) followed by ten days of penitence that prepare for the holiest day of the year, the Day of Atonement (Yom Kippur). An absolute new beginning is made; a complete cleansing takes place.

The trumpet signaled the jubilee year: after "seven weeks of years, seven times seven years . . . you shall send abroad the loud trumpet on the tenth day of the seventh month; on the day of atonement you shall send abroad the trumpet throughout all your land" (Lev. 25:8-9). The jubilee proclaimed liberty. All property was restored to original owners, debts were absolved, the land left fallow, slaves set free. Jesus' first sermon in the Nazareth synagogue took a text from Isaiah and announced that the jubilee year had begun: "The Spirit of the Lord is upon me . . . to set at liberty those who are oppressed, to proclaim the acceptable year of the Lord" (Luke 4:18-19). A. Stobel argues that A.D. 26-27 was a jubilee year, and that Jesus' citation of the Isaiah text took account of this actual jubilee year, when the trumpets were sounding throughout the land and the Levitical liberation traditions were remembered again.[7]

Some in St. John's congregations would still remember the long-ago days when they had worshiped in the Jerusalem temple. Trumpets, for them, would arouse memories of the rich sounds and sights of temple worship. There, "trumpets were blown at the daily sacrifice, as soon as the dismembered lamb was thrown into the altar-fire. But the lamb could not be thrown in, nor the trumpets blown, until the priest offered incense on the golden altar within the Temple. He went in with his attendants; the congregation in the court waited quietly for his reappearance; then the sacrifice proceeded and the trumpets blew."[8] The same pattern and sequence they had seen practiced on earth, they now see taking place in heaven. Prayer pulls the actions of heaven and earth into correspondence.

The earliest New Testament writing, St. Paul's Letter to the Thessalonians, connects the trumpet with Christ's coming: "For the Lord himself will descend from heaven with a cry of command, with the archangel's call, and with the sound of the trumpet of God" (1 Thess. 4:16). Resurrection of the dead and rapture of the living follow that trumpet blast. Jesus had earlier promised that at the end, the Son of Man would "send out his angels with a loud trumpet call, and they will gather his elect from the four winds, from one end of heaven to the other" (Matt. 24:31). Both Jesus and St. Paul were preaching from a text in Isaiah: "And in that great day a great trumpet will be blown, and those who were lost in the land of Assyria and those who were driven out to the land of Egypt will come and worship the Lord on the holy mountain at Jerusalem" (Isa. 27:13).

The images fuse: a thorough cleansing, a mighty conquering, a final coming. There is a new year and a new kind of living. There is a new land and a new place of blessing. Prayer lands us in the new life, within and without, in our hearts and in our country. We have a restored relationship with a holy God; we are sent forth as a holy people into a promised land. The trumpets proclaim what God is doing in answer to our prayers and wake us up to participate in his action on our behalf. They prevent us from sleeping through the revolution. They keep us alive to every act of judgment and salvation.

The mood of the trumpets is of fresh beginnings and victorious actions. This contrasts with the content of the visions that issue from the trumpets, for the content has to do with judgment and repentance. Jericho, jubilee, Jerusalem, and Jesus (salvation) are juxtaposed with Moses' Egyptian plagues and Joel's locust armies (judgment). The poet puts unlikely images alongside one another and lets them work in our imaginations, as cross-fertilizing metaphors.

The medieval imagination loved to meditate on the Hebrew stories as archetypes of the soul's journey. The act of prayer discovers analogies to the Christian's discipleship everywhere, in likely and unlikely places. The imagination of Richard of St. Victor's is representative when he counsels:

But first we must leave Egypt behind, first we must cross the Red Sea. First the Egyptians must perish in the waves, first we must suffer famine in the land of Egypt before we can receive this spiritual nourishment and heavenly food. He who desires that food of heavenly solitude let him abandon Egypt both in body and heart, and altogether set aside the love of the world. Let him cross the Red Sea, let him try to drive all sadness and bitterness out of his heart, if he desires to be filled with inward sweetness. First the Egyptians must be swallowed up. Let perverse ways perish lest the angelic citizens disdain an ignoble companion. First the foods of Egypt must fail, and carnal pleasure be held in abomination before we may experience the nature of those inner and eternal pleasures.[9]

St. John directs the praying imagination, full of the hope that the trumpets evoke, to attend to what God does in response to our prayers, so that in lives of thoroughgoing repentance we may be free for the new life. The trumpet plagues reconstruct the exodus plagues. The exodus plagues were not punitive but purgative, sent not simply to make Pharoah miserable, but to get him to change his mind, to repent. The purpose continues here, as the praying imagination prepares to apply the trumpet plagues to our lives. The first trumpet plagues show that there is safety in neither earth nor sea nor sky (Rev. 8:7-11). Salvation comes from God and only from

God. When we become complacent in "Egyptian" routines, God intervenes. Nothing is secure but God. No relationship is firm except in faith.

The poisoning of the waters (Rev. 8:10-11) is a contrast to the freshening of the waters when Moses threw a tree into the pool at Marah "and the waters became sweet" (Exod. 15:22-25). Evil, and especially pretentious evil, has poisonous effects. The early fathers, delighting in the correspondence of images, loved to join story to story; here they saw the tree of crucifixion thrown into the wormwood pool of our sin so that a well of living water is made fresh in us.

The darkening of the luminaries — sun, moon, stars — throws a shadow over all of life (Rev. 8:12). Now all the elements (earth, salt water, fresh water, heavens) are under judgment. Genesis made it clear that everything we see is a result of God's creative will; Revelation makes it clear that everything is subject to God's creative judgment. When any of the great elements of creation get between us and God, becoming idols, judgment topples them and restores us to simple trust and adoration. Every misplaced trust and every mistaken devotion is called into question.

Still, we do everything we can to make light of judgment. We use every stratagem we can find to avoid dealing with the consequences of sin. But God will not let us off. He will not indulge our inattention. He will be taken seriously. In a pause between trumpet blasts, an eagle cries its warning (Rev. 8:13). However practiced we become at tuning out sounds that we do not want to hear, including the sound of God's displeasure at sin, God finds new ways to penetrate our defensive deafness. The eagle cry catches us off guard.

Then come the locusts (Rev. 9:1-11). Enmity with God is a ferocious assault on humankind. Joel's locust prophecy is recast to show the terrible consequences of a life that refuses the way of repentance. Only in repentance are we saved from the terrors of sin. With the introduction of Apollyon (Rev. 9:11), the picture becomes surrealistic, nightmare figures in a grotesque scene: the angel of the bottomless pit is captain of the locust army. Still, destruction, terrible as it is, is not ultimate — it is named and therefore under the command of him who "fixed their bounds which cannot be passed" (Ps. 148:6).

In contrast to the sixth day of creation when the life of God was breathed into the form of man, and in parallel to the passover plague when the Egyptian firstborn were slain by the death angel, the sixth angel's trumpet signals death for some and life for others (Rev. 9:13–19). Death is the "last enemy." It marks the boundary of our relationship with God. Just as pain is a way to healing, and hurt a goad to health, so judgment is a means towards repentance. But it is not a guarantee. "The rest of mankind . . . did not repent (Rev. 9:20–21). Neither did Pharoah repent after experiencing the ten plagues of judgment. We are forced to look within ourselves for the persistent stubbornness that dismisses divine invitations and overlooks spirit reminders.

Between the blowing of the sixth and seventh trumpets, St. John introduces another subject (Rev. 10–11). Before completing this series, he involves us in his next series. We are not to arrive at a conclusion prematurely. There are many next-to-last things before the last things. But for now let us proceed directly to the seventh trumpet (Rev. 11:15–19), which opens a heavenly scene of answered prayer: the faithful who have prayed the Lord's Prayer, "Thy kingdom come, on earth as it is in heaven," now learn that "the kingdom of the world has become the kingdom of our Lord and of his Christ." Their prayers are answered. The rule is complete. The reign is glorious. God's temple in heaven is opened and the ark of his covenant is seen there accompanied by loud sounds of victory.

We are once more in Jericho. When Jericho fell, the Ark of the Covenant had been carried in the trumpet-led parade around the pagan city that was walled against God's people and against God's work. The Ark was the sign of God's presence with his people. Later it was captured by the Philistines and still later rescued by David's army. It had been placed in Solomon's temple, but in the destruction of that temple (586 B.C.) had been lost. Where had it gone? And where was God? For centuries the people had prayed, "Thy foes have roared in the midst of thy holy place; they set up their own signs for signs . . . We do not see our signs; there is no longer any prophet, and there is none among us who knows how long. How long, O God, is the foe to scoff?" (Ps. 74:4, 9–10). Now St. John shows his praying people that the Ark has not been destroyed. It has been all along where it was supposed to be, in the heavenly temple where all prayers are consummated.

"Turn your Bible into prayer" wrote Robert Murray McCheyne to a young confirmand. That is what St. John did on his knees on Patmos on the Lord's Day.

8. The Last Word on Witness
Revelation 10 and 11

I have told the glad news of deliverance
in the great congregation;
lo, I have not restrained my lips,
as thou knowest, O Lord.
I have not hid thy saving help within my heart,
I have spoken of thy faithfulness and thy salvation;
I have not concealed thy steadfast love and thy faithfulness
from the great congregation.

PSALM 40:9–10

And I will grant my two witnesses power to prophesy for one thousand
two hundred and sixty days, clothed in sackcloth.

REVELATION 11:3

I had to return to myself, to learn how to outline my own hidden convictions, my own real faith, and through this to pay witness. It's a lot of work
and I haven't yet learned how to do it.

CZESLAW MILOSZ

Antipas, from the Pergemene church, lost his life in the persecution. He was called "my faithful witness," *ho martus mou ho pistos
mou* (Rev. 2:13). Earlier, Jesus had been described in the nearly identical phrase, "the faithful witness," *ho martus ho pistos* (Rev. 1:5).
Unlike Antipas "who was killed among you," which he certainly
was, Jesus is also described as "first-born of the dead" (Rev. 1:5).

It is both difficult and dangerous to tell the truth. People who tell
the truth not infrequently get killed. The word used in the first
Christian century for telling the truth about God in a given situation, *martus*, has come into our language as "martyr," the person
who loses his life telling the truth.

Biblical people from the beginning were committed to telling the
truth. The truth of God had been revealed; now it must be said –
honestly, boldly, accurately. In contrast to other religions in the

ancient world that went in for idol-making and temple-building, the biblical faith prized the truth-telling word. Other religions used rite and ritual to manipulate gods and goddesses; words were not used to *say* something, but to cast spells or give incantations, that would move the will of the deity. Biblical faith, in defiant contrast to that, insisted that God spoke and that we must listen and give answer. "Witness" was a personal report on the conversation. Prophets and apostles carried on a tradition of fearless speaking. It was high-risk work. The work, at least in Israel, was accompanied by a high mortality rate. In addition to the named Antipas, how many unnamed? Later in the Revelation, St. John sees the great whore "drunk with the blood of the saints and the blood of the martyrs of Jesus" (Rev. 17:6). Most families in the late first century would have friends or relatives among those saints and martyrs.

Out of the silence in heaven in which the prayers of the Christians are heard, God prepares to speak. He speaks. His speaking is, in some mysterious but unmistakable way, connected with the prayers. The history-making, kerygmatic speech of God is trumpeted by the angels. Terrific consequences follow. But there is another, more modest speech that is also important. The words we speak to God (the incense-prayers) are powerful; we are assured of that. The words God speaks to humankind (the trumpet-preaching) are awesome; we are convinced of that. But how about the words we speak that report on our God-directed speech, and God's earth-targeted gospel? In comparison with such praying and such preaching, can it mean much that I stutter out God's word in my daily conversational encounters among people who would rather hear almost anything else? That is the hesitancy addressed by Revelation 10 and 11, and the answer is emphatic: by all means, yes!

Just as the seventh unsealing was delayed until there was comprehensive assurance that the workaday Christian community, up to its elbows in the evils of history, was itself ordered and secure (Rev. 7), so the blowing of the seventh trumpet is delayed until the significance of ordinary Christian witness can be assured. For the Christian community has always placed the highest value on the most mundane conversations. What people of faith say to one another and to those outside the faith is not as central as what we speak to God through Jesus Christ (in prayer), and not as impressive as the angel-trumpeted proclamations of the gospel (in preaching), but it has its essential place, and that place must be occupied.

The chief difficulty in maintaining Christian witness is timidity. The life of the world is gaudy, noisy, and assertive. The life of faith is modest, quiet, and unassuming. What can an ordinary Christian say that will stand a chance in the brash shouting of money and pleasure and ambition? Or in the wailing laments of boredom and depression and self-pity? In a society in which the thesaurus of metaphor and symbol has been ransacked by cynical advertisers, faithless artists, and indulgent entertainers to condition us to a maniacal but brainless devotion to me and now, how can the imagination be renewed so that we can say, honestly and personally, without necessarily raising our voices, who God is and what eternity means?

St. John's apocalyptic angels are one way. Not the plump darlings of the Rubens' oils, or the giggling, tinsel-fringed girls in Christmas plays, but real angels, apocalyptic angels—vast, fiery, sea-striding creatures with hell in their nostrils and heaven in their eyes. Angels are a biblical means for representing the invisible. When the invisible, intricate and complex, rich and luxuriant, is alive to the minds of men and women, references to angels abound. The belief in angels represents a recognition that "God's world . . . is far richer than what can be seen on our planet." The Bible speaks freely of angels as ministering spirits, "sinless inhabitants of a world in which spirit is not hampered by matter but uses it freely, without limitations; at the same time they are creatures who, in spite of and with their sense of higher order, serve the cause of redemption, protection, and direction of earthly humanity."[1]

Angels are presented to us in two ways in scripture. They come in the form of ordinary persons, undistinguishable from the man or woman next door. The angel is the agent of the supernatural, an instance of the direct working of God in everyday life, but in appearance natural. Three men appeared to Abraham and Sarah and only afterwards did they realize that their visitors were angels (Gen. 18). The writer to the Hebrews urges the practice of hospitality to strangers on the grounds that "some have entertained angels unawares" (Heb. 13:2). If we ever do see an angel, we will not know it at the time. Angels have a penchant for appearing incognito. The other way in which angels are presented is in visions, and then they are presented extravagantly, immense figures filling the skies, with constellations in their hair and wielding swords the size of comets.

The Christian mind can discern the divine wisdom in the forms in which angels are present to us. To the half-converted mind, hankering after miraculous visitations and supernatural sensations, God says, "Nothing doing. I am supernaturally present with you, but you will only know it through the duties and responsibilities of the immediate life around you." But to the devout Christian, intent on faithful intercessions and patient burden-bearing, the Spirit on occasion gives visions and dreams to fortify the faithful with the knowledge that we are surrounded and supported by heavenly hosts in our warfare.[2] Angels are for encouragement, not for entertainment.

The loss of angels to the language of faith is not so much because of an atrophy of the ability to believe as of an anemia of the capacity to imagine, for, as Berkhof remarks, "A generation like ours which assumes (without proof), in its theories and science-fiction literature, the existence of conscious beings on other planets who are interested in this earth can hardly find the belief in angels strange."[3]

What we need is a hearty infusion of imaginative red cells into the circulatory system of our faith. If ordinary, daily Christian conversation is not to congeal into a sodden mush of platitude and cliché, it needs to be in touch with the rich, vibrant reality of the supernatural, the invisible vitalities of God who, Psalm 18 tells us, "rode on a cherub." It is impossible to imagine that cherub as a rosy-cheeked infant. The mind requires something more like a magnificent centaur, with a comet streaming from the socket of one eye.

Emily Dickinson complained, "This timid life of Evidence/Keeps pleading—I don't know."[4] The Apocalypse responds with a robust life of imagination that dares to see angels clothed with the sun and in consequence is bold to witness, "I believe." St. John's strategy for guiding us from timidity to witness is to fill the backgrounds of our imagination with the vision of an angel projected on the screen of faith, a mighty angel descending out of heaven, cloud-clothed, rainbow-crowned, face ablaze like a sun, bestriding ocean and earth on legs that are great columns of fire (Rev. 10:1-2).

St. John and the people to whom he is pastor are being prepared for the work of witness, the daily conversational use of words in the service of the gospel. But some things must not be said, at least not yet. The mighty angel opens his mouth in a lion roar; the response is meteorological—seven thunders answer back. St. John, quite naturally, prepares to write down the message of the seven thunders (*that* will impress the cultured despisers!) but is forbidden. The first thing we learn in witnessing is not to tell everything. Witnessing is not blabbing. Jesus had similarly warned against casting pearls before swine (Matt. 7:6).

The thunderous Psalm 29 tells us as much as we are ever likely to know about what the seven thunders said: seven times in that psalm the voice of the Lord (*qol Yahweh*) thunders in creation and judgment, with all creatures in heaven and earth responding in worship: "glory!" It is a psalm in the style of the Revelation. If we are directed by the precedent of Psalm 29 in understanding what the seven thunders said, it would seem that the reason St. John is commanded to seal up the message is not that it must remain secret but that the unbelieving world is not yet capable of hearing it.

Witness, apparently, does not mean telling everything we see and hear, breathlessly and indiscriminately. Reticence is as much a part of witness as expression. Jesus, descending the Mount of Trans-figuration with the three disciples, instructed them "tell no one the vision" (Matt. 17:9), not because it must never be known, for it came to be known, but because that was not the right time. There are numerous instances in Jesus' life when he forbade those who were healed to tell about it. This was not because they had been initi-ated into a secret society, but because they were being trained in the exacting and difficult Christian skill of witness, in which there is "a time to keep silence, and a time to speak" (Eccl. 3:7).

But if St. John is forbidden to say one thing (what the seven thunders said), he is commanded to say another. The strong angel who has descended from heaven stands before him and presents him with a book. This is the second appearance of the strong angel. The first time he was standing before the sealed book inquiring urgently if there was anyone capable of unsealing it (Rev. 5:1-2). Here he is holding the same book, but now it is unsealed—the meaning has been shown by being preached. (There will be a third, and final, appearance of the strong angel, holding not a book but a great millstone: unrepentant Babylon hardening her heart to the words of the book, is hardened into a stone and thrown into the sea of judgment [Rev. 18:21-24]).

St. John takes the book presented to him by the angel. "Book" means intelligible revelation; the history in which we live has meaning, plot, and purpose. This book is open, unsealed, for Christ has unsealed it. We do not come to God by guesswork. The open book is accompanied by the announcement that there is to be no more delay: revelation is complete (Rev. 10:6). Christ has fulfilled all the promises of God. "Today is the day of salvation." Procrastination— the chief mischief introduced by predictors and fortune tellers of all kinds ("if the truth is still in the future, I do not have to deal with it today")—is abolished. We live in an intense, eternal Now. Witness embraces the openness and immediacy of God's word. Witness is wary of discussions. It opposes an aloof objectivity that claims to preserve scientific truth by discouraging personal participation. Witness plunges into radical subjectivity and invites others to do likewise. Witness demands an alert mind (to read the open book) and an immediate response (for the time is up).

St. John is told not only to take the open book but to eat it. Eating a book takes it all in, assimilating it into the tissues of your life. Witnesses first become what they then say. If witness is to be anything more than gossip about God, it must be the word internalized. Most people have opinions about God which they are not hesitant to voice. Such talk is worthless, or worse. Just because a conversation (or sermon!) has the word *God* in it, does not qualify it as Christian witness. St. John is not instructed to pass on information about God, he is commanded to assimilate the word of God so that when he does speak it will express itself artlessly in his syntax just as the food we eat is, when we are healthy, unconsciously assimilated into our nerves and muscles.

St. John takes the book. But the word that designates the book presented to him is not the same word describing the book that he took. The heavenly voice says, "Go, take the open book [*biblion*] that is in the hand of the angel." He approaches the angel and says, "Give me the little book [*biblaridion*, the diminutive of *biblion*]." In chapter 10, verse 10, he reports, "and I took the little book [*biblaridion*] from the angel's hand." "Booklet" in English, gives the sense.

St. John, being prepared for the work of witness, is presented with a gospel that is deep, powerful, complex, and awesome: "For who has known the mind of the Lord" (Rom. 11:34). The message is eternal and encompassing. We who dare to witness are painfully aware that we are only on "the outskirts of his ways" (Job 26:14). No mere person is qualified to be spokesman for such a message. But St. John does not avoid the work of witness by pleading inadequacy; he takes what he can, a booklet instead of the book.

The exchange of words suggests a kind of modesty in the work of witness. We know that we are presented with the complete meaning of the divine life as it is directed to us, and we know that we are required to announce that meaning in our conversations. But we know also that we cannot tell it all. Our minds boggle at its immensity. Our own lives by their smallness betray its largeness. Our vocabulary cannot begin to cover the ground. But we are not therefore speechless. There is something, after all, that can be said, and we will say it. But in the word of witness we are aware of the difference: the opened book is that which we are presented, the little book is what we manage to get hold of and assimilate. However much we say, we say only part of it. However well we speak, we know that it is a halting, abbreviated version of the fullness that is the word become flesh. But our inadequacy does not incapacitate us. Because we cannot say it all does not mean that we are exempt from saying what we can. But it does suggest a certain humility, which is not always evident in persons who dare to witness to their Lord.

Continuing to follow instructions (for we are never on our own in the work of witness, but always attentive apprentices), St. John eats the book. He had been told what to expect: "it will be bitter to your stomach, but sweet as honey in your mouth" (Rev. 10:9). He then experienced what he was told: "It was sweet as honey in my mouth, but when I had eaten it my stomach was made bitter" (Rev. 10:10).

St. John will have remembered, as we do, the story of Ezekiel. It is a story that the Spirit etches in the understanding of every person who embarks on the work of witness. Ezekiel had also been given a book and commanded to eat it. He said "it was in my mouth as sweet as honey" (Ezek. 2:8–3:3). Ezekiel's experience is common among all who incorporate the word of God in their speech. The servant of God, meditating and savoring the word of God, enjoys and delights in what is provided. "O taste and see that the Lord is good!" (Ps. 34:8). God's word is sweet to the taste, like honey in the mouth. But—and this is the irony of the sweet word of witness—the word is often not received but rejected, and the witness of the word experiences in the pit of the stomach the bitterness of rejection. Ezekiel's congregation was a "rebellious house" (Ezek. 2:7). He spoke the immensely attractive word to his people and then reported, "They are not willing to listen to me; because all the house of Israel are of a hard forehead and of a stubborn heart" (Ezek. 3:7). Jeremiah, Ezekiel's near contemporary, fared no better. He received the word in a most moving and delightful way (Jer. 1:10). He spoke it with poetic passion in sentences of tensile strength and metaphors of blazing clarity. But the people rejected it, and what he experienced was anguish and pain: "For the word of the Lord has become for me a reproach and derision all day long" (Jer. 20:8). No biblical witness that we know of—not Moses, not Elijah, not John the Baptist, not our Lord himself, is unacquainted with this bitterness.

Every witness experiences the polarity of sweetness and bitterness. The word is sweet when it is received from God; it is bitter when it is rejected by others. It is irresponsible to describe the work of witness as all sweetness. There are some who persist in doing just that, who tell us that if we are bold to speak the word of truth skillfully and sincerely we will invariably meet with success. There are some who say that the only barrier between the searching God and a lost humanity is clear communication; when we get the word "out" all will be well. There is no biblical warrant for that. Biblical witnesses were motivated by the promised sweetness of the word, but they were also warned of the bitterness of rejection. It is a great message to taste: "Come to me all who labor and are heavy laden, and I will give you rest" (Matt. 11:28) – but it is a difficult message to stomach: "Put to death therefore what is earthly in you . . . On account of these the wrath of God is coming" (Col. 3:5–6).

Difficult or not, it must be done. Successful or not, it must be done. God wills that his redemptive activity in history and among persons be known. The book is, after all, open and open at great cost – it was only the *slain* lamb who was found capable of opening it. And so there is a command: "You must again prophesy about many peoples and nations and tongues and kings" (Rev. 10:11). Witness is not an option. It is not a special assignment given to the especially articulate, or the brashly insensitive. The Spirit uses the same word of command to St. John that launched Jeremiah in his witness (Jer. 1:10), but with a slight addition, the little word "again." The addition of "again" (*palin*) is a creative misquotation – a deliberate change in the original to ensure fresh participation. It is easy to imagine St. John applauding all that was shown to him up to this point regarding witness, and responding, "Yes, Lord, I will pass all of this on to the people in my churches. I know from experience that everything you say is true. I will tell the Christians what you are showing me so clearly." Then the Spirit replays the message, "You must again prophesy" and St. John counters with the inevitable, "But Lord, I have put in my time; I have paid my dues; I have been through this bitter business time and time again. Just let me spend the few years I have left as a senior consultant in the church's work of witness." The Spirit is inflexible: "Listen carefully to what

I said, John, I said, '*Again* prophesy.' You must not suppose that I have a bad memory and carelessly misquoted Jeremiah 1:10. I didn't misquote; I knew what I was doing when I added the word *again*. There are no *emeriti* in the work of witness."

It is the Spirit's style, while preparing the Christian for the long work of endurance, to interrupt with interludes of assurance. The Christian faith is not unrelieved testing. In fact, the Christian faith is mostly participation in the life of grace, a "sabbath rest." All the same, the Christian faith is embattled, and it would be fatal to ignore the dangers of tribulation and temptation. The Revelation is, in large part, a provisioning of the imagination to take seriously the dangers at the same time that it receives exuberantly the securities, and so to stand in the midst of and against evil. Disciplines are developed that rekindle the glow of first love (Ephesus) and renew the ardor of zestful service (Laodicea) in a world whose sacredness is trampled by unbelief. So just as the sixth unsealing led to an assuring vision of the safely sealed Christians, so here, in the midst of developing the difficult work of witness, there is a brief respite under the metaphor of measuring the temple.

This measured place, fenced in, so to speak, is a visual representation of the Christian community at worship, listening to God's word preached ("Go and make disciples of all nations . . .") and offering up prayers ("Deliver us from evil . . ."). Moral and spiritual order is carved into the chaos of tribulation. The lines are clean, the dimensions specified—the place is measured. Christians at worship find their place in a cosmos of redemption, the lines drawn against the devil's anarchy. The exactly measured temple, altar, and worshipers are like Wallace Stevens' "jar in Tennessee" that took dominion of the "slovenly wilderness" simply by being set on a hill. Even though completely unostentatious ("the jar was gray and bare"), it forces us to see sprawling Tennessee in relation to the shaped jar and not the other way around.[5] Order, if only a jar, if only a liturgy, quietly subjects disorder to itself. The picture is little more than a vignette: a reminder that the place of worship is established, inviolate, so that we can gather energy for the tough life of witness to which we are commissioned.

The place of worship is protected, but the place of witness is not. The court of the gentiles, where witness takes place, is not measured. There the holy things and the people who speak of them are treated with contempt. Witness takes place in the face of hostility. There is no banked chorus of singers providing background support to the witness. There is no one to introduce the witness with an impressive listing of credentials that will give his or her testimony weight with the audience. Witnessing is not like that at all. The witness may be a hero to Christians, but in the world the witness is solitary, suspect, ignored, and occasionally abused.

The contribution of the Revelation to the work of witness is not instruction, telling us how to make a coherent apology of the faith, but imagination, strengthening the spirit with images that keep us "steadfast, immovable, always abounding in the work of the Lord" (1 Cor. 15:58). Instruction in witness is important, but courage is critical, for it takes place in pitched battle. In the work of witness in which we "fight not against flesh and blood, but against the principalities, against the powers" (Eph. 6:12), we are "surrounded by so great a cloud of witnesses" (Heb. 12:1). We are among an elect company, well-furnished with heroes. But we don't see them. It is St. John's task to make them visible.

He uses the transfiguration of Jesus as a base. That story is well known in the Christian community, since St. Matthew, St. Mark, and St. Luke each tell the story. The event occurs at a critical place in Jesus' ministry as he is transferring his authority into the hands of his disciples. St. Peter has just recognized Jesus for who he really is and confessed his lordship. Jesus has begun to train his followers in the difficulties that lie ahead. He has embarked on the journey that will take them, in a few days, to Jerusalem where he himself will experience rejection, suffering, and death for his witness. As part of the training he takes three disciples to a high mountain for prayer. They see him transfigured before them. As the glory of heaven shines through the form of Jesus, two witnesses, Moses and Elijah, converse with our Lord attesting (witnessing) that he is the Messiah. They are enveloped in a cloud. A voice from heaven confirms the witness: "This is my beloved Son, listen to him." The cloud clears, the two witnesses are gone; now, they, Peter, James, and John, are the witnesses.

St. John's vision recasts that story to show the importance, the danger, and finally, the inviolability of Christian witness. The vision of the two witnesses drawn out of the story of the transfiguration emphasizes the significance of each particular act of witness in which we engage. The unnamed witnesses of Revelation 11 are the named witnesses of the transfiguration, Moses and Elijah. The two men, great in their own right, through the centuries accumulated symbolic greatness: Moses, giver of the law, and Elijah, exemplar of prophecy. Between them these two direct the attention of all humanity to Christ as Lord and Savior—God in our history for our salvation. Law and prophecy are the content of all witness.

Law (Moses) is the revelation of God's truth. God wills us to know what is real. There is intelligibility in creation, and God shows it to us: intelligibility in rocks and weather, in morality and thought, in prayer and worship. Nothing is arbitrary. Nothing is haphazard. We do not make up an explanation of reality as we go along; it is given to us by God. That is the importance of the Mosaic law: God speaks to us in such a way that we comprehend the intelligible givenness of reality. The universe is not a whim. Things do not occur by a throw of the dice. There is reason and order and sense. Our minds, of course, cannot take it all in, but whatever we can take in makes sense. The man who denies meaning in life writes out his denial in a grammer that he is sure will make sense to those who read it. We cannot escape this vast sense of givenness in which everything fits. The work of witness attests to this. When we witness we do not unpack the contents of our own emotional suitcases for the titillation of voyeurs, we point to what *God* has revealed.

Prophecy (Elijah) is the immediate application of God's truth in current and personal history. Truth is not only an objective reality "out there," it involves us in an act of participation "in here." Prophecy is the call to *live* the revealed truth, not merely acknowledge it, and to discover new ways to live it in every aspect of life—while brushing my teeth, dialing the telephone, pulling a lever in a voting booth, signing a check. It is a proclamation that

God's truth, evident in the "things that are made" (Rom. 1:20), must be embraced as the truth of my life in details, not just in general.

Prophecy points out connections between dailiness and God's eternity and calls us to choose to live these connections. We cannot live apart from these choices. We cannot be human apart from appropriate responding. Prophecy is the part of witness that says this. We are not animals that live by sheer instinct; we are not angels that live by sheer intelligence; we are human beings who consider and reflect and decide. Prophecy addresses our wills with an invitation to participate in God's will. When we witness we do not recruit or propagandize; we clear the ground where decisions are made, try to throw some little light on the intersection between time and eternity, and invite entrance into that clarity where the "narrow way" begins.

Law tells us how God is involved in our lives. Prophecy tells us how we are involved in God's life. Law and prophecy are the systole and diastole of witness. There can be no witness if either is omitted. The two witnesses point to the Christ who reveals all of God to us, and to the Christ who is our total response to God.

These two witnesses are at work in the world as long as there is a world (the 1,260 days of Rev. 11:3). There is a remarkable power in their witness. The fire that pours from their mouths destroys enemies, and the key that locks the heavens so that no rain falls, shows us that witness is not a kibbitzing voice on the sidelines of life, chirping out moral advice. These voices articulate what is deepest in reality itself. The work of witness is backed up by heaven and earth: "From heaven fought the stars, from their courses they fought against Sisera. The torrent Kishon swept them away, the onrushing torrent, the torrent Kishon. March on, my soul, with might!" (Judg. 5:20–21). Those who oppose the word of witness, oppose reality itself, outwardly and inwardly.

But the two witnesses are also grossly humiliated. They are murdered and their exposed corpses are mocked in the city streets. This is not entirely unexpected, for the rebellious nature of humanity has a long history of rejecting God's word in both its revealed and applied forms, wanting desperately to set up shop on its own, desiring to be "as gods." When it looks as if it might work (as it does from time to time, for brief intervals in history), there is festive celebration: "Moses is dead—no more do we have to be reminded of the purpose of creation; Elijah is dead—no more do we have to be reminded of the destiny that awaits us! We are free to exploit the earth, oppress our enemies, manipulate our friends, indulge our emotions, pamper our bodies. 'Come, let us build ourselves a city . . . let us make a name for ourselves.'" But their party is always interrupted before it is well underway. "After three and a half days" the two witnesses are on their feet again. The work of witness cannot be stopped. The life of the two witnesses is reproduced in every act of witness.

The two witnesses, like Moses and Elijah in the transfiguration, disappear with God in the cloud, and the seventh trumpet is blown. The seven trumpets are now a complete cycle. They began by announcing the Egyptian plagues, preparing the way for redemption. The world's hardness of heart is purged of its evil by the plagues. The task that was never accomplished by holy wars, righteous indignation, moral reform, or political liberation is carried forward by God's prayer-blown trumpets.

The work of witness takes place in the pause between the six trumpets and the seventh, as the seven thunders resound. Heaven is antiphonal with great sounds. When Moses was on Sinai we are told that "there were thunders and lightnings, and a thick cloud upon the mountain, and a very loud trumpet blast" (Exod. 19:16). After the Egyptian plagues came the Sinai revelation. On the mountain "the sound of the trumpet grew louder and louder, Moses spoke, and God answered him in thunder" (Exod. 19:19). The great conversation was a dialogue between trumpets and thunders. It is in that context that our words of witness are placed. We speak our words of witness accompanied by God's trumpet-proclamations. Answering voices from heaven validate the witness in the song of the twenty-four elders (Rev. 11:15–19). "On earth as it is in heaven" is present experience.

Everything that has been heard and seen of God finds its way in one way or another into the words of witness. All scriptures find their way into the ordinary speech of the Christian. Daniel's Gabriel holding Ezekiel's scroll commands St. John to preach Moses' revelation and behold Elijah's fire come down from heaven. The scriptures, pondered and assimilated in Christian witness, are reexpressed in fresh and surprising ways, and result, cumulatively, in "loud voices in heaven" (Rev. 11:15).

9. The Last Word on Politics
Revelation 12–14

Some boast of chariots, and some of horses;
  but we boast of the name of the Lord our God.
They will collapse and fall;
  But we shall rise and stand upright.

PSALM 20:7–8

Here is a call for the endurance of the saints, those who keep the commandments of God and the faith of Jesus.

REVELATION 14:12

Politics always competes with religion (joining it, tolerating it when it must,
and absorbing it when it can) in order to promise, if not a life beyond, then
a new deal on this earth, and a Leader smiling charismatically from the
placards.

ERIK ERIKSON

The people who were taught to pray, "Thy kingdom come, on earth
as in heaven" have just been told, "The kingdom of the world has
become the kingdom of our Lord and of his Christ, and he shall
reign for ever and ever." (Rev. 11:15). Really? In the climax context
of the seven trumpets, the believers' work of prayer is confirmed.
But when they walk out the door to work the next morning, they
will deal with the kingdom of Rome that hadn't "become" anything,
except maybe worse. What does St. John have to say to that?

The gospel of Jesus Christ is more political than anyone imag-
ines, but in a way that no one guesses. The "kingdom of God," an
altogether political metaphor, is basic vocabulary in understanding the Christian gospel.[1] It is, at the same time, responsible for
much misunderstanding. The political metaphor, "kingdom,"
insists on a gospel that includes everything and everyone under
the rule of God. God is no religious glow to warm a dark night.
Christ is no esoteric truth with which to form a gnostic elite. The

Christian faith is an out-in-the-open, strenuous, legislating, conquering totality. God is sovereign: nothing and no one is exempt from his rule.

The political metaphor of kingdom invites misunderstanding because all the politics that we know require the exercise of power, either through the manipulation of force (militarism) or the manipulation of words (propaganda), and usually both. We quite naturally assumed that if there is a Kingdom of God there will also be coercion by God, and will not be hesitant in exercising some of it ourselves, either verbally or physically, on his behalf.

Jesus announced the presence of the Kingdom of God. The word was often on his lips. At the end, he accepted the title King in that kingdom. He clearly intended that everyone know that the rule of God was comprehensive, established over body as well as soul, over society as well as individual, in our external behavior as well as our internal disposition, over cities and nations as well as in homes and churches. He just as clearly repudiated the accustomed means by which that rule was exercised: he rejected the devil's offer of a position in government, rebuked the brothers Boanerges for wanting to call down fire from heaven to incinerate their enemies, ordered Peter to put up his sword, reassured Pilate that the governor's job was in no danger, and finally, to make sure no one missed the point, arranged that his coronation take place on a cross.

All the same, people, Christians among them, keep missing the point. It is not as if the politics of Jesus are less visible than the politics of Rome, for they have received adequate coverage in the history books. But they are so much less pretentious and promise so little in immediate reward, that it is difficult to persevere in their practice. It is especially difficult to persevere without using the ordinary means of politics when Jesus' way doesn't seem to be working at all and Rome's way is working all too well.

Politics involves two elements: the exercise of ruling power and the means by which that power is exercised. People love to hear that God is powerful and that he rules; they are not as enthusiastic when they discover the means by which he exercises his ruling power. So sources are used selectively: Isaiah's prophecy is read to inspire trust in God's powerful rule in the universe; Machiavelli's *Prince* is read to find out how to rule effectively in this world. The two sources are edited and combined to provide manuals that will keep the church both religious (Isaiah) and relevant (Machiavelli).

Two temptations exert a powerful pull on the Christian community. One is to retain the political dimensions of the gospel and to take up the usual political means, namely, force. Instead of riding that silly donkey, Jesus should have charged into Jerusalem on a stallion and let a few heads roll. The other is to give up the political and have a nice little fellowship—cultivate a faith that more or less abandons the world of government, economics, culture, and society, and settle for saving a few souls.

These temptations are exacerbated when the people who practice the politics of Jesus are bullied over a considerable period of time by the politicians of Rome, and things are getting worse, not better. St. John discerns the lines of temptation. He deals with them at the center of his Apocalypse by constructing a formidable defense of imagery, enabling the Christian community to maintain all the political dimensions of the Kingdom of God while resisting all the political demons.

He begins with an imaginative retelling of the nativity of Jesus, the least political, it would seem, of all the gospel stories. The ear-splitting blast of the seventh trumpet has already pulled the sleeping world out of bed (Rev. 11:15). The roused world hears the victory song of the twenty-four elders and sees through a fissure in the skies the temple of God, its doors open so that the Ark, material evidence that God's rule connects with our salvation, is plainly visible (Rev. 11:15–19). A fusion of lightning, thunder, earthquake, and hail marks a scene change (nobody leave your seats!) and a woman appears in the sky theater. She is dressed in a diaphanous garment woven from the rays of the sun, each thread lambent. Twelve stars, pulsating white and red fire, are a crown on her head. She stands on the moon. And she is pregnant.

This statuesque beauty rivets our attention and then collapses into the travail of childbirth. The robust hymn of the twenty-four voice all-male chorus, its harmonies still echoing in the night, is drowned out by the cries of the woman in labor. Suddenly a dragon appears, ugly as the woman is lovely. The reptile is a crimson gash, violating the sky, its seven heads poised to devour the infant coming from the womb. The birth-giving woman and the death-dealing dragon are the light-year limits of the best and worst we can imagine. The moment the child appears, the dragon lunges. We shut our eyes, too terrified to witness the outrage. And then, at the last possible moment, there is rescue. The infant is seized and lifted to the throne of God. The mother escapes to a place of safety and is cared for.

In the split-second interval between birth and rescue, as the dragon is robbed of his prey, we recognize this child by means of St. John's description, "one who is to rule all the nations with a rod of iron." This is the one who will rule the world as it has never been ruled before, establishing a politics that will end all politics, the fiercely prophesied Messiah of Psalm 2. St. Matthew, using Isaiah 7:14, drew our attention to the intimacies of Jesus' birth. St. John, using Psalm 2:9 as his text, involves us in its politics.

The immediate consequence of the birth is not Christmas carols, but a great war spread across the heavens. The marvelous Michael, captain of the angels, joins battle with the dragon and his demon horde. Back and forth across the skies the contest rages and then, as suddenly as it began, it is over. The dragon and his hosts, no match for Michael and his angels, falls out of the sky in a heap. "Bounced" is more like it (*eblēthē*) – unceremoniously tossed out. The terrorizing names – Great Dragon, Ancient Serpent, Devil, Satan, Deceiver-of-the-Whole-Earth – are a pile of dirty laundry on the ground.

> Arrived! salvation and power;
>   our God's kingdom,
>   his Christ's authority.
>
> The Arch-Accuser, accusing our friends
>   day and night before God
>   is out, cast out.

They conquered him
  through the Lamb's blood
  and their witnessing words.

So rejoice, heavens
  and you who live there!

But woe, earth and sea!
  the devil has landed
  in a furious rage;
  he knows his time is up.   (Rev. 12:10–12)

Isaiah's vision is confirmed: "How you are fallen from heaven, O Day Star, son of Dawn! How you are cut down to the ground, you who laid the nations low!" (Isa. 14:12). Jesus' perception is elaborated: "I saw Satan fall like lightning from heaven" (Luke 10:18).

This is not the nativity story we grew up with, but it is the nativity story all the same. Jesus' birth excites more than wonder, it excites evil: Herod, Judas, Pilate. Ferocious wickedness is goaded to violence by this life. Can a swaddled infant survive the machines of terror? Can promise outlast horror? We want him to live, we long for this rule, but is it possible in this kind of world? Are not the means lacking? But we overestimate the politics of Rome and underestimate the politics of grace. St. John's imagination is adrenaline to us of little faith, and we are again dauntless, unimpressed by dragon bluster, sure of God's preservation. The child survives, salvation is assured. God's rule is intact.

It is St. John's Spirit-appointed task to supplement the work of St. Matthew and St. Luke so that the nativity can not be sentimentalized into coziness, nor domesticated into drabness, nor commercialized into worldliness. He makes explicit what is implicit in the Gospel stories. The messianic birth takes place out of the womb of God's people in a cosmos resplendent with wonder. The entire creation is clothing for God's people who are, Eve and Mary, mother to Messiah. The visibilities of creation and the invisibilities of salvation cohere in the action. The splendors of creation and the agonies of redemption combine in this event, this center where God in Christ invades existence with redeeming life and decisively defeats evil. It is St. John's genius to take Jesus in a manger attended by shepherds and wisemen and put him in the cosmos attacked by a dragon. The consequence to our faith is that we are fortified against intimidation. Our response to the Nativity cannot be reduced to shutting the door against a wintry world, drinking hot chocolate, and singing carols. Rather, we are ready to walk out the door with, as one psalmist put it, high praises of God in our throats and two-edged swords in our hands (Ps. 149:6).

Grounded, the hapless dragon tries again. The assault this time is on the mother. The snake vomits a cataract of water towards the woman to drown her. But the earth is no more hospitable to the dragon's designs than the heavens had been: the ground opens up, swallowing the river that was to have swallowed the woman. The dragon is deprived a second time of its victim. Is there anyone left to attack? As a matter of fact there is—we Christians "who keep the commandments of God and bear testimony to Jesus" (Rev. 12:17). Is there any reason to suppose that he will be more successful with us than with our Lord and his mother? Hardly. By this time the dragon appears a bit bedraggled. St. John, it seems, is having a little fun at the devil's expense.

The failed dragon stands on the shore of the sea and contemplates his failures. Obviously, he needs help. If he is going to wage war on the people who "keep the commandments of God and bear the testimony of Jesus," he needs a means by which he can either conquer or subvert their life of faith. He will attempt both. The dragon's quarrel is not with the race of Adam, as such, but with the people of faith whose lives are marked by God-obedient actions and Jesus-witnessing words. Since it is not against creatures that he will mount his assault but against creatures of Christ, he requires a stratagem that will deflect their obedience and falsify their witness. He will frighten them into disobedience; he will deceive them into illusion.[2]

He recruits help from the underworld, two beasts, one out of the sea, the other out of the earth, to execute his malign will within the believing community, these people whom God commands and saves. St. John's scripture-reading congregations have no trouble recognizing the animals; the beasts are Leviathan and Behemoth, portrayed in God's whirlwind speech to Job as the ultimate in ferocity (Job 40–41), but also known to be crushed and disposed of, no longer any threat to God's rule.[3]

Leviathan and Behemoth were awesome, but there is also an unmistakable touch of the ludicrous in St. John's description. The sea beast is a patchwork job, assembled from left-over parts of leopard, bear, and lion. The land beast is a fake lamb, a clumsy counterfeit of the magnificent true Lamb (Rev. 5:6, 7:17). St. John allows for their capacity to strike terror still, but he also shows them as considerably shopworn. The old beasts have been around too long and are starting to lose their stuffing.

Politics reaches into dimensions of behavior and belief. The authority of government is exercised to maintain order, defined in civic and criminal law (otherwise there is babel). Most political systems, ranging from family to empire, combine the elements of government and religion, as the Romans did. American democracy separates them. But combined or separate, the two elements are still there, parallel in their political importance.[4] St. John's visionary analysis of what the Christian is up against when confronted with the exercise of coercive force by means of police and propaganda, seems to me equally on target for both Rome and America on a large scale, and for families and congregations on a smaller scale.

Dissenters in a society are as dangerous as criminals to the political establishment. This is obviously true in totalitarian regimes, subtly true in democratic societies. Our socially expressed behavior and religiously expressed beliefs are equally political. If the devil's design is to separate our behavior and our belief from the rule of God, politics will be a field in which he deploys his picked troops. The beasts from the sea and earth are the images by which St. John will show us the satanic will covertly at work in these large areas of government and religion. With the sea beast, the dragon will frighten us into disobedience (make war on the saints and conquer them" [Rev. 13:7]); with the land beast he will deceive us into illusion ("deceives those who dwell on earth" [Rev. 13:14]). The respective powers of the two beasts, to intimidate and to deceive, are countered by the words of admonition that St. John gives to his parishioners. Each beast vision concludes with a succinct pastoral counsel; these counsels direct our Christian progress through the political dimensions of our lives, shown by the beast visions to be under threat.

After presenting the sea beast in his violence, St. John counsels: "Here is a call for the endurance and faith of the saints" (Rev. 13:10). There is no question but that we may lose our lives by violence in this world. But death is not defeat. Death is not the worst thing that can be done to us. This is difficult counsel to follow. St. John, knowing how difficult, and how often our ears simply do not hear what it is difficult to hear, takes particular pains to ensure a full hearing. He introduces his counsel by repeating Jesus' attention-arresting formula: "If anyone has an ear, let him hear!" He follows it with an attention-getting misquotation. His prophet predecessor, Jeremiah, in a likewise difficult time, had written,

> Those who are for pestilence, to pestilence,
> and those who are for the sword, to the sword;
> those who are for famine, to famine,
> and those who are for captivity, to captivity (Jer. 15:2)

The seventh-century prophet's immediate context was different, but the words are exactly right for St. John's purpose, so he takes the last line from that series and writes: "If anyone is to be taken to captivity, to captivity he goes"—not an exact quote, but close. He follows it with, "If anyone slays with the sword, with the sword he must be slain." But that is not at all what Jeremiah wrote.

In Jeremiah the "sword" sentence ("those who are for the sword, to the sword") is exactly parallel to the "exile" sentence. Why did not St. John do the obvious and follow the first line quoted from Jeremiah with an emphatic second, driving it home? Why, in the middle of this admonitory stream, does he shift rhetorical horses? We know his task: he must fortify his people to face the worst. In a political world of sea beast violence, he must bring into the open what may be ahead for any one of them: exile, death, persecution, torture. He knows that when named, fears lose half their potency. He will make sure that no disaster inflicted by the evil power will be unheard of in his congregations. Knowing what to expect, they at least will not be surprised into cowardice.

But there is a parallel difficulty. When we live in a world of violence long enough, it is easy to adopt violent means ourselves, especially when we know that our cause is righteous and the opposition is evil. Religious faith, especially when zealous, is no stranger to the exercise of violent force. And so St. John, having set down his counsel to endure, yokes it with a warning to not defect into violence. That would be just as bad as defecting into cowardly compliance. Had not Jesus, in as violent a scene as any of us will find ourselves, said, "Put your sword back into its place; for all who take the sword will perish by the sword"? (Matt. 26:52). Killing the opposition is the sea beast's way of solving its problems. It is not ours. Ours is endurance and faith.

This combination, endurance and faith, is not dumb passivity. Nor is it timid advice such as Josephus a few years before had given the Jews of Palestine: to abstain from fighting because they will certainly lose. This is not prudent counsel to cut their losses, cowardly caution that is unwilling to risk the cut and thrust of violence. St. John's exiles and martyrs were terrifically active in their suffering. The Christ-followers had learned something profound about sacrifice and death: endurance and faith are aggressive forces in the battle raging between God and the devil. It requires high energy to meet the sword with willed suffering, with embraced sacrifice.

Next is the land beast, characterized by the capacity to deceive. After painting a picture of the animal, St. John gives his counsel: "This calls for wisdom: let him who has understanding reckon the number of the beast, for it is a human number, its number is six hundred and sixty-six" (Rev. 13:18). St. John expects the deceit of the land beast to be penetrated by the Christian mind: hard, critical thinking. The land beast is, more than anything else, religious. It has a Christ-like quality; it is "like a lamb" (Rev. 14:11), but it is a parody, not a derivation, of Christ. Its main task is to get people to worship. In order to subvert our religious life, it uses religious means with all the trappings of the miraculous. When a person or movement is religious, appears to be on good terms with the supernatural, and urges us to engage in religious acts, we let our guard down. There is something seemingly incompatible, on the surface anyway, between a skeptical mind and religious faith. For people whose habit is faith, whose disposition in matters of God and the supernatural is towards acceptance, it is easy to be deceived by religious leaders. There is, in fact, no part of life in which deceit is more prevalent than in religion (just as there is no part of life in which violence is more prevalent than in the state). Organized behavior is prone to violence; organized belief is prone to deceit.

How do we protect ourselves from organized deceit? St. John is blunt; use your heads. Figure out what is going on. Most of the conspicuous religion that is in vogue at any one time in the country derives from the land beast. Expose these religious pretensions. This religion has nothing to do with God. Get its number: it is a *human* number. This is not divine mystery, but a confidence man's patter: it is religion that makes a show, religion that vaunts itself, religion that takes our eyes off of the poor and suffering and holy Christ. In the language of numbers, 666 is a triple failure to be a 777, the three-times perfect, whole, divine number. It is a recurring characteristic of this land-beast religion that it is commercialized. It requires huge budgets to maintain itself. It manipulates us economically, getting us to buy and sell at its bidding, marketing advice, solace, blessing, solutions, salvation, good feelings. The devil's strategy here is not the black mass, but the mass market.

Israel's basic creed, taught her by Moses and passed on to Christians, was "Hear, O Israel: The Lord our God is one Lord; and you shall love the Lord your God with all your heart, and with all your soul, and with all your might" (Deut. 6:4–5). This was the barebones belief and behavior of God's people—the confession of one God and the command to love him. They were taught this belief and trained in this action. One way they maintained attentiveness to this *shema* ("hear!") was to take parchments on which these words were written, roll them into small capsules (phylacteries) and fasten them with a thong to their foreheads and on the backs of their hands

THE LAST WORD ON POLITICS / 127

(Deut. 6:8). These brief, simple yet profound words ordered the content of their minds and directed the action of their hands. Belief and behavior were commanded and coordinated by the word of God: the Lord is one . . . love the Lord. But when the summary creed (mark) of the land beast replaces the *shema* on forehead and hands, religion becomes consumption—people become gross parodies of the gospel, buying all they can to show they are blessed by God, bowing down before every display of success. The buying and selling of religion is the mark of the beast.

St. John with his beasts mocks the seriousness with which authority, whether in government or religion, takes itself. The moment either or both begin to act godlike, they earn our contempt. These beasts, when St. John is done with them, are not awesome but ridiculous. Their pretensions are not to be taken seriously. We must laugh them out of court. Psalm 2 provided the jab of recognition that identified the dragon-threatened infant as the world-subduing Christ (Rev. 12:5); it also sets the mood for dealing with any authority, governmental or religious, that usurps Christ's rule as priest and king: "He who sits in the heavens laughs; the Lord has them in derision" (Ps. 2:4).

Christians are not contemptuous of authority as such. The early church managed to maintain a simultaneous respect for government ("honor the emperor" [1 Peter 2:17]) and contempt for every element in it that tried to substitute for God and his Christ (any "mouth uttering haughty and blasphemous words" [Rev. 13:5]). A Christian can be a good citizen under a bad government; a Christian can maintain a holy witness in a corrupt church. But prayer for the emperor (president, bishop, revivalist, pastor, pope) doesn't preclude lampooning the evil that St. John helps us discern.

Dragon, sea beast, and land beast are a satanic trinity that infiltrates the political world in order to deflect our worship from the God whom we cannot see to the authorities that we can see, and to deceive us into buying into a religion or belief-system that has visible results in self-gratification. St. John presents this infiltration as fearsome but not indomitable; the dragon was bested by Michael, the sea beast can be resisted, the land beast can be figured out.

Thus the larger-than-life political world is reduced to manageable terms. The Christian, with St. John's help, is not overwhelmed by big government, by sensational religion, by gigantic threats, by colossal odds, by breathless claims. The temptation to use the methods of satan to counter the force of satan is considerably weakened. The lies of the enemy, clever as they are, are not so clever that they cannot be found out. Jesus' triple victory over similar temptations is material for depth analysis.[5]

St. John's Apocalypse does not underrate the satanic—we *are* opposed by great power and deception. All the same a lot of it is sheer bluff, and the caricaturing visions reduce the satanic trinity from what it puffs itself up to be, to what it merely is. This is not supernatural power before which we are helpless; it is more like paranatural power that we are not used to. But trained by St. John's pastoral imagination, we are equipped to stand fast and discern.

The *tour de force* exposé of the three beasts of damnation is matched by three visions that show the forces of salvation at work behind the scenes on our behalf. The beast visions penetrated the hoax of evil; the salvation visions reveal the support system that backs up the life of endurance and discernment. We are not, that is to say, in a strictly defensive posture against the "principalities and powers." There is aggressive action underway on our behalf, even though we are not always aware of it. The three salvation-assisting visions are first, the Lamb leading worship on Mount Zion (Rev. 14:1–5); second are three angels preaching sermons from a pulpit in mid-heaven (Rev. 14:6–13), and third is the Son of Man harvesting the fields that are "white unto harvest" (Rev. 14:14–20). The visions show us that while we are doing our best to worship God and not the powers of the world, to understand our faith and not be misled by the devil's religious flimflam, and to cultivate a life of holiness in a weed-filled society, we are being helped to do each task.

Worship

Worship is our response to the Lamb's action among us, the action that redeems us from our plight. Our voices are augmented into song as we join creation's praise of the creator, Israel's thanks for salvation. Worship is the act in which our misunderstood and misspoken words are corrected and arranged into an expression of the whole truth of ourselves and our God; it is the act in which we find our fragmented lives corrected and arranged into a whole and perfect offering to God—by the action of the Lamb, we become "spotless."

But nothing *happens* in worship. In a political world where the power brokers are maneuvering their way to influence and control, where every word is a counter for gaining a following or shaping a response, how can people who are serious about their lives even think of gathering simply to be in adoration, to sing songs, to say and be who they are in God? Is this not neglecting moral duty? Is this not to abandon the field to the enemy? We are apt to think so— until we find that these nonactions of worship are the very acts that are backed up by the leadership of the Lamb, who is in the thick of history inaugurating the Kingdom in his nativity and consummating his rule in the crucifixion and resurrection. If worship is not a waste of time for the Lamb, it cannot be for us (Rev. 14:1–5). "Excessive activism is typical of those who do not live by grace."[6]

Preaching

Preaching is the act in which the word of God is proclaimed in awe and adoration among those who worship (first angel). It is also the speech in which the doom of the beast world is announced (second angel). And it is the discourse by which guidance is given for holy living (third angel). This many-dimensioned, world-making, salvation-shaping, reality-orienting word of God is always under threat of being silenced or muffled. It is silenced by closing the book in which it is written. It is silenced by the sound and fury of the daily traffic. It is silenced by the buzzing of ambition and covetousness in our own brains. Preaching gives the silenced word sound again, making it resonate in our ears so that we deal with God not as a memory but as immediately and personally spoken to us.

But preaching tells us nothing we don't already know. It has all been said so many times. And it is after all, written in the scriptures where we can look it up at our convenience. In a political world in which so many things are happening at once—wars, alliances, negotiations, tragedies, new leaders announcing hope, study groups coming up with plans that will solve the problems of famine and war—it is certainly urgent that we keep up with the news so that we can be informed and act responsibly in the world. And with so much news to attend to, who has time for preaching, which is the furthest thing from news? We are apt to think so—until, in the middle of the battle we find our courage flagging and our commitment wavering, and realize that the world is not primarily a place where information is stored and retrieved, but a moral and spiritual contest in which we are embattled. Then we are grateful for a proclamation from some midheaven pulpit, telling us again what God says about what is happening, turning information into command or promise, translating moral memories into spiritual urgencies (Rev. 14:6–13).

Holy Living

Holy living is the action by which we express in our behavior and speech the love and presence of our Christ. Holy living is posited on the conviction that everything we do, no matter what we do, however common and little noticed our lives, is connected with the action of God and is seed that becomes either a harvest of holiness or a vintage of wrath.

But there is nothing in our actions by which they can be empirically perceived to have such consequences. And there is great pressure to select our actions and words according to their effectiveness in getting something done, now. Not many question that a certain amount of morality is required, lest anarchy make commerce impossible; but behind that minimum we need to calculate our actions on the basis of what we want to get, not on any consideration of who we are or what God wills, factors that carry no weight in the market. We are apt to think so, anyway—until getting what we want goes stale and trickles into boredom. Maybe actions and words are for something beyond me, something of more value than I can price. Maybe they have some meaning within them that matures, like a seed, and comes to some kind of full-grown fruit, in as far off and unlikely connection with its source as an oak tree with its acorn. "True victories happen slowly and imperceptibly, but they have far-reaching effects. In the limelight, our faith that God is the Lord of history may sometimes appear ludicrous; but there is something in history that confirms our faith"? When I realize that, I am grateful for someone who guides me in holy living, directs me in words and acts that, when they leave me, become a crop that will be harvested for some great eucharistic banquet, and not its dread opposite (Rev. 14:14-20).

These are the three activities by which we survive and flourish politically: engaging in worship, listening to the proclaimed word, the practice of holy living. We find fortification for them in the Lamb leading worship, the angels preaching, the Son of Man harvesting a crop of deeds. Do these seem poor political weapons against the power and propaganda of the dragon and his beasts? But the proof is in the history books: "It was largely due to the propagation of such resolute ideas as are expounded in the Apocalypse that Christians were kept loyal to their faith and that, without a tear in their eye or a sword in their hand, they were able eventually to change the face of the world by enforcing the recognition of their claims at the hands of the empire."[8]

There is no avoiding politics. The moment one life impinges upon another politics begin. And our lives do impinge on others whether we will it or not. We are centers of power – power that can curse or bless – and are responsible for managing and directing that power. Power doesn't disappear or diminish when we enter the way of faith. If we are naive with power or disdainful of it, we will certainly either misuse it or allow it to be used by others who are neither innocent or scrupulous.

No action or belief is private. The more religious or value-charged, the less private. Matters associated with Christ and Antichrist are, then, the least private and therefore the most political of all. Everything we think gets out of our skulls and everything we do goes beyond our skins, entering into a crisscrossing network of complex interaction. Our actions and beliefs connect with others and gather momentum for justice and peace, goodness and holiness, war and oppressions, blasphemy and desecration – a confounding intermixture of means and motives.

The politics of the Lamb takes the ordinary and basic elements of our obedience (offering our adoration in worship, listening to the proclaimed word, practicing a holy life) and develops them into the ultimate and eternal. The politics of the Lamb, by showing that the plainest details of our daily faith are significant factors in a cosmic drama, protects us from hubris and guides us into the maturity that pours intelligence and energy into what is before us, making a work of holy art out of the ordinary.

The politics of the dragon takes the superficial and the pretentious and inflates them into promises of dominion and reputation, seducing the ego and exacerbating pride. The politics of the dragon, by manipulating wish and fantasy, is always dealing with abstractions removed from the actual circumstances in which people's lives are fashioned for good and evil, thereby involving people in unreality. Abstractions are great breeding places for evil: a glorious generality hides a multitude of sins.

Every community is set down in the middle of this conflict of politics. Christian communities of faith have St. John's vision by which to distinguish the politics of the dragon from the politics of the Lamb. We are in a crossfire of blustering dragon-pretension and powerful Lamb-meekness. They are equally concerned with the operation and use of power. We choose: we follow the dragon and his beasts along their parade route, conspicuous with the worship of splendid images, eleborated in mysterious symbols, fond of statistics, taking on whatever role is necessary to make a good show and get the applause of the crowd in order to get access to power and become self-important. Or we follow the Lamb along a farmyard route, worshiping the invisible, listening to the foolishness of preaching, practicing a holy life that involves heroically difficult acts that no one will ever notice, in order to become, simply, our eternal selves in an eternal city. It is the difference, politically, between wanting to use the people around us to become powerful (or, if unskillful, getting used by them), and entering into convenants with the people around us so that the power of salvation extends into every part of the neighborhood, the society, and the world that God loves.

The parish is a microcosm of this conflict. Politics is the management of power, whether in marriage and family, business and trade, congregation and committee, legislature and convention, school classroom and executive board room. We are in politics whether we want to be or not, whether anybody votes for us or not. It is essential that we discern the lines of influence as we practice politics in these shifting forums. St. John's visions provide pastoral wisdom for this work. Will it be the power of coercion or the power of grace? Will it be a politics of Abstraction consisting of grand images and programs, unconnected with who we are, that force conformity on others in impressive amphitheaters and spectator-filled stadiums? Or will it be a politics of Incarnation, consisting of adoring God, listening to his word, and obeying his commands in the detailed and dense dailiness of our easily dismissed and frequently despised Galilee?[9]

One sentence (Rev. 14:13) in St. John's six-vision series on politics links our politics directly with the politics of Jesus. Jesus, on trial before the political powers of government and belief, the Jewish high priest and the Roman governor, was convicted on a charge of blasphemy and sent to his death. In that setting he said,

> Henceforth [ap'arti] you will see the Son of Man
> sitting on the right hand of power,
> and coming on the clouds of heaven.   (Matt. 26:64)

St. John's Christians, some of whom will be (and any of whom might be) condemned on similar counts of blasphemy, are included in Jesus' political stand with the bold-print (grapson, "write!") blessing, "Blessed are the dead who die in the Lord, henceforth (ap'arti)."

The locution, ap'arti, "henceforth," is not a common construction.[10] The repetition calls attention to itself and links Martyr and martyrs; the King of the Kingdom in the very act of practicing the means of the Kingdom is linked with the subjects in the Kingdom as they in their turn practice the means of the Kingdom. This identification is confirmed by the Spirit:

> Yes! that they may rest from their labors,
> for their works do follow after them.   (Rev. 14:13)

The immediately following vision furnishes imaginative validation by showing the works following after them as the harvester Son of Man, coming on a cloud as he had promised (Matt. 26:64), reaps the good grain from the fields of their works, after which his angels harvest the vineyards of wild grapes, the vintage of the grapes of wrath.

I recite the blessing, "Blessed are the dead who die in the Lord, henceforth!," at the death (none so far by violence) of every Christian to whom I am pastor. The twentieth century is in direct continuity with the first. The dragon politics that battered St. John's Christians, batter mine. The Lamb politics that we are covenanted to practice require sinewy endurance and sapient discernment. The details of the difficulties in which we live change, but the gravity does not: we must persevere in submitting to the powers of the Kingdom, practicing the means of the Kingdom.

10. The Last Word on Judgment
Revelation 15–18

For not from the east or from the west
  and not from the wilderness comes lifting up;
but it is God who executes judgment,
  putting down one and lifting up another.
For in the hand of the Lord there is a cup,
  with foaming wine, well mixed;
and he will pour a draught from it,
  and all the wicked of the earth
  shall drain it down to the dregs.

PSALM 75:6–8

All nations shall come and worship thee,
for thy judgments have been revealed.

REVELATION 15:4

Majestically, the Bible is based on three divine 'No's.' The first is Man's
Fall, called his fall, made into his fall by God's judgment. The second is
the Great Flood, judging the World of Tribes. And the third is the Exodus, the leaving of the temples and fleshpots of Egypt, and the condem-
nation of everybody connected with the witchcraft of Egypt.

EUGEN ROSENSTOCK-HUESSY

St. John's images enter us as the ringing of a tower full of church
bells. The ancient English craft of change-ringing used to fill par-
ishes with immense sounds to the glory of God, as the ringers
pulled on the bell ropes in their church towers. Serious campanol-
ogists scorned to play mere tunes on their bells—their passion was
for something more demanding and complex: the rhythms of tuned
bells wove in and out of one another, first one taking the lead, then
handing it over to another of different timbre and pitch, and then
another, on and on, working out close mathematical permutations
and combinations. Modern ears, unused to such intricacies and
dulled by the clatter of machinery, hear only noise and complain

to town councils to get them stopped. Failing to distinguish art they are only aware of clangor.[1]

The modern imagination, flattened by the tramping hobnail boots of fact and information, has similar difficulties with St. John's images. We are neither used to or comfortable with these complexities. We like ideas, especially our religious ideas, laid out neatly and in order—in singable tunes. But St. John introduces image after image, and keeps them "ringing" at once, counterpointing the rhythms, inventing new combinations. His purpose is to draw us into the multi-layered intersections where God's will joins our experience of good and evil, assent and denial, Christ and Antichrist. He both delights our praising minds and deepens our enduring faith in the incredible coordinates of grace. He wants to get the entire drama of God's ways with us, before us, and within us. We want that too. And so we submit our believing imaginations to the logically absurd but imaginatively commonplace exercise of "hearing the vision." We restrain our impulse to explain his poetry and let the images do their own work in us, connecting old scripture memories with recent experience, gathering the scattered bits and pieces of thought, emotion, and behavior, and working them into the most inclusive and coordinated of all lives, the life in Christ.

We have been aware for a long time in these pages of the tolling of judgment. The sound became clarion when the fifth seal was opened and the souls under the altar cried, "O sovereign Lord, holy and true, how long before thou wilt judge and avenge our blood on those who dwell upon the earth?" (Rev. 6:10). "How long?" is a question with a long history. The desire for judgment, often escalating into a demand, is deeply imbedded in the life of God's praying people.

> How long, O Lord? Wilt thou forget me for ever?
> How long wilt thou hide thy face from me?
> How long must I bear pain in my soul,
>   and have sorrow in my heart all the day?
> How long shall my enemy be exalted over me? (Ps. 13:1-2)

That fourfold "How long?" is repeated and elaborated in every conceivable circumstance in the salvation story—in sickness and exile, in doubt and defeat, in pain and bereavement. Now the question is put the final time.

The call for judgment that arrives at a climax in the Apocalypse is not abstract or juridical, a concern for ethical decorum and a just society. It is not a "concern" at all, it is a cry: hurt people want relief, the bullied want fairness, the pushed around want dignity. The question "How long?", prayed by the slaughtered souls under the altar, effloresces into a questioning: how long is it to be permitted that goodness and beauty and truth are wantonly violated by mindless and godless schemers? How long do we have to put up with might-is-right arrogance?

The question echoes through cultures, reverberates through centuries. The injustice is not always blatant, and the cries for redress are not always broadcast. For every major martyr killed in courageous confrontation with the wicked, there are a million minor martyrs under that altar who persevere through lifetimes of injustice, crying silent prayers.

The desire for judgment develops. The frustration of delay deepens. All the raw material of injustice is served up in the ordinary experience of being female or male, being child or parent, being husband or wife, being employer or employed. We don't have to wait around for a war, or go to the ghetto, or get caught in a pogrom. In the daily places of love and work we come up against seemingly irremediable injustice. The world is not a good place for justice. We learn this early. Children, with instinctive moral sense, ignorantly but accurately paraphrase scripture, "It's not fair." Nobody gets what they deserve, whether in reward or punishment. The consequences of both virtue and vice are far out of line with their causes. Sometimes we get less than we deserve and know we are exploited, sometimes more and feel lucky (or guilty). Most of us, through the years, develop moral callouses and get on as best we can. Then a radical injustice erupts—political terrorism, domestic abuse—and the question is fresh and urgent again: How long? For St. John, the radicalizing event was the martyrdom of some of his parishioners.

It is notable that St. John's pastoral method here does not involve the balm of comforting words. He doesn't smooth things over, reminding us that it could be much worse. He doesn't so much as suggest that "to understand all is to forgive all." He does not put things in proportion so that we will not feel the outrage so keenly. On the contrary, he intensifies whatever sense of injustice we already have: in answer to the cry "How long?" martyred souls are told to wait a little longer "until the number of their fellow servants and their brethren should be complete, who were to be killed as they themselves had been" (Rev. 6:11). The combination, added instances of injustice accompanied by a further delay, is salt, not balm. But surely this has gone on long enough? Surely, after all these centuries it is time to call a halt to the whole rotten business, call the perpetrators of these cruelties on the carpet and wipe the condescending smiles off their faces with a once-for-all judgment?

It is disconcerting that there is no biblically straight answer to the straight question, "How long?" Yet, even though no date is ever put on the court calendar, a lively belief in God's judgment continues to be firmly held by millions of Christians. What accounts for this persistent belief among people who continue to live with the unanswered questions? For it is most remarkable that communities of faith, in the face of acccumulating and not-yet-avenged injustice, persevere in believing that God is just and will judge. The persistence of the prayer "How long?" issues, apparently, from a deep, unshakable conviction that God will bring an end to injustice, even though he shows no signs of calling the court room to order. How did this conviction get so deep into God's people? How did it acquire its unshakable anchorage? How does it? There is no empirical documentation to support it. Judgment appropriate to the deed and meted out on the spot is rare, biblically: Annanias and Sapphira, Judas, Herod; that's about it. It is no less rare in our lives. Mostly we live through a lifetime of moral ambiguity, acquiring longsuffering to endure the unjust behavior of others, experiencing mercy in the delay of judgment on our own sins. Confined to the data of our diaries we would almost certainly tire out and drift into the cynicism that Yeats expressed: "Some think it a matter of course that chance/Should starve good men and bad advance."[2]

So what accounts for the incredible persistance of the cry? In the general abandonment of prayer, in which great crowds of people give up on God and plunge into the streets to get what they can with their fists, what accounts for the remarkable minority who do not, but who stay, and cry, and wait? We are accustomed by now to St. John's answer, namely, worship. Worship provides the context for the paradoxical simultaneities of believing in justice while experiencing injustice, just as it has provided the context for everything else that has been lifted out of our everyday lives and brought into this vision. The long-delayed but now imminent judgment takes shape in an act of worship (Rev. 15:1-8). Seven angels of judgment get ready for their work while the congregation sings a hymn.

In St. John's arrangement of his theological poem, this judgment scene is the fifth of his six sections.[3] It corresponds to the transition from the fifth book of Moses to the sixth which is designated with the name Jesus (Joshua) and tells of the occupation of the promised land. (The Bible of the early church was the Septuagint, the Greek translation of the Hebrew original. Where we read the Hebrew name "Joshua" in our Bibles, they would read the Greek translation of it, "Jesus").

The two names, Moses and Jesus, are linked at the conclusion of the fiercely-phrased judgment poem, Deuteronomy 32, where it is said that this song was taught to Israel by Moses and Jesus (Deut. 32:34). St. John develops the emphasis by designating the congregational hymn that is sung while the action of judgment is being prepared as the "song of Moses . . . and the song of the Lamb," that is, Jesus (Rev. 15:3).

The hymn text (Rev. 15:3-4) is a much-abridged version of Deuteronomy 32. But there is enough to bring to mind the awesome position in which we find ourselves as a saved people, set down in a dangerous world. Just as Israel, "bought with a price" and trained in the rough disciplines of the wilderness years, purged and toughened by the judgments of God, is ready to enter into the promised land, so are we—conquering and to conquer.

> Your works are immense and terrific
>   Lord God, all powerful,
> Your ways are right and clear,
>   O King of the nations,
> Who is not in awe of you, Lord,
>   does not celebrate your name?
> You are holy—the one and only!
>   the nations have come, every one.
> They see your judgments in plain sight
>   and are prostrate in adoration! (Rev. 15:3-4)

The Revelation began with a vision of the Christ whom we worship (Rev. 1) and was followed up with a vision of God's people at worship (Rev. 4-5); it will conclude with the newly created heaven and earth fashioned into a place of worship, a sanctuary, and filled with worship (Rev. 21-22). St. John, an exiled pastor with responsibility for seven congregations of Christians subject to a barrage of violence and propaganda from without and infiltrated within by cunningly attractive lies, can think of nothing better than to call them to worship. His insistence on contextualizing everything that they think, experience, and feel in the act of worship is not the fussiness of a liturgiologist who cannot bear the mess of ordinary life and so escapes into the arranged beauties of incense, chant, and ritual. No spiritual leader has shown as much evidence as St. John has of being in touch with and responsive to the manifold difficulties of living a difficult life in a difficult world. St. John's recurrent representations of worship are not pious, escapist fictions, but theological convictions. The conviction is that God's action, not the world's action, is what we want to be involved in. The world is not the context for dealing with God; God is the context for dealing with God (and the world). In a world in which we are constantly subject to dizzying disorientations, worship is the act in which we are reoriented contextually.

Worship is the essential and central act of the Christian. We do many other things in preparation for and as a result of worship: sing, write, witness, heal, teach, paint, serve, help, build, clean, smile. But the centering act is worship. Worship is the act of giving committed attention to the being and action of God. The Christian life is posited on the faith that God is in action. When we worship, it doesn't look like we are doing much—and we aren't. We are looking at what God is doing and orienting our action to the compass points of creation and covenant, judgment and salvation.

In the press of world events that oscillate between the glamor of celebrities and the violence of terrorists, worship seems an absurdity. Most Christians feel the absurdity. Some feel it to the point of abandoning it. Surely this cannot be the right thing to do for human beings of strength and goodwill and intelligence? Surely it is a waste of good energy to hand around a loaf of bread and a chalice of wine? The more a person is aware of the many-dimensioned catastrophes (moral, ecological, nuclear, etc.) that threaten human existence, the more the act of worship is called into question. The people who quit worshiping are not, for the most part, people who do not care about the world, but precisely those who do. It is not for lack of moral energy that worship is slighted by many, but exactly because of it. They desert the place of worship with the best of motives, in order to *do* something about the world's condition. The people with whom they have been worshiping all these years—some of them not too bright, many of them nice enough as neighbors, most of them sleepily unaware of the gravity of our condition—all at once seem unpromising allies, and they leave them in search of moral intensity and intellectual rigor.

There are others who do not desert the place of worship, but in staying do something worse: they subvert it. They turn it into a place of entertainment that will refresh bored and tired consumers and pump some zest into them; or they turn it into a lecture hall on the assumption that what they know, they then do; or turn it into a platform for launching good works, shooting rockets of righteousness behind the enemy lines. Attention is subverted from what God is doing to what we are doing. And some, of course, absent themselves from worship out of sloth or indifference, long ago having lost interest in the question "How long?"

But the significant absentees are those who, impatient with the deferred answer, see no point in waiting any longer and leave to do something on their own. The dangerous attendees are those who, restless with the nonaction of worship, subvert it into something that will make something happen. It is for these, those who quit worship and those who subvert it, that St. John's demonstration of the organic continuity between God's actions and our witness and praise, (which is worship), and out of which God shapes his action among us and in the world, is cogent. Nothing that we do has more effect in heaven or on earth.

The action of worship out of which judgment develops is arranged around the waters of baptism, "a sea of glass mingled with fire" (Rev. 15:2). Pulpit, table, and font are the furniture of Christian worship. At the font we are washed from our sins; at the table we are fed the body and blood of Christ; at the pulpit the word of God is given authoritative utterance. The pulpit (throne) received its emphasis in the worship scene of Revelation 4 and 5. The table (altar) oriented the liturgy of Revelation 8; now the font of baptism is central. The worshiping congregation (including in its heavenly dimensions the slaughtered souls from under the altar who had complained of the deferred judgment), gathers around the waters of baptism, singing the judgment hymn.

It is particularly appropriate that the place of baptism furnish the context as the judgments of God come into focus. In the waters of baptism, as St. Paul puts it, we go down to our death and come up to our life: "We were buried therefore with him by baptism into death, so that as Christ was raised from the dead by the glory of the Father, we too might walk in newness of life" (Rom. 6:4). At baptism a life of sin—rebellion against God, refusal to serve his lordship, rejection of his love—is drowned, and new life in Christ resurrected out of it.

The waters of baptism are, first of all, the waters of judgment. But they are, simultaneously and most emphatically, the waters of salvation. All the biblical experiences with water are gathered into Christian meditation on baptism: the watery chaos over which the spirit of God moved, brooding creation; the catastrophic waters that cleansed the earth of its degeneracy into continuous evil and carried Noah and his family to salvation; the Red Sea waters that sank the Egyptian horses and riders and from which Moses marched Israel into freedom; Solomon's great brass tank ("sea") of water used to purify the priests as they administered the temple worship; the Jordan waters into which St. John Baptist dipped crowds of repentant sinners and out of which Jesus rose, proclaimed and proclaiming God's kingdom.

No one standing before the baptismal waters is going to be able to think of judgment exclusively as something that happens to others: *I* have undergone this also, and here I am — despite the judgment, or more likely, because of it — alive, saved. Setting judgment in the context of baptism guards against self-righteous gloating.

From this company, the seven angels, their bowls filled with God's wrath, leave to pour out their judgments. As they empty their bowls and we see the consequences, we realize that this is nothing new but is continuous with what God has been doing all along if we had only had eyes to perceive it. In particular we remember the ten judgment plagues on Egypt, because each of the seven bowls (and this was true of the trumpet plagues earlier) repeats an aspect of judgment long known through that critical episode in the salvation story. This clear link with Egypt reinforces St. John's emphasis on worship, for we recall that the ten plagues were not visited on the Egyptians because they were an extraordinarily evil people, but for a single reason which had no apparent moral content to it at all: they were determined to prevent Israel from worshiping God.

Moses' task, and it is the same for every spiritual leader, was to shape a worshiping people before the Lord. When he came out of his Midian exile in obedience to God's call and presented himself and his message to his people, their spontaneous and uninstructed response was worship: "And the people believed; and when they heard that the Lord had visited the people of Israel and that he had seen their affliction, they bowed their heads and worshiped" (Exod. 4:31). Most of the book of Exodus, after the story of getting out of Egypt has been told, is a training manual for worship (Exod. 24–40).

The celebrated negotiations between Moses and Pharaoh had a single theme: worship. Moses' opening petition to Pharaoh was, "Let my people go, that they may hold a feast to me [God] in the wilderness . . . let us go, we pray, a three days' journey into the wilderness, and sacrifice to the Lord our God" (Exod. 5:1,3). Each renewal of his petition repeated the reason, "Let my people go that they may serve (i.e., 'worship' [*latreuo*]) me."[4] Two variants pick up phrases from the original petition: "sacrifice to the Lord" (Exod. 8:27) and "hold a feast to the Lord" (Exod. 10:9). Moses' task was to lead his people in worship. Pharaoh's sin was that he prevented them. The judgment plagues are visited over this issue, and this issue alone. The greatest evil that people of faith face from outside is the obstruction of worship. The greatest evil that they face from inside is the subversion of worship. This is what we have most to fear. This is what St. John gives continuous attention to. And it is on this evil that the judgments are visited.

The cry for and questioning of God's judgment, "How long?" is now established in its proper context, the act of worship. Judgment is no longer a matter of getting clarifying information or mending a personal grievance; it is *experienced* as the long-ago launched, deeply worked out, thoroughly accomplished action of God which we entered into through our baptism, the consequences of which we share in our salvation, which we participate in by means of our worship, and the completion of which we already celebrate by means of word and sacrament.

The judgment theme is completed in the portrayal of the "great whore" (Rev. 17–18). First there is a narration of her destruction (Rev. 17); then there is a song on the same subject (Rev. 18). This sequence, story followed by song, is taken from Exodus and reinforces our perception that judgment is enacted in order to set people free to worship, and when the people are set free, the order of the day is worship (Rev. 19). Exodus 14 tells the story of the judgment on Egypt, which was at the same time the salvation of Israel; Exodus 15 sings a song on the same subject. St. John uses this identical said/sung pattern, but substitutes the Great Whore and her lovers for Pharaoh and the Egyptians. We know that God's judgment came upon Pharaoh because he obstructed Israel's worship. We realize that the Great Whore is judged under the same indictment.

The task of the apocalyptic imagination is to provide images that show us what is going on in our lives. "If there are mysterious powers around," a character in a Saul Bellow novel says, "only exaggeration can help us to see them. We all sense that there are powers that make the world—we see that when we look at it—and other powers that unmake it."[5] But these things that were once obvious to us, get muddled as we pick our way through the world's traffic. What was at one time clear in faith gets blurred and distorted through the smudged window glass of our culture. St. John's apocalyptic images clarify in two directions. The world of revelation, the 2000 years of experience (4000 for us) of being God's people is clarified. None of it is obsolete or irrelevant. We do not make up the life of faith on the spot as we have need for it. We do not innovate salvation in moments of desperation. We have ancestors. Our Christ was slain "before the foundation of the world." Faith is rooted in history and grounded in geology. Our poor memories and distracted affections have obscured the connections; St. John's images reconnect us.

The other clarification is local: our daily encounters with bank tellers, post office clerks, and gas station attendants are, each one, elements of sin and grace. All of these people and each of these encounters is a significant detail in the life of faith. But we are not aware of it. Most of the time we are not living in a crisis in which we are conscious of our need of God, yet everything we do is critical, to our faith, and God is critically involved in it. All day long we are doing eternally important things without knowing it. All through the day we inadvertently speak words that enter peoples lives and change them in minor or major ways, and we never know it. Is there a way to train us in an awareness of the glories pulsing in every willingness, of the evils pregnant in every willfulness? The apocalyptic vision is a way.

The Great Whore symbol of everyday experience is a very nice city to live in. The woman and the scarlet beast on which she sits comprise the streets we walk daily, the shops where we buy our vegetables while making small talk with the proprietor. Flannery O'Connor, in answer to a question about why she created such bizarre characters in her stories, replied that for the near-blind you have to draw very large, simple caricatures.[6] The Great Whore is one of these large, simple caricatures. It is an image that can bring to never-again-to-be-forgotten awareness the powerfully seductive presence of those who would obstruct or subvert our worship of the slain and risen Lamb.

The worship of God in Christ is the most important and the most difficult thing that Christians do. Because it is so difficult, we are always ready to go for something easier, especially if that something seems to include all the essentials of worship. But we had better not. The Great Whore, sunk like a millstone in the sea, is our warning. Whore is a sexual term. But in Revelation 17–18, the Great Whore image is not about sex, it is a metaphor for worship gone wrong. St. John has nothing to say about the sexual conditions in the late first century; his business is with the conditions of faith. His pastoral responsibility is to prevent his Christians from quitting the enduringly arduous life of worship in favor of something which appears just as religious, looks a lot better, and is a lot easier. He tells them about the Great Whore to open their eyes to the differences between the worship of the Lamb and this other worship, which is not worship at all, but keeps us from worship. Whoredom is sex connected with money. The physical union of the sexes is given a price tag. When the intercourse has been paid for, the relationship is at an end, until whatever time it is paid for again. The coupling is sexual, the relationship is commercial.

The terrible thing about the whore is not that she takes strangers to bed with her (that is the one arguably decent thing that she does), but that once getting them there she uses her body to lie about life: there is no joining of lives, only of genitals. The exploration and development of our unique human identity, of which sex is the physical means, is replaced by elaborate and deceiving fantasies. A fundamental impoverishment of person is accomplished behind a seductive spell of perfumes, silks, and flatteries. Whoredom uses sex to lie about life: the truth of life is that love is a gift, that relationships are commitments, that sexuality is the sacrament of spirituality. The whore's lie is that love is purchased, that relationships are "deals," that sexuality is appetite. Whoredom is the use of good to do evil; the use of a good body to demean the person, the use of the means of realizing our identity to depersonalize identities. The great wrong in whoredom is not sexual immorality but spiritual sacrilege.

Worship under the aspect of the Great Whore is the commercialization of our great need and deep desire for meaning, love, and salvation, for the completion of ourselves from beyond ourselves. Whore-worship thrives by naming the worst things about us—our pride, our lust, our envy, our greed, our anger—with the designation "God," and gathering depersonalized and depersonalizing crowds to pursue these divinized defects religiously. The great danger that the world poses for us is not in its gross evils, but its easy religion. The promise of success, ecstasy, and meaning that we can get for a price is Whore-worship. It is the diabolical inversion of "you are bought with a price" to "I can get it for you wholesale."

The Great Whore is presented in implicit contrast to the Virgin Bride. After the judgment of the Whore is complete, the contrast will become explicit at the marriage supper of the Lamb (Rev. 19). The Bride is as sexual a metaphor as the Whore, but it forms an absolute contrast. For the Whore, sex is in the service of commerce; with the Bride, sex is devoted to love. For the Whore, sex is a contract; for the Bride, sex is a life commitment. For the Whore, sex is a calculation; for the Bride, sex is an offering.

We are sexual beings deeply, thoroughly, and inescapably. In the experience of our sexuality we know another, and, indirectly, ourselves. It is also in our sexuality that we know, or don't know, God. Whore-worship is a matter of moments and occasion. Bride-worship gathers every part of life into union. Whore-worship is practiced on the principle of attraction and pleasure; Bride-worship is for better and for worse, in sickness and in health, till death do us part. Bride-worship is always at an immediate disadvantage in competition with Whore-worship, for Whore-worship is indulgent and lusty getting, while Bride-worship is sacrificed and faithful giving. That is why Whore-worship is such a continuous threat to Bride-worship. And why we need St. John's violent caricature of the religious advertising that endangers our endurance and faithfulness.

Whore-worship brings us great gain: we get what we want when we want it. Bride-worship is an offering: we give ourselves and don't know how long we will wait for fulfillment. Throughout the Revelation, the great scenes of worship show God being served—the people come to him, giving themselves in praise. At no place does he entice them with easy promises. In the great lament of Revelation 17 over the Great Whore's demise, the longest and most detailed lament is from the merchants and sea traders (Rev. 17:11–19): in Whore-worship they got everything they wanted, their lives overflowed with things, and now it is gone, wasted, up in smoke. They are bereft of everything they were promised and invested in and enjoyed. It is not their businesses that have collapsed, but their religion, a religion of self-indulgence, of getting. Now it is gone: salvation-by-checkbook is gone, god-on-demand is gone, meaning-by-money is gone, religion-as-feeling is gone, self-as-(temporary)-god is gone. They are left with nothing but themselves, of whom after a lifetime in the whorehouse, they know nothing.

But the judgment of God reaches its conclusion not in the laments but with a hymn of hallelujahs. The biblical book that the Revelation most resembles, the Psalms, is brought to a formal conclusion with this identical word, *hallelujah*. Parallels between the Psalms and the Revelation abound. Both books are oriented in the act of worship. Both give voice to an enormous range of trouble; the enemy holds a conspicuous place in the experience of the psalmists and St. John alike. The longing for a fairly rendered judgment is passionately prayed. And it is all gathered to a conclusion with the word *hallelujah*!

The word *hallelujah* occurs in Revelation for the first time in Chapter 19, verse 1. The timing is exactly right, protecting our gratitude and relief for judgment from degenerating into gloating over the judged. As judgment is enacted in the cannibalizing and cremation of the whore, we are exposed to the great danger of denunciatory glee. Longing for judgment is only a step removed from a demand for revenge. The desire for God's judgments always totters on the edge of wanting to see our enemies writhe in pain. The saint, wanting God's judgments to set things right, has a way of slithering into the sadist who takes pleasure in seeing his tormenters punished. Four hallelujahs pull us from the edge of gloating over pain and back to the act of worship where we are humble and adoring in the presence of the Glory.

The first hallelujah (Rev. 19:1) celebrates the truth and righteousness of God's judgments on the Great Whore, that image that summed up every temptation to abandon God, every trap to betray Christ, every ambush to our endurance, every seduction to our faith.

Hallelujah!

> The Salvation, the Glory, the Power
>   all belong to our God.
> The Judgments are accurate and right.
>
> He judged the Great Whore!
>   the earth ruined with her cheating sex,
>   and God's servants' blood spilled by her hand
> He restored to rightness! (Rev. 19:1-3)

The second hallelujah (Rev. 19:3) is breathed gratitude as the billowing smoke of her incineration disperses in the air.

Hallelujah!

> Her smoke ascends
> endlessly, endlessly. (Rev. 19:3)

The third hallelujah (Rev. 19:4), spiced with an affirmative amen, is spoken by the twenty-four elders and four creatures, the resident liturgical community around the throne, the splendid choir invisibly present to our rag-tag gatherings for worship each Lord's Day, and then answered antiphonally, out of the throne itself.

Amen! Hallelujah!

> Praise our God
>   all his servants.
> Everyone in awe before him:
>   all the small people!
>   all the big people! (Rev. 19:4-5)

The fourth hallelujah (Rev. 19:6) is a thundering congregational response to the call to worship that issued from the throne and called everyone to praise God. It goes on to announce the celebrative meal that brings Christ and his people into an eternity of shared love, the marriage supper of the Lamb.

Hallelujah!

The Lord rules,
   our all-powerful God
Let us be glad, let us celebrate,
   let us offer the glory to him.
For the Lamb's marriage has arrived
   His bride has dressed herself
in the wedding gown he gave her
   a gown of linen, lambent and clean. (Rev. 19:6-8)

In the Psalter, four hallelujah Psalms (Ps. 146-149) gathered all the pain and lament of Israel out of the mud of unfinished judgments into a detailed elaboration of praise, and then fused them into the mighty Psalm 150, with its thirteen salvos of praise, cannonading hallelujahs through Israel and church. Here the four hallelujahs gather the broken bodies and spilled blood of the church out of the judged world into the great Eucharist to which all our eucharists are sacramentally linked, and pronounce a blessing on the guests.

11. The Last Word on Salvation
Revelation 19 and 20

Thou preparest a table before me
  in the presence of my enemies;
thou anointest my head with oil,
  my cup overflows.

PSALM 23:5

"Hallelujah! For the Lord our God the Almighty reigns.
Let us rejoice and exult and give him the glory,
for the marriage of the Lamb has come,
and his Bride has made herself ready;
it was granted her to be clothed with fine linen,
bright and pure"—
for the fine linen is the righteous deeds of the saints.
And the angel said to me, "Write this:
Blessed are those who are invited
  to the marriage supper of the Lamb."

REVELATION 19:6–9

When the danger is greatest, the saving power also increases.

FRIEDRICH HÖLDERLIN

Jesus, the name with which St. John begins and ends the Revelation (Rev. 1:1 and 22:21), means "the Lord saves." The first person in scripture to carry the name was Joshua, son of Nun, the Hebrew general who led a saved people to take possession of the country of their salvation. Twice now, St. John has taught us salvation songs that celebrate the triumph of God's work (Rev. 7:10 and 12:10). His third and final salvation song did double duty: it concluded the judgment vision and introduced the salvation vision:

Hallelujah!

The Salvation, the Glory, the Power
  all belong to our God.
The judgments are accurate and right.

>   He judged the Great Whore!
>   the earth ruined with her cheating sex,
>   and God's servants' blood spilled by her hand
>   He restored to rightness! (Rev. 19:1-3)

The salvation songs and images that St. John sets before us are placed against a background of catastrophe. Salvation is the answer to catastrophe. The dimensions of catastrophe are understood, biblically, to exceed human capacity for recovery. All parts of creation—Arcturus and the Mississippi, Lebanon cedars and English turnips, rainbow trout and parula warblers, eskimos and aborigines—have been jarred out of the harmonious original and are in discord. The transparent complementarity of male and female is darkened into rivalry and accusation. The cool evening conversation between God and humans is distorted into furtive evasions. The "fit" between heaven and earth, between creation and creature and Creator, is dislocated: form no longer matches function, result no longer flows from purpose. Instead there is pain, travail, sweat, death.

Nothing is exempt from the catastrophe. Nothing is innocent in the catastrophe. Heaven and earth are implicated. Bacteria foul the bloodstreams, sickening sinner and saint. Hailstones plummet out of the skies and flatten a wheatfield, fragile and elegant, ready for harvest. Liquid fire rips through the earth's crust, incinerating tigers and trees in volcanic fury. Rebel angels, disbarred from practicing in the courts of heaven, infiltrate invisible world realms, twisting the glories of intelligence into patterns of deception. And human beings, created in "the image of God" discover within themselves, often in shocked horror, a "heart desperately wicked."

The catastrophe is beyond calculation. Still, there is so much beauty in the wreckage, such deep goodness, so much moral zest, such blessing, so much active intelligence, that it is possible to live for stretches of time, sometimes quite long stretches, honestly unaware of the extent of the disaster. But then, either by a slow accumulation of evidence carefully observed, or by a sudden, crisis-evoked recognition, it is inescapably before us, and we are inescapably in it: we are separated from our origins, separated from our God, separated from parents and cousins and siblings, from bears and hawks and coyotes. We are, in Walker Percy's blunt report, "lost in the cosmos."[1] We don't know where we are. We don't know who we are.

The catastrophe was caused, Christians believe, by a primeval act of rebellious disobedience that attempted to circumvent or displace God. But that is not the popular belief. The popular belief is that however bad things seem from time to time, there is no catastrophe. To face the fact of catastrophe would involve, at some point or other, dealing with God. Anything seems preferable to that. So the devil doctors the report, the world edits the evidence. People reduce their perceptions of catastrophe to a level that is manageable without getting God into the picture in any substantial way. And so the same act that caused the catastrophe, perpetuates it.

If there is no accurate perception of catastrophe, there can be no adequate perception of salvation, for salvation is God's action that deals with the catastrophe. There has been nothing puny in St. John's perception of catastrophe—it requires a strong stomach to stay on the scene while the seals are broken, the trumpets blown, and the bowls poured out. By the time these sequences have been completed, many people have deserted St. John and taken up with milder views, something that they can browse through in a condensed version and contemplate to the beat of a Scott Joplin rag. It is too bad, because now they have no context for appreciating St. John's correspondingly energetic rendition of salvation.

The root meaning in Hebrew of "salvation" is to be broad, to become spacious, to enlarge. It carries the sense of deliverance from an existence that has become compressed, confined, and cramped.[2] Salvation is the plot of history. It is the most comprehensive theme of scripture, overtaking and surpassing catastrophe. Salvation is God's determination to rescue his creation; it is his activity in recovering the world. It is personal and impersonal, it deals with souls and cities, it touches sin and sickness. There is a reckless indiscriminateness about salvation. There are no fine distinctions about who or what or when—the whole lost world is invaded, infiltrated, beckoned, invited, wooed: "for God so loved the *world* that he *gave* his only Son." God takes on the entire catastrophe.

The world's alternative to salvation is optimism. Optimism is a way of staying useful and being hopeful without having recourse to God. It requires, of course, a much reduced perception of catastrophe if it is to maintain credibility. Optimism comes in two forms, moral and technological. The moral optimist thinks that generous applications of well-intentioned goodwill to the slagheaps of injustice, wickedness, and the world's corruption will put the world gradually, but surely, in the right. The technological optimist thinks that by vigorously applying scientific intelligence to the problems of poverty, pollution, and neurosis, the world will gradually, but surely, be put right. Neither form of optimism worships God, although the moral optimist sometimes provides ceremonial space for him. Optimists see that there are few things left to do to get the world in good shape, and think that they are just the ones to do it.

It seems ungracious to be unenthusiastic over such an enormous expenditure of intelligence and good will. These people, after all, are at least doing something. But the biblical discernment is that a spiritual evil motivates their good actions. It is the evil of ignoring or circumventing or denying God. Their efforts to live well, to help others and improve the world are fueled by a determination, conscious or unconscious, to keep God out of who they are and what they are doing. As long as they can rationalize, fantasize, or interpret the catastrophe as something considerably less than catastrophe, they can deny their need of God for salvation, either for themselves or others or the world. This optimism is so pervasive, advertises itself so attractively, and chalks up so many awards, honors and achievements, that it is difficult not to be impressed, and then, in the general euphoria, to go along with it. It is certainly a lot easier, for then we do not have to deal with God.

St. John's pastoral task is to keep his Christians dealing with God. One part of his task is to keep us scrupulously honest before the catastrophe: if the sharp details of evil blur into the background, in five minutes we are devising our own rescue operations for saving the world, or at least the neighborhood. But another part of his task is to keep us believing participants in God's action of salvation. Salvation is a larger subject than catastrophe. He shows us the largeness of the action and the nature of our participation in it in the great salvation vision of Revelation 19 and 20.

St. John's salvation vision is composed of two elements, a meal and a war. The meal and the war represent the polarities of salvation. It is as necessary that we explore the immensities of salvation as that we not draw back from the enormities of catastrophe. We are, it seems, even more fainthearted before grace than before evil. St. John's salvation images of the meal and the war are the devices by which he will draw us as deeply as he can into the country of salvation.

Unused to living beyond ourselves, out of control, by faith, the great danger is that we timidly retreat to the kind of religion that we can manage. The commonest reductions that we make as we attempt to get God's salvation down to a size that we are comfortable with is to reduce it to subjective devotion, or reduce it to ethical decorum, or work some combination of the two. But salvation is the action of God. It is always far more than we think it is, far more than we are experiencing at any one time. We are forever stopping short and defining it in terms that we understand right now. But such understandings are always premature, and therefore reduce this large action that we have so much more to learn in, so much more, by God's grace, to get in on. "Having begun in the Spirit are you now ending in the flesh?" was St. Paul's slightly acidic comment on our reductionism. St. John's pastoral approach is through visions: he opposes the reduction of salvation to the spiritually subjective by showing us a meal; he opposes the reduction of salvation to good manners by showing us a war.

The four hallelujah songs linked the scene of judgment, showing the dimensions of catastrophe (Rev. 15-18), with the vision of salvation. The first song proclaimed salvation, the second and third expanded the theme, and the fourth announced salvation as a marriage between Jesus (the Lamb) and Christians (his Bride). The songs have precipitated us into the pulsating center of salvation.

The image of marriage immediately develops into an image of a marriage supper: the saved are not only the Bride, they are guests at the ceremony that celebrates the unique joining of intimacy and faithfulness that is marriage. In St. John's Gospel, Jesus' first sign is given at a marriage supper in Cana, where he turned the waters of purification into the wine of blessing; his last meeting with his disciples was a resurrection breakfast on Galilee beach. St. Mark shows Jesus at supper with sinners, scandalizing the sensibilities of the Pharisees. In St. Luke's Gospel, the Easter evening supper at Emmaus reveals the Savior to Cleopas and his friend. Jesus was fond of using the common setting of meals, dinners, and wedding suppers both for telling stories and engaging in conversation. It was over a meal that Zaccheus learned of salvation. At the last meal Jesus ate with his disciples, he commanded its repeated continuation, so that they might accurately remember what they had experienced in him ("do this in remembrance of me") and unwaveringly expect what he was yet to do ("until I come").

We know that Jesus worshiped in synagogues and temple, the standard places where God was worshiped and scripture taught. But most of his teaching and prayer took place in streets and fields, on the mountains and in the homes where he gave and was given meals. When he established a way for his followers to maintain what they had experienced, received, and been commanded by him to do, he did it by telling them to have a meal together of bread and wine. They did it. And we keep doing it.

Considering the overall faithlessness and forgetfulness characterizing Christians through the centuries—the general squalor of our conduct, our propensity for heresy—one of the truly incredible exceptions is the persistence with which this meal has been eaten. There is no single element of continuing obedience that is more impressive than this. From age to age, different doctrinal emphases come into ascendancy while others slip into abeyance. Through the centuries, cultural accommodations to the radicalness of the gospel are made here in one direction, there in another. The worship of Christians has found architectural expression in all sizes and shapes of buildings. All through these differences, changes, and conflicts the meal has been eaten: the same words always spoken, the same elements of bread and wine always consumed. There have been, it is true, arguments about what the words meant, what the elements are—but the arguments have never interrupted the obedience.

The salvation vision opens with an invitation to this meal:

> Happy is everyone invited
> to the Lamb's marriage supper!

The power of this eucharistic meal to keep us participant in the essentials of salvation is impressive. This is the primary way that Christians remember, receive, and share the meaning of our salvation: Christ crucified for us, his blood shed for the remission of our sins. This is where we affirm the action of our salvation. What we know and believe of Christ in his incarnation, and what we expect and hope of Christ in his coming again, brackets our present lives: in this large context, and in this ordinary setting, we celebrate our salvation. Every eucharistic meal that we eat reintroduces us into this large country of the one for whom St. John coined the grammatical name "is and was and is to come" (Rev. 1:4, 8). Significantly, he puts the present tense first ("is"), and then shows that present comprehended by his past and future ("was" and "is to come"). This grammatical collapsing of all the tenses into one takes place sacramentally at the eucharist. The many-dimensioned reality of salvation is preserved not by a truth that we must figure out, or by an ethical behavior that we must carry out, but in a meal to eat. Not everyone can comprehend a doctrine; not everyone can obey a precept; but everyone can eat a piece of bread, drink a cup of wine, and understand a simple statement—my body, my blood. I maintain continuity with the killed and raised Jesus who is salvation, not be learning something or by performing something, but by eating a meal.

The eucharistic meal uses everyday elements of the common life to connect me with the extraordinary and unique crucifixion and resurrection of Jesus. Eucharist is at one and the same time ordinary and extraordinary, the repetition of the commonplace and the celebration of the unique. Meals, in all cultures, seem to have this capability of stretching from the ordinary to the extraordinary and interpenetrating them. The three meals of our ordinary days are routine. But when we want to celebrate a great occasion, wedding or birthday or anniversary, we do not find it unnatural to use the meal as the means for expressing intensity, ecstasy, and consummation.

Salvation, on the one hand, is Christ on the cross and risen from the tomb; on the other hand, it is eating bread and drinking wine. In the eucharistic meal, these cannot be separated: salvation is both Christ on Golgotha and Christ in me.

The eucharistic meal does more: it maintains the social shape of salvation. Eating together is an act of trust and love among friends and strangers, an accepted invitation to equality with one another before God. We do not customarily, or if we can help it, eat alone. We come together with others, with family and friends. We demonstrate basic courtesies at the table. It is the place we learn consideration and forgiveness. It is also the place to which we invite strangers, hospitality being the means by which we bridge suspicion and loneliness, gathering the outsider into the place of nurture and acceptance. The eucharistic table incorporates the evangelistic thrust of salvation that Jesus insisted upon: "And men will come from east and west, and from north and south, and sit at table in the kingdom of God" (Luke 13:29).

Every invitation to the eucharistic meal and every setting down to it is an implicit defense against reducing salvation to the spuriously spiritual—a devotional transaction that takes place in the strict privacy of the soul. The meal makes it impossible to keep salvation as a private preserve between God and us in the interior depths of one's soul. The snobbish cultivation of devout feelings of salvation that withdraws from mingling with unsavory people and trafficking with everyday things comes to grief at the eucharistic table. It is impossible to preserve a devoutly pure subjectivity when you have to deal with spilled wine and bread crumbs. Nor does the meal make it easy to experience salvation primarily as the cozy manipulation of spiritual feelings in carefully arranged settings with people we like a lot, insulated from the grosser aspects of the world. The eucharistic meal will not accommodate these reductions: the people at the table are those the Lord invites, not the ones I like; the elements on the table are material bread and wine, not spiritual thoughts and devout feelings. At the meal we listen to the unvarnished words of Jesus; at the meal we eat and drink under the straightforward command of Jesus.

The second element in St. John's salvation vision is a war. First the image of the Bridegroom Christ married to his Bride Christians was expanded into the image of the Lamb Christ providing himself as the eucharistic meal. This is now juxtaposed to the image of the Warrior Christ riding into the great war, Armageddon. The contrast between meal and war could hardly be more extreme, but it is complementarity, not contradiction, that we experience as we submit to the images. Salvation is the intimacies and festivities of marriage; salvation is aggressive battle and the defeat of evil. Salvation is neither of these things by itself. It is the two energies, the embrace of love and the assault on evil, in polar tension, each defined by the other, each feeding into the other.

The war vision shows Jesus on a white horse, splendidly and victoriously robed, leading Christians in a triumphant rout of the dragon and his two beasts, which is to say, all the variations on evil that come to us and that we can experience.

> I saw heaven wide open;
>
> Look! a white horse!
> Faithful and true
>
> Is riding the horse
> judging and warring
>
> in righteousness. (Rev. 19:11)

St. John's details of the battle-scene tantalize us with complexities that escape a neatly diagrammed summary. There is more here than meets the eye; the action spills off the map. But there is no room for misunderstanding: salvation is being won. The two beasts, responsible for so much confusion and suffering are disposed of, "thrown alive into the lake of fire that burns with sulphur" (Rev. 19:20). A millennium later the dragon, evil source of catastrophe from Eden to Egypt, and from the crucifixion of Jesus to the martyrdom of Christians, is thrown in with them (Rev. 20:10). Why all three are not dumped in the lake together is one of the, to me, unanswerable but minor ambiguities that keeps the vision from being reduced to a diagram. The last word, though, is that every form and source of evil is banished from history.

Salvation comes into being, the vision informs us, in the face of furious opposition. Much of the opposition is hidden and does its work obscurely. One function of the vision is to train our perceptions so that we will never again overlook it. At the same time the vision raises our adrenalin level, so that we bring our energetic best to the high spiritual drama that we participate in every day as we confess the lordship of Christ. Once having seen this, we are not likely to fight a halfhearted war against a wholehearted enemy.

We do not live in a benign or neutral world. There is malign opposition, an evil will at work to deceive and destroy us. Salvation attacks an enemy. "Our salvation is a drama played out with the devil, a devil who is not simply generalized evil, but an evil intelligence determined on its own supremacy."[3] When Jesus taught us to pray, "Deliver us from evil," he was arming us for a life of salvation. St. Paul, preaching salvation, did not organize ethical societies around the Mediterranean basin; he fought battles and developed an extensive vocabulary to name the evil opposition: powers (Rom. 8:38), rulers (1 Cor. 2:8), thrones (Col. 1:16), dominions (Eph. 1:21). He didn't seem to be in the least bit intimidated by these ominous forces. He was always working from a stance of accomplished victory, since Jesus on the cross "disarmed the principalities and powers and made a public example of them, triumphing over them in him" (Col. 2:15). There is, apparently, nothing to fear in the act of fighting. Danger here is all in the not-fighting. The safest place is on the battlefield, for it is there that Christ is active, riding the white horse.

St. John's Armageddon thrusts this dimension of salvation forcibly into our awareness, and thereby enlists our faithful participation in the action of salvation. The only way we can dodge the pastoral intent of the vision is by projecting it into the future as an end-of-the-world war. It *is* an end-of-the-world war, but it is the world of temptation and injustice and deceit in us and our communities that is coming to an end. St. John uses the vision of the great war to actively engage our faith and participation in all aspects of salvation that require alert, obedient, courageous engagement. If we suppose (which many seem to) that salvation is a diploma that qualifies us for eternity, a diploma we can frame and hang on our bedroom wall, then we have it all wrong. It is battle. The moment we walk away from the Eucharist, having received the life of our Lord, we walk into Armageddon, where we exercise the strength of our Lord. Readers of the gospels are accustomed to this aggressive dimension of salvation. Jesus' attacks on the forces of evil and the deceits of hypocrisy are as common as his gregarious meals with sinners, prostitutes, and friends.

The "strong man's house" (Mark 3:27) that Jesus entered and so energetically plundered of its goods—the souls of the sin-enslaved, the bodies of the sickness-oppressed—is Armageddon. The seventy disciples, returning from their first day in Armageddon, were exhilarated, "Lord, even the demons are subject to us in your name!" Jesus's response anticipated St. John's vision: "I saw Satan fall like lightning from heaven. Behold, I have given you authority to tread upon serpents and scorpions, and over all the power of the enemy; and nothing shall hurt you. Nevertheless do not rejoice in this, that the spirits are subject to you; but rejoice that your names are written in heaven" (Luke 10:17–20). Jesus confirmed their euphoria, but he also set it in a larger context: the core of salvation was not what they were doing ("spirits subject to you") but the work *he* was accomplishing ("your names are written in heaven"). Their work was ancillary to his; to keep their focus sharp, they should aim their rejoicing at his accomplishment on their behalf. We are the recipients and participants in salvation, not its makers and shapers.

The term Armageddon was introduced when the sixth plague bowl was emptied of its contents (Rev. 16:12–16). This is the only occurrence of the name in scripture. It means in Hebrew "mountain [Ar] of Megiddo." Zechariah in a parallel context shows God victorious over all opposition at the site of Biqathmeggedon, plain of Megiddo (Zech. 12:10). Megiddo, whether as mountain or plain, served the prophetic imagination as a place to muster and concentrate our faith, lest we be indolent in the crisis. Other places serve similarly for other writers. Malcolm Cowley has written of his experience, fighting with his righteous friends against the evil fascists in the 1920s: "there were moments in France when the senses were immeasurably sharpened by the thought of dying next day, or possibly next week."[4]

Meggido was a large fortress city, strategically placed at the base of the Carmel range of mountains, sentinel over the plain of Esdraelon and Valley of Jezreel, the historical battlefields of Israel. Occupying a correspondingly strategic position across the diagonal of the plain was Mount Tabor where Deborah and Barak mustered the tribes for their triumphant assault on the Canaanites. Down the plain to the East was Gilboa where Saul came to doom. Josiah died on this field, fighting Egyptians. Jehu's furious and bloody chariot chase traversed this ground. On the mountain rising behind Meggido, Elijah won his contest with the Jezebel-sponsored priests of the evil worship that seduced Israel from faithfulness to her Lord. Just over the rim of mountains across the plain was the Nazareth in which Jesus grew up.

It is no part of my task here to account for the difficulty posed by a holy God working his salvation through those ancient battles. But there it is: we are dealing with something larger than ethics. God works with what is at hand, and war was at hand—evil but not incapable of being used to good purpose by God: "Surely the wrath of men shall praise thee; the residue of wrath thou wilt gird upon thee" (Ps. 76:10). It will hardly do for us to be more scrupulous than God. Novelist Doris Lessing, who carries no brief for the Christian cause, nonetheless is wry in her observation of people who have the habit of dismissing great tracts of the Bible because "Jehovah does not think or behave like a social worker."[5] The fact is that salvation is war. Moses led his people into battle against the

Amalekites, Joshua led his people into battle against the Philistines. By the time of Jesus, words have preempted swords as the primary weaponry, but the fact of war has not changed: Jesus leads his people into battle against the dragon and the two beasts, every malign force that diminishes our lives and damns our souls. Every day of our lives we face Sisera and Jezebel and Necho. Salvation wins back the territory lost to the invasion of evil, and restores the country to the believing, enduring, and worshiping people of God.

In the apocalyptic perspective of St. John's vision, the vaunted pretensions of diabolic evil are brought to our surprised awareness in the forms of dragon, sea beast, and land beast, but at the end evil can only express itself in the comic ugliness of three frogs (Rev. 16:23–24). St. John's vision takes evil seriously, but not too seriously. St. Teresa of Avila had a similarly healthy respect and lively awareness of evil. But she was impatient with people who were over-wrought by it: "a fig for all the devils . . . I don't understand these fears, 'the devil! the devil!,' when we can say 'God!' 'God!' and make the devil tremble . . . I pay no more attention to them than to flies. I think they are such cowards that when they observe that they are esteemed but little, their strength leaves them."[6]

By setting Armageddon before us as a vision of salvation, this pastor prevents us from thoughtlessly reducing salvation to good behavior, supposing that the consequence of salvation is to make us nice, install good manners in everyone, and make us all docile consumers. It is difficult to see how people who read scripture for very long can come up with such a tame view of salvation. There is, of course, a great deal of ethical instruction in scripture, but the instruction is not the action; *salvation* – at Gibeon, at Elah, at Kidron – is the action, and the one prominent characteristic in this action is an aroused ferocity against evil. There is simply no margin left for misunderstanding salvation as an Ivy League honor code. "I am persuaded," says Bishop Aulen, at the end of his book *Christus Victor*, "that no form of Christian teaching has any future before it except such as can keep steadily in view the reality of evil that is in the world and go to meet the evil with a battle song of triumph."[7]

At the same time, it is patently clear that this war is like no war that has ever been fought, or will be fought, by human armies. The warrior Messiah, seated on the white horse, "learned the art of war-fare," as St. Hillary so neatly put it, "when he overcame the world."[8] He has a single weapon, his word. He wages war by what he *says*, which is an articulation of who he is. His name is written on gar-ment and thigh: he is well-identified.

This is the identical war that St. Paul found himself in: We battle not against flesh and blood but against principalities and powers. "For though we live in the world we are not carrying on a worldly war, for the weapons of our warfare are not worldly but have divine power to destroy strongholds. We destroy arguments and every proud obstacle to the knowledge of God, and take every thought captive to obey Christ" (2 Cor. 10:3-5). When the sword-word came from Jesus' mouth in the Capernaum synagogue, the demoniac was not slain, but delivered (Mark 1:21-28). When the sharp sword-word issued from Jesus's mouth in the Gaderene cemetery, the demoniac, Legion, was not slaughtered but saved (Mark 5:1-20). We who accompany Jesus across the mountains and through the valleys of salvation are permitted no other weapons. When St. Peter, eager to fight the evil forces that were sweeping Jesus towards the cross, bared his weapon and with an awkward swing managed to cut off the ear of the high priest's slave, Jesus put an immediate stop to it–"no more of this!"–and repaired the damage with his healing touch.[9] Wendell Berry's quiet sarcasm, "Did you finish killing/every-body who was against peace?"[10] exposes the folly of using the weap-ons of destruction to wage the war of salvation.

William James campaigned for a "moral equivalent of war"–something that would arouse all the prowess that war evokes in us, but without the carnage and the waste. Nothing much came of his campaign. St. John had much the same idea, but his was a spiritual rather than a moral equivalent, and went much deeper. His vision arouses aggression against wickedness without using any of the weapons of wickedness. It has not eliminated the use of those weapons by others, it is true, nor is it likely to, but it has recruited millions into the action of salvation. It is impossible to calculate the large tracts of salvation that have been recovered from evil dominion without anyone's blood being spilled, except by martyred Christians in voluntary sacrifice.

One of the unintended and unhappy consequences of St. John's Armageddon vision is that it has inflamed the imaginations of the biblically illiterate into consuming endtime fantasies, distracting them from the daily valor of dogged obedience, sacrificial love, and alert endurance. This is exactly what St. John did not intend, as even a cursory reading of his Revelation makes evident. When people are ignorant of the imagery of prophets and gospels, and untutored in the metaphorical language of war in the story of salvation, they are easy prey for entertaining predictions of an end-time holocaust at Mount Meggido in Israel, conjured up from newspaper clippings on international politics. Jesus told us quite clearly that the people who make these breathless and sensationalist predictions are themselves the false Christs and false prophets that they are pretending to warn us against (Matt. 24:23-26).

But the suppression of the vision would be too large a price to pay to prevent these irresponsibilities. A better antidote, if more difficult, is to let St. John's vision resonate with Jesus' gospel-reported actions, and St. Paul's epistle-promulgated teachings, and then trust the stories and instructions and visions to work their complementarities in our imaginations, pulling us into the terrifically energetic confluence of, as Professor Goppelt has it, the "already and the not yet" which is salvation.[11]

All of St. John's vision sets the present demands of living by faith in Jesus Christ in the context of everything else that is going on, the past flowing into this present, the future rushing into this present. Sin introduces divisions into our perceptions, categorized separations into our understandings, especially between what we can see (the historical) and what we cannot see (the eschatological).[12] St. John assumes the correspondence of these two dimensions in the eucharistic meal, and continues the assumption in the war of Armageddon. The Armageddon war sets our daily conflict with evil in the context of the cosmic conflict, or vice versa. What we put asunder, St. John puts together. This is what good pastoral work is. This is what every sermon attempts. St. John's Revelation is one of the great moments, on Patmos and in the seven congregations in Asia, when the eschatological and the historical are fused. How many times has this fusion been accomplished? As many as every Lord's day? Perhaps.

Salvation, then, is not simply something that God does: it is something that God is doing, and not only for us but with us, enlisting us in the saving action. Eating a meal shows salvation at work in ordinary life, strengthening the people of faith; fighting a battle shows salvation at work defeating the opposition and converting all who, whether knowingly or ignorantly, are deepening the catastrophe by opposing, avoiding, or denigrating God's word and rule. St. John's salvation vision follows the meal and battle pattern that was set down in Jesus' passion. On the night in which he was betrayed, he had a meal with his disciples that initiated our weekly Eucharists. It was succeeded by his arrest, with soldiers pouring into Gethsemane with swords and staves and torches. This meal and this war are the polarities of saving action: the meal is the act in which we are together in friendliness, sharing that which brings us life; the war is the act in which we confront evil with hands trained for war, fingers for battle (Ps. 144), fighting "the good fight of faith." The meal is leisured and joyful. The war is strenuous and determined. The meal deals with the ordinary, the war with the extraordinary. Salvation is both. We cannot choose one over the other. If we are going to be with our saving Lord, we must regularly and often sup with him; and we must be ready, at a moment's notice, to enter the fight with him.

A couplet in Psalm 23 could have served as a text for St. John's vision of salvation. Maybe it did. The Revelation and the Psalms are often in correspondence in their language and images, their intensities and extravagances. Both books are mostly prayer and poetry; it should not surprise us when correspondences resonate.

> Thou preparest a table before me
> in the presence of my enemies.

The Lord presides over a meal as a host; a war has rendered all enemies powerless to harm. Psalm 23 and Revelation 19 are companion pieces in the exposition of salvation, showing forth the two elements: rescue from the catastrophe of the shadow of death; hospitality at a table where we are made whole with the intimacies of goodness and mercy. Rescued and healthy: *saved*, both now ("all the days of my life") and always ("in the house of the Lord forever").

12. The Last Word on Heaven
Revelation 21:1–22:5

Therefore my heart is glad, and my soul rejoices;
   my body also dwells secure.
For thou dost not give me up to Sheol,
   or let thy godly one see the Pit.
Thou dost show me the path of life;
   in thy presence there is fulness of joy,
   in thy right hand are pleasures for evermore.

PSALM 16:9–11

And I saw the holy city, new Jerusalem, coming down out of heaven from God, prepared as a bride adorned for her husband; and I heard a great voice from the throne saying, "Behold, the dwelling of God is with men. He will dwell with them, and they shall be his people, and God himself will be with them.

REVELATION 21:2–3

Delete the thought of heaven from man's lexicon and he is soon reduced to a one-dimensional environment, living without any invisible means of support.

PAUL MINEAR

St. Matthew tells us that when Jesus came up out of the waters of his baptism, the heavens opened and the Spirit, in appearance like a dove, came through the opening and descended on him. The sight was accompanied by the sound of a voice, also out of heaven, "This is my beloved Son, with whom I am well pleased" (Matt. 3:16–17). St. Mark and St. Luke repeat the story with slight variations. The opening of the heavens, they agree, is the opening of Jesus' ministry on earth. In his Apocalypse, St. John uses the identical vocabulary when he tells us that he saw a door opening into heaven and a voice speaking out of heaven (Rev. 4:1).

When the heavens are open, we are able to see and hear what we did not see and hear before, God's rule in operation, God's words in our language. The gospel writers tell us that is what happened as Jesus began his ministry. St. John's Patmos vision parallels the Palestine revelation: the gospel narratives and the Apocalyptic visions have the same subject, Jesus, and use the word heaven in the same way. Heaven, in gospels and the Apocalypse (and thoughout scripture) is the metaphor that tells us that there is far more here than meets the eye. Beyond and through what we see there is that which we cannot see, and which is, wonderously, not "out there" but right here before us and among us: *God* — his rule, his love, his judgment, his salvation, his mercy, his grace, his healing, his wisdom.

Calling the word *heaven* a metaphor does not make it less real; it simply recognizes that it is a reality inaccessible at this point to any of our five senses. The Hebrews and Greeks made one word do the work for which English employs two. *Shamayim* (Hebrew) and *ouranos* (Greek) mean either the visible sky over us or the invisible realm of God invading us, with the context determining which sense is being expressed. But whichever sense is at the fore, the other is whispering in the background, making its presence felt. English, by using "sky" for what we see and "heaven" for what we don't see, eliminates the whispers. Clarity improves, but comprehension thins out. We eliminate ambiguity, but we also erase the irradiating lines of metaphor that shoot out illumination in several directions at once. The biblical "heaven" (*shamayim/ouranos*) doing double duty for the visible and the invisible, keeps our imaginations at work making connections between what we see and do not see, both of them equally real, each a reminder of the other.

St. John's final vision is of heaven. It is not an ending, as we might expect, but a fresh beginning: "Then I saw a new heaven and a new earth" (Rev. 21:1). The biblical story began, quite logically, with a beginning. Now it draws to an end, not quite so logically, also with a beginning. The sin-ruined creation of Genesis is restored in the sacrifice-renewed creation of Revelation. The product of these beginning and ending acts of creation is the same: "the heavens and earth" in Genesis, and "a new heaven and a new earth" in Revelation. The story that has creation for its first word, has creation for its last word: "The end is where we start from."[1]

"The heavens and the earth" means, simply, everything. "Heavens," literally, is skies—the great dome of lights that is over us and beyond us, the dazzling theater in which we watch the fine-tuned choreography of constellations and the wildly beautiful raging of storms. We know these heavens through our senses—we see the stars and hear the thunder—but we cannot handle or shape or control them. "Earth," literally is that which is beneath and around us, that which we are in touch with, can handle, shape, and, up to a point, control. It is the sure ground under our feet, the greeny asphodels we pick, the fields we plow, plant, and harvest. It is more extensively physical than we are able to follow with our five senses. Even with the help of devices that greatly extend our sensory perceptions—telescope, microscope, radar, sonar, radio, television, and instrument-laden space capsules—we have not yet come anywhere close to a complete accounting for and cataloguing of the seemingly endless combinations of electron and proton that stretch from Betelgeuse in Orion to Birmingham jail in Alabama. The two words *heaven* and *earth*, together tie us to a material creation that, as far as our senses report it to us, never ends.

We are immersed in materiality from start to finish. At the Genesis beginning we are immersed in materiality; at the Revelation ending we are reimmersed in materiality. Between these boundaries nothing takes place apart from geology and history, geography and weather, incarnation and sacrament. Our existence is framed in matter. Nothing in the gospel is presented apart from the physical, nor can it be understood or received apart from the physical. That is not to say that there is nothing but matter, for that would deny most of what living by faith asserts. But it does mean that nothing can be experienced apart from matter. The great invisibles, God and the soul, are incomprehensible apart from the great visibles, heaven and earth.

Things unseen are only apprehended by means of things seen. The gospel is the enemy of all forms of gnosticism. The gospel does not begin with matter and then gradually get refined into spirit. The revelation of God does not begin with a material universe and a flesh and blood Jesus and then, working itself up through the grades, finally graduate into ether and angels and ideas.

Heaven and earth are polarities: they designate the two poles of one material reality, neither of which can exist without the other (like north and south) and which together hold everything material between them. Heaven and earth, which is to say, *materiality*, are the inclusive context in which we exist. Materiality does not cease with resurrection. The gospel writers insisted on its continuation by their witness to the body of Jesus, and the creed writers in their formulation, "resurrection of the body." There is no use trying to sneak out of it through some unattended back door or secret fissure. We are not angels.

One great danger in life is that we will reduce everything to matter, eliminating spirit; an equally great danger, and one to which people who live by faith are especially prone, is that we will shortchange matter and indulge ourselves in an immaterial world of idea and fantasy. If we want to maintain alertness to what God is doing, we must keep our eyes and ears open in the place that he is doing it. Creation, heaven and earth, is God's workplace. It is particularly necessary to insist on this when we drop "earth" from the phrase "heaven and earth" and attend to, simply, heaven. Our unregenerate nature has a way of slipping the leash of the physical and running away like a disobedient dog into all kinds of lush spiritualities. But all dematerialized spiritualities are vacant lots. The frequency with which St. John's vision of heaven is bloated by make-believe into an antibiblical fantasy is one of the wonders of the world.

St. John, along with his biblical colleagues, freely mixes his literal sky and metaphorical heavens (God's realm). But when he brings his final vision before us, the meanings more than ever interpenetrate. St. John was a pastor to a praying people who were engaged in the hard task of discerning the action of God in the seductively fraudulent commerce of their cities, picking the word of God out of the blasphemous words of politics and religion that daily bruised their ears. His vision of heaven answers to the first table of petitions in the Lord's Prayer: he shows us God's name being hallowed, his kingdom coming, his will being done "on earth as it is in heaven." Heaven is not remote, either in time or space, but immediate. Heaven is not what we wait for until the rapture or where we go when we die, but what *is*, barely out of the range of our senses, but brought to our senses by St. John's visions. We are now able to look upon the events around us not as a hopeless morass of pagan deception and human misery, but as the birth pangs of a new creation and a beckoning to participate in God's remaking of God's creation.

The vision of heaven is an affirmation of correspondence: that which we have begun to experience corresponds to what we will completely experience.[2] The vision of heaven is not the promise of anything *other* than what we have already received by faith; it does, though, promise *more*, namely, its completion. In her character-istically earthy way, St. Teresa of Avila says in her commentary on the Song of Songs, "The pay begins in this life."[3] There are intri-cate and deep continuities between earth and heaven, between what we see and what we don't see. Just as the actions of earth flow into heaven, so the actions of heaven descend to earth. Heaven is as actual as earth.

It is important to have a convincing rendition of this. Otherwise we settle for too little: we interpret heaven in terms of earth, instead of interpreting earth in terms of heaven. If we interpret in the wrong direction, we live either in mediocrity, unaware of the glories just past our perceptions, or in dreams that are useless to the lives we have. Heaven is not simply a dream to retreat to when things get messy and inhospitable on earth. Heaven is not fantasy. We have access to heaven now: it is the invisibility in which we are immersed, and that is developing into visibility, and that one day will be thor-oughly visible. As the poet Robert Browning put it, "Earth's crammed with heaven."

When St. John obeyed the command, "Write this, for these words are trustworthy and true" (Rev. 21:5) he rewrote Genesis and Isaiah, Ezekiel and Jesus. He confirmed the promises and perceptions interwoven through centuries that show that the action and pres-ence of God, the entire realm of God's rule, has invaded our world and our lives.

Heaven is also more, far more. But the "more" is the completion of what is, not an escape from it. It is the wholeness of what we now see in part, not the repudiation of it. The vision of heaven is thus thoroughly practical—it keeps us convinced of the reality of all the acts and words whose good sense is disputed by the age we live in. Heaven is not a purple passage tacked onto the end of the Apocalypse to give a flourish to the rhetoric, but an immersion in the realities of God's rule in our lives that has the effect of reviving our obedience, fortifying us for the long haul, and energizing a courageous witness. By using the stuff that is in our lives right now— places and people, sights and sounds—the invisible and visible parts of our lives are connected in a fresh way. Heaven is an affirmation and confirmation that the beauties and sanctities of the visible creation—tree and rock, Jesus and Eucharist—are not illusions that trick us into what cynics think of as the naive, useless, and silly practices of love, hope and faith, but are realities that are in strict correspondence with what has been begun in us and will be complete in us.

The surprise in St. John's rendition of heaven is that it comes in the form of a city: "And I saw the holy city, new Jerusalem, coming down out of heaven from God, prepared as a bride for her husband" (Rev. 21:2). It should not be as much of a surprise as it is, for Isaiah also saw it this way (Isa. 65:17–66:24), but Isaiah's vision is less intense, permitting our attention to drift. There is no mental drifting as St. John elaborates his vision of heaven.

Other religions describe heaven as the restoration to the natural—to a formal, gardenlike paradise, or an unspoiled wilderness like Arcadia. That seems like the right way: when we want renewal and restoration of mind and spirit, want to recover intimacies in family and marriage, our usual practice is to leave the city for the country, or wilderness, or resort—some variation on Eden or paradise or Arcadia that we are apt to call "heaven on earth." And there seems to be biblical precedent for it. Our sin resulted in expulsion from a garden, shouldn't salvation be a restoration to it? Gardens are quiet. In gardens we stroll and contemplate, smell the roses, pet the unicorns, and commune with God in the cool of the evening. A garden is life blessed and ordered by God. Paradise is a garden in Genesis. Love is a garden in the Song of Songs.

But cities are noisy with self-assertion, forgetful and defiant of God, battering and abusive to persons. The first city, Enoch, was built by the first murderer, Cain, and destroyed in the Noachic flood. The second city, Babel, was built in an arrogant attempt to storm heaven and was abandoned in a tangle of broken languages. When St. John gave us his vision of judgment, it was a city that was destroyed: "Fallen, fallen is Babylon the great!" (Rev. 18:2).

Heaven surely, should get us as far away from that as possible. Haven't we had enough of cities on earth? Don't we deserve what we long for? Many people want to go to heaven the way they want to go to Florida—they think the weather will be an improvement and the people decent. But the biblical heaven is not a nice environment far removed from the stress of hard city life. It is the invasion of the city by the City. We enter heaven not by escaping what we don't like, but by the sanctification of the place in which God has placed us.

There is not so much as a hint of escapism in St. John's heaven. This is not a long (eternal) weekend away from the responsibilities of employment and citizenship, but the intensification and healing of them. Heaven is formed out of dirty streets and murderous alleys, adulterous bedrooms and corrupt courts, hypocritical synagogues and commercialized churches, thieving tax-collectors and traitorous disciples: a city, but now a holy city.

And not only a city, but the city of Jerusalem—a cramped, thousand-year-old city, quite without splendor. True, there had been moments of great worship, great preaching, great temple-building, and great revelation here, but the accumulation of stories among a biblically-informed people made it intractible to idealization: this was the city that David captured from the pagan Jebusites and then dishonored with adultery and murder. This was the city that became infamous for its child sacrifices and unlawful sorceries. This was the city that mocked the saintly integrity of Jeremiah and turned a deaf ear to the powerful preaching of Isaiah. This was the city twice destroyed in judgment, first by the God-directed armies of Babylon, later by the Christ-prophesied Roman soldiers under Titus, and between the destructions only shabbily rebuilt by Nehemiah. When Jesus came to the city he wept: "Would that even today you knew the things that make for peace! But now they are hid from your eyes" (Luke 19:41), and he lamented: "O Jerusalem, Jerusalem, killing the prophets and stoning those who are sent to you! How often would I have gathered your children together as a hen gathers her brood under her wings, and you would not! Behold, your house is forsaken and desolate" (Matt. 23:37–38). Isn't this the most unlikely of cities to serve as a model for heaven? Yet here it is.

This city-shaped vision that the Spirit brought to St. John to pass on to his city congregations can only mean one thing: heaven is quarried out of the marble and granite of our self-will, our self-assertion—all our brother-hating (Enoch), God-defying (Babel), Christ-rejecting (Jerusalem) cities. No city, of course, is unmixed evil, and there is always much that is good and beautiful and true in the worst of them. Still, all our city-building is, in the long run, a conspicuously unsuccessful attempt to live in peace, in justice, and in joy. What living in cities is good for is making money, acquiring power, practicing deceit. Now, descending out of heaven we see the city as a community in adoration, ready to receive God's love in faithfulness, a bride adorned for her husband! Heaven is a holy city living in harmony with God; heaven is a virgin bride, alive in intimacy with God; and the city and bride are us.

The city is described as having twelve foundation stones and twelve gates. The gates are inscribed with the names of the twelve Israelite tribes, the foundation stones with the names of the apostles. With these two sets of names, St. John further develops our sense of correspondence: our flawed and faithless ancestors give access and foundation to heaven. In yet another way, now, our participation and hope in heaven is prevented from tearing lose from the hard city life of faith in Thyatira, Pergamum, and Ephesus; in Pittsburgh, Minneapolis, and Reno.

The twelve tribes of Israel are unlikely material for gates into heaven. It is possible, I suppose, to idealize these names and use them as symbolic representations of holy ancestors, but only for people who are ignorant of the life stories. But we know that the early Christian communities were not ignorant on that score. They were avid readers of scripture, and the scriptures they read were the Hebrew scriptures, in Greek translation. The marvel in the stories of those twelve sons of Israel was not their sanctity nor their heroism but that God willed to use such intractable and unattractive human lives to lay the groundwork for the great salvation work that he completed in Jesus. The father of the twelve, Jacob/Israel, has little to commend him, and his seed did not improve in his sons. We have stories of brutality, fraud, violated and violent sex, cowardice. But in and through those life stories, God persistently brought about the salvation of wretches that didn't deserve to be saved, and revealed his glory.

Our stories of the twelve apostles are not as extensive as those of the tribes, but what we do have does no more to encourage pride in our spiritual genealogies. These also are a random gathering of ordinary hopeful and fearful, sacrificing and grasping, courageous and inconstant human beings. The remarkable thing is that Jesus spends his life in their company, patiently and mercifully teaches, trains, forgives, rebukes, travels with them, and loves them to his death. Only of three of them (Peter, James, and John) do we know very much. For another four (Andrew, Philip, Thomas, and Matthew) we have only an anecdote or two. The remaining five are storyless: James son of Alphaeus, Bartholomew, Thaddeaus, Simon the Cananaean, and Matthias, who replaced Judas Iscariot. By the last decade of the century, when St. John's Asian Christians were leaving home, taking up their crosses, and following their Lord, half of the apostolic names had acquired some luster, but the other half were sunk into unremembered obscurity. All twelve were part of the foundations of the city.

We are not, apparently, to think of heaven along the lines of Valhalla: great heroes carrying trophies, swept into heavenly honor in a swirl of breathtaking legend. If heaven is for such people, it will not have much to do with my life. But nothing in the life of faith or the vision suggests that. Simeon and Reuben (surely not them!)

are building materials for heaven, as are Bartholomew and Thaddeaus (who are they?). Such being the case, there is nothing so evil in my unfaithfulness and nothing so obscure about my life that is not, even now, being fashioned into the foundation stones and entrance gates of heaven.

When St. John saw the names of the twelve tribes inscribed in the gates of pearl, and the twelve apostles inscribed on the foundation stones, he knew, and makes us know, that everything in history is retrievable. It is an insight that has been elaborated metaphysically by Martin Heidegger: the past has to be seized and broken open, as it were. It becomes significant for the future, and, in the moment of *vision* and *decision*, is integrated into the future.[4] We arrive from all directions through Israelite access; we live, on every side, on apostolic foundations. Everything ventured in Israel and church is complete before our eyes. Heaven is an intricate system of completions.

The striking visual features of heaven are its symmetry, its light, and its fertility. It is perfectly proportioned, it is light-filled, and it is life-producing. The symmetry is a realization of entire holiness. We are being fashioned into holiness: holiness is perfectly proportioned wholeness. Heaven is described geometrically as a cube — the cubic holy of holies designed for Solomon's temple (1 Kings 6:20), extravagantly enlarged from 2,700 cubic feet to 3,225,000 cubic miles. These numbers may not overwhelm people used to the light-year calculations of astronomers and the deep-time reckoning of geologists, but they might conceivably jar our imaginations loose from confining holiness to a box in the church or sky.

The intended effect of these numbers on the imagination, though, is not to stagger us with size, but to give us a feel for the enormous wholeness, the vast holiness that reduces every desecration and blasphemy around us to puniness. Everything is proportionate to everything else. Nothing is awkward. Balance, harmony, proportion prevail. Everything fits. Nothing is out of place. Galileo quipped, famously, that the intention of the Holy Ghost is not to teach us how heaven goes, but how one goes to heaven.[5] The "how," here, is holiness.

Lewis Mumford in his book, *The City in History*, shows how the city is an extension of the skin and functions as the skin functions, to keep together that which belongs together.[6] The building of a city wall creates group consciousness and interrelatedness. The two symbolic cities of the Apocalypse, Babylon and Jerusalem, show this, Babylon is the self-consciousness and interrelatedness of evil. When evil reaches its highest density it forms a whore-city. That city is a concentrate of evil and is destroyed. Likewise, when God-consciousness and the interrelatedness of love reach their highest density, a bride-city is formed. That city is the concentrate of people worshiping in spirit and in truth. The way we live (spirit) is proportionate to the God of our lives (truth). But our Sunday worship and Tuesday faith and Thursday love do not continue symmetrical for very long: the trajectories hook and slice, the proportions are knocked askew. By Wednesday, one gate is hanging loose on its hinges, and on Friday we see that a foundation stone is badly chipped. What do we do then? Abandon the vision and accommodate ourselves to a Babylonish life? Or affirm the vision of Jerusalem and in worship, prayer, and obedience let the symmetry press itself into us, let the holiness proportion itself into our assymetrical days?

The arranged architectural symmetries of our sanctuaries and the synchronicities of our liturgies are not alien and artificial arrangements by which we temporarily stay the chaos, but true representations of the holy city into which we are being built, a "building from God, a house not made with hands, eternal in the heavens" (2 Cor. 5:1).

The second visual feature of heaven is that it is light-filled: "they need no light of lamp or sun, for the Lord God will be their light" (Rev. 22:5). Light is our fundamental visual experience; light is that by which we are able to see anything at all. The first work of creation was the making of light. The first vision of the Revelation shows Jesus as the light of the world, standing in a sea of lights. Now, the last creation shows heaven filled with light, awash in brightness.

Christians believe that the light we perceive and follow in Christ conquers darkness. We believe that the night (*nux*) into which Judas plunged in his betrayal of Jesus (John 13:30) is overcome in the glory (*doxa*) of Jesus' resurrection (John 13:31). St. John's heavenly vision affirms this: "the glory (*doxa*) of God is its light . . . and night (*nux*) shall be no more (Rev. 21:23, 22:5). But there is more here than the affirmation of light and the disposition of night. The city is founded on twelve precious stones, and these stones go beyond merely affirming the light: they show its plenitude. Light is a gathering of colors; the stones separate the colors and hold them up, one by one, for emphasis and praise.

Commonly, we walk through the "valley of the shadow of death" and don't see the light. Often our eyes are clouded by sin, and we don't discern the colors. We live through dark ages of history. We are plunged into dark nights of the soul. What do we do then? How will St. John direct us? Perseverance is required. Singlemindedness must be cultivated. But "the greatest problem is not how to continue but how to exalt our existence. The cry for a life beyond the grave is presumptuous if there is no cry for eternal life prior to our descending to the grave. Eternity is not perpetual future but perpetual presence. He has planted in us the seed of eternal life. The world to come is not only a hereafter but also a herenow".[7] Nothing can be so destructive to the maturing of faith than when endurance is reduced to grim, gray, stoical determination. St. John gives us a vision of heaven, for if we have no vision of heaven, we will almost certainly be leveled to a monochrome existence—colorless do-gooders who see everything in terms of black and white, whose lives are drab with moral drudgery. But the life of grace and the love of Christ are nothing if not extravagant. There is an excess of reality beyond anything that we have yet experienced; not only light, but light refracted into twelve colors. The extravagance streams out of heaven in a kaleidoscopic blaze of color and illuminates the steps of our pilgrimage.

Precious stones are precious not because of their cost, but because of their capacity to show color. Light comes to us in a fusion of colors. As it strikes objects, some of the colors are absorbed and others reflected back to us. By the time the light gets to our retinas, bounced off of skin or bark or flower, the edge has been taken off

the original brightness. But certain stones do just the opposite—
they select particular colors out of the general light and present
them to our eyes with an intense and burning purity. Some artists
do something similar with their paints. They make us aware of yel-
low as we never knew it before (van Gogh), or give us an experience of blue that had previously been diluted by competing colors
and distracting forms (Mondrian). The twelve stones do this: separate the colors of light and show them purely. The light of heaven
is not the blur of a forty watt bulb, hanging naked in the night; it
is *colors*, light that reveals the specific hue and texture of everything
in creation. In the light we see not only objects, but also their dazzling, light-charged beauty. In the darkness nothing is visible, in
the dusk "all cats are gray," but in the light we are surrounded by
and washed in an exuberant Niagara of color.

George MacDonald, in his novel, *Castle Warlock*, describes a treasure trove of unset precious stones, poured into a patch of evening
sunlight on a bare floor. His description is a commentary on St.
John's city:

Into the pool [of light] began to tumble a small cataract of shredded rainbows, flashing all the colours visible to the human eye—and more. The
stream that flowed from it . . . a silent motionless tempest of conflicting
yet utterly harmonious hues, with foamy spray of spikey flashes and spots
that ate into the eyes with their fierce colors . . . There pulsed the mystical glowing red-heart and lord of colours; there the jubilant yellow-light
crowned to ethereal gold; there the wide-eyed spirit blues—the truth
unfathomable; there the green that haunts the brain—storeland of Nature's
boundless secrets . . . All the gems were there—sapphires, emeralds, and
rubies; but they were scarce to be noted in the glorious mass of new-born,
every dying colour that gushed from the fountains of the light-dividing
diamonds[8]

We are particularly aware of the invasion of heaven's light into
earth's shadows in acts of worship, as the various lights of revelation
unexpectedly illuminate dark corners in the world and heart. That
is fitting, for St. John got his twelve precious stones from Aaron's
breastplate, the garment the high priest wore when presenting the
people before God and God before the people in worship (Exod.

28:17-20). The dazzling colors of heaven are not reserved for heaven. "Small cataracts of shredded rainbows" pour out daily from the heaven-started acts of praise and obedience. "And hope of heaven's vision/Will light our pilgrim way" is an oft-confirmed experience.[9] The effect of these stone-emphasized colors on earth is substantial. Each act of enduring faith and sacrificing love, frequently begun in the dark and long continued in the shadows, somewhere in the course of its enactment, flashes with the color of its final plenitude.

The third visual feature of heaven is its fertility. Life is abundant: "then he showed me the river of the water of life . . . on either side of the river, the tree of life with its twelve kinds of fruit, yielding fruit each month" (Rev. 22:1-2). The river and the orchard orient us in the conditions that nourish our humanity into abundance. Water and food, two basic necessities of life, are presented in abundance as river and orchard. Heaven shows the conditions sufficient to our creation, conditions under which we get what we need to be who we are. Our need for the basics is endless—far more extensive than we ever realize, for we have hardly begun to realize what it means to be human, human as Adam and Eve were human, human the way our Lord was human. None of us has laid eyes on a person fully human. The saints, some of them, give hints of it. How do we live deeper into our created and redeemed humanness? How do we acquire nutrients that energize the exhausting birth pangs and growing pains (Rom. 8:22!) in which we are becoming like him? Learn a new meditation technique? Follow the latest guru? Collect art? Fight communists? Vacation in China? Climb Kilimanjaro? Learn acupuncture? Try glossolalia? Practice Zen?

Our sin-corrupted imaginations get everything backwards. We attempt to improve life by means that, in fact, diminish it. Earlier in his Apocalypse, St. John gave us a vision of famine. The rider on the black horse mocked us by advertising unaffordable prices for daily bread, while the luxury items of oil and wine were abundant. Evil does that. It starves us of what we need to live, while it surfeits us with what we don't need, masking our need. Shockingly anemic with malnutrition and weak from dehydration, people oil their skins with costly ointments and stock their cellars with

182 / REVERSED THUNDER

vintage wines. This is proclaimed as progress. Society gets richer and richer—and sicker and sicker. A dehumanized people compensate for lack of vitality with an overlay of cosmetics (oil) and expensive dainties (wine). Biblical people may scorn neither oil nor wine in puritan contempt or ascetic fervor, for the story of Jesus cannot be told accurately except by affirming both.[10] But the clarifying images of heaven prevent oil and wine from being mistaken for nourishment. The elements necessary to our vitality are water and fruit. These images restore us to the conditions that quietly nourish our God-created beingness, and distance us from the feverish promotion of our sin-incited role playing. When our basic needs are met, God doesn't then give us something we don't need, he gives us more of the same, for life is so profound that we never come to the end of it and never cease needing what fuels the energetic work of becoming ever more abundantly ourselves.

The human body and soul are God's creation, which he proclaimed good. As such they cannot be improved upon. God's "good" cannot be improved to "better" or "best." Heidegger always insisted that it is a fallacy to believe that life begins in some backward condition, weak and helpless. The opposite is true. The beginning is the strongest and mightiest. What comes afterward is not development, but the flattening that results from mere spreading out.[11] It is the inability to maintain the beginning. The beginning is emasculated, and then exaggerated into a caricature of greatness by multiplying numbers and bloating size, like the Romans, stumbling after their Greek predecessors—unable to make things beautiful, they made them big.

Heaven reasserts the beginning. It clarifies the conditions of our basic humanity by putting us in touch with the abundant, creative sources of strength and health, water of life and tree of life. We never graduate from life and what maintains life. Heaven is not an advance over the basic, but a deepening of it. And what is basic, water and fruit, is also abundant. Our lives flow in a river. Our lives ripen into fruit.

In such ways St. John's vision of heaven provides images of the conditions that support and promote vigorous growth in Christ and steady maturation in discipleship. We are already, in Christ, "new creatures" (2 Cor. 5:17) and in our life of faith are presently "being changed into his likeness from one degree of glory to another" (2 Cor. 3:18). We are, therefore, in one sense "in heaven"—part of and participant in the new creation, the holy city in which God is ruling and having his way. But the conditions in the cities in which we get our mail are not entirely propitious to glory. Most of the letters and magazines in our mailboxes are in service to images that saturate us with illusion and fraud. We need a means for discerning the glory. The images of heaven are heuristic: they are a means for discovering the real in the tangle of illusion, of sorting the fraud out of the revelation and trashing it.

This can be seen in some detail by noting the numerous correspondences between St. John's messages to the city congregations and the images of the heavenly city. Paul Minear has given particular attention to these correspondences, tracing the lines between what Christians in the cities need (Rev. 2 and 3) and the images provided to them in the heavenly city (Rev. 21 and 22).[12] Heaven, in other words, is functional. By means of this vision, we come to know that heaven is not what we passively wait for, but that it is (among other things) the activity that furnishes images by which we achieve clarity regarding the conditions propitious to our sound development as creatures in Christ.

Prominent among these conditions, as we have seen, are a holiness that is neither cramped or distorted, but spacious; an illumination that goes beyond the minimum of showing what is true by showing it extravagantly beautiful; a nourishment that is the healthy feeding of our lives, not the frivolous adornment of them. The *dimensions* of the city make our lives ample in holiness (for holiness is amplitude), the *lights* of the city make our lives beautiful (for truth is many-splendored), the *food* of the city makes our lives robust (for life is abundant). There is an implicit rejection in the visions of versions of holiness that are squinty and contorted, versions of truth that are dull and drab, and versions of growth that are decorative or effete.

Can the vision convince us? One frequent criticism of St. John's vision of heaven is that it is not very interesting.[13] If substantiated, that is a fatal criticism, for if heaven does not correspond to what is deeply real and passionate for completion in us, it is certainly false. Has St. John misled us? Such critics can be countered by referring them to the rivers and trees of Genesis, the breastplate gems of Exodus, the heaven and earth and city of Isaiah, the measuring rod of Ezekiel, the crucifixion and resurrection of Jesus, and the metaphor-strewn letters of St. Peter and St. Paul. If the critics have never submitted their minds to the power of these narratives, never acquired a feel for the images, never been battered by the stormy paradoxes and crushing contradictions only to emerge, surprised and healed, in the still waters of faith, then St. John's heaven might very well seem dull. For St. John is a master of allusion; if our minds and experiences are vacant of all that he alludes to, he will have been addressing empty kegs.

But given an open mind and good will in the critics, such a deficiency can be repaired. The kegs can be filled. A more likely reason for the dismissive treatment is that St. John has done nothing to appeal to our illusions. He is a master of allusion, but a strict abstainer from illusion. He will not appeal to our fantasies. He is a pastor. He is not a salesman promoting an interest in heaven by using the bait of our lust, or greed, or avarice, or pride. And we, unused to appeals based on anything other than self-interest, do not know what to make of it.

Robert Browning's too often quoted "A man's reach should exceed his grasp, or what's a heaven for"[14] is both right and wrong, but in the context in which it is usually quoted, mostly wrong. It is right in that heaven does correspond to our desire for fulfillment; our being requires completion. It is wrong when it suggests that ambition has its terminus in heaven. It is wrong when it legitimizes discontent with what we have here and now. It is wrong when it encourages a prideful contempt for limits and stimulates an arrogant pushing past conditions and over persons that confine us. Most people who quote Browning use him as a text to authorize grasping for more on earth as a down payment on bigger barns in heaven, where they can grasp to their heart's content. To the person who simply wants more, who is impatient of limits, who is bored with what he or she has and wants diversion from it, St. John's vision of heaven will not serve well. This is not a paradise for consumers. St. John's heaven is not an extension of human cupidity upwards but an invasion of God's rule and presence downwards. Heaven in the vision, remember, *descends*. The consequence is that "the dwelling of God is with men." If we don't want God, or don't want him very near, we can hardly be expected to be very interested in heaven.

13. The Last Words

Be pleased, O Lord, to deliver me!
   O Lord, make haste to help me!
As for me, I am poor and needy;
   but the Lord takes thought for me.
Thou art my help and my deliverer;
   do not tarry, O my God!

PSALM 40:13, 17

He who testifies to these things says, "Surely I am coming soon" Amen.
Come, Lord Jesus!

REVELATION 22:20

To live in the past and future is easy. To live in the present is like thread-
ing a needle."

WALKER PERCY

The visions come to an end. St. John, dazed in adoration, falls at
the feet of the revealing angel, prostrate in worship. The angel
rebukes the misplaced devotion: "You must not do that! I am a fellow servant with you and your brethren the prophets, and with
those who keep the words of this book. Worship God" (Rev. 22:9).
This is the second time that St. John has tried to worship the
revealing angel instead of the revealed God (Rev. 19:10). Why is he
having such a hard time getting it right? Why do we? Because it is
easier. It is easier to indulge in ecstasies than to engage in obedience. It is easier to pursue a fascination with the supernatural
than to enter into the service of God. And because it is easier, it
happens more often. We have recurrent epidemics of infatuation
with religion. People love being entertained by miracles. A religion of angels is a religion of supernatural excitement, of miraculous ecstasy. It is heady stuff. Around it for very long, any of us
are apt to get swept off our feet and carried along in the general
delirium. Revealing angels have always proved more popular
than the revealed God.

It is not surprising that from time to time we find ourselves in awe, worshiping some particularly attractive messenger of the divine. St. John was not exempt, falling on his face twice by failing to worship rightly. Still, it is not to be treated indulgently. Rebuke must be immediate and stern: Get up. Get on your feet. Worship God, and only God. Angels, prophets, and fellow Christians stand on the same level and kneel together on the same ground— as *worshipers*.

The way St. John's Book of Revelation has been treated by many of his readers is similar to the way he himself treated the revealing angel, but without the promptly heeded angelic rebuke. It is difficult to worship God instead of his messengers. And so people get interested in everything in this book except God, losing themselves in symbolhunting, intrigue with numbers, speculating with frenzied imaginations on times and seasons, despite Jesus' severe stricture against it (Acts 1:7). The number of intelligent and devout people prostrate before the angel, deaf to his rebuke, is depressing and inexcusable. For nothing is more explicit in this book than that it is about God. It is the revelation of Jesus Christ, not the end of the world, not the identity of antichrist, not the timetable of history. The use of the "I" throughout the text makes this unmistakable: Jesus Christ as Lord, and the God of Jesus Christ, speak in the first person to tell us who Jesus is ("I am the Alpha and the Omega," in the opening proclamation, or to tell us what he does ("Behold, I make all things new", in the closing proclamation). Nothing in the book is comprehensible except through faith in Christ. Nothing has meaning apart from his lordship. There is not a line here that is not rigorously theological. But, "because we have an unhealthy curiosity, a deficient comprehension, because we are always attracted by the spectacular and the emotional, in the Apocalypse we generally become interested in what is only an envelope."[1]

What God is up to in the world and what goes on in the world because of it has now been revealed to us in a succession of stunning images. God creates in ways past finding out, with energy and in beauty exceeding anything that we have eyes and ears for. Nothing that we encounter from birth to burial merely *is*. It is the marvelous result of God's making. There is a verb behind every noun, the first verb in cosmos and scripture: create. God saves in ways past finding out, with a persistence and wisdom exceeding anything we can will or understand. No person we meet from the moment we open our eyes in the morning till we shut them in sleep at night is *finished*. Each person is a tragic-comic soul whom God is saving. Implicit in every personal name (explicit in baptism) is the Holy Trinity, that intricate coming into being of persons-in-relationship in a not-to-be-fathomed eternity.

But this creating is taking place in a world that is visibly in decay; this saving is taking place in persons who are visibly damned, which is to say that the creation and the salvation are not obvious. St. John is showing us what is not obvious but is nevertheless deeply true. These are not the big stories that editors arrange in print and film to tell us what is going on in the world and what we are up against. There was one moment, though, when the creating and saving were perfectly obvious, the moment of Jesus Christ. The actions weren't obvious for very long, or to very many people, but for the few hours that spanned the crucifixion and resurrection of Jesus, for the few men and women who were his disciples—for those few hours among those few believers—everything was in focus: God creating, God saving, in and through Jesus Christ.

Then the focus blurred. The clarity of creation blurred and the created world became merely things to be bought and sold, used and discarded. And the sanctity of persons blurred, so that individuals became simply people we liked or didn't like, who made our lives better or worse, whom we wanted to get close to or get away from. Was there any way to recover the focus? Restore to obvious visibility the creating and redeeming Christ? There was: there was worship. The imperative was clarion: worship God. Obedience was widespread: believers did it in faithful regularity. First-day worship shaped their week and their lives. They retold the story of Jesus; they reenacted those focused hours of clarity and sanctity in the eucharistic bread and wine; they recovered a focused attention on the creation that was under all that they looked upon, the salvation interior to all whom they met.

The effort to keep the focus is always at risk. The command requires repetition, again and again. St. John repeated it: worship God. He is one of the world's masters in calling Christians to worship. I described him earlier as a fusion of pastor, poet, and theologian. As pastor he accompanied the people of faith through all the parts of their ordinariness, and through his prayers, conversation, and witness showed every detail in their work and love as extraordinary in grace. As poet he used the common language of commerce, courtship, and school with such care and skill that words became windows into interiors where love was realized, truth affirmed, and Christ recognized. As theologian he moved through the highly charged world of hunger and thirst after righteousness, winnowing the chaff illusions of idols from the wheat reality of God, teaching believers how to distinguish the revelation of Jesus Christ from the frenzy of their own unbridled religious imaginations. The work of pastor, poet, and theologian achieved a synthesis in the act of worship.

Worship God. He did it himself on Patmos and trained his Christians in it in their weekly assemblies. All his mastery in what he learned and practiced is elaborated in his Revelation, and then compressed in the command that he himself obeyed: worship God. Worship recovered the focus of Jesus Christ. It is a complex work, more complex even than the brilliantly arranged sights and sounds, proportions and actions, numbers, and animals in this pastor's theological poetry. The work of worship gathers everything in our common lives that has been dispersed by sin and brings it to attention before God; at the same time it gathers everything in God's revelation that has been forgotten in our distracted hurrying and puts it before us so that we can offer it up in praise and obedience. All of this does not take place merely in a single hour of worship. But, faithfully repeated, week after week, year after year, there is an accumulation to wholeness. And that is why the imagination is so important. For the imagination is that capacity within us to gather, arrange, and connect all the data of existence into something whole and right. The intellect is not to be slighted in this work, but it is the imagination that does the lion's share of the work in worship.[2] As St. John's redeemed imagination, under the protection of inspiration, draws to a conclusion he commands and enables our practice of his practice: worship God!

The whole work of the world against the community of faith is to insinuate that the Christian life is nice in its way, but peripheral to the real world of human action. The conspiracy of the gang that runs Babylon is to eliminate contemplation from the life of the average person so that unless something is illuminated by klieg lights, no one will notice it, and unless someone speaks into a battery of microphones, no one will listen. The devil's plot is to banalize Jesus into a pale Galilean who certainly must be taken seriously and quoted reverently whenever we take time out, as we should from time to time, to discuss great ideas. The satanic strategy is to normalize Christians into a homogenized Roman pudding of good citizens who really should try to get along with each as best they can. When this work is successful, everyone becomes a Christian in such a way that it makes no difference.[3]

The front line work of Christian communities is up against this work of the world. It is not against unbelief, but against dulled belief; not against misbehavior but against blurred behavior. No one has given better leadership to this work than St. John. His visions, for those who submit their worshiping imaginations to them, make it impossible ever to countenance the bland and vapid in either Christ or Christian.

Alongside worship, urgency is commanded. The urgency is explicit in the opening lines of the Revelation, "show to his servants what must soon take place" (Rev. 1:1); it remains intact in the last lines, "show to his servants what must soon take place" (Rev. 22:6). But "soon" is an insipid rendition of St. John's *tachei*. The tone of the Greek word is caught in English by, "Taxi! Taxi!" When we hail a taxi, we summon a driver and his vehicle to tend to our immediate need to get somewhere. We shout, get in, and are on our way. We do not make an appointment with the driver for later in the week. No delay is anticipated. "Taxi!" Everything that St. John writes is immediately relevant. Nothing is held back for future application.

The cause and context for this urgency is the second coming of Jesus Christ. Jesus had promised "the Son of Man coming in clouds with great power and glory" (Mark 13:26), and had counseled urgent readiness: "Take heed, watch" (Mark 13:33). St. John now recalls the saying: "Behold, he is coming with the clouds, and every eye will see him" (Rev. 1:7), and twice repeats the necessity for alertness, first in the message to Sardis, "I will come like a thief, and you will not know at what hour I will come upon you" (Rev. 3:3), and again as the judgment scene approaches its climax, "Lo I am coming like a thief! Blessed is he who is awake" (Rev. 16:15). Isolated from their contexts, these sayings have unhinged the imaginations of many, leaving them easy prey to fear and fantasy. But St. John is nothing if not careful about context. When Jesus promised his return, he did not intend to scare us out of our wits, or license a guild of prophets who would earn a comfortable living by making book on the time. He placed himself firmly ahead of us, as end, just as he had established himself at the beginning. We have a "deep need for intelligible Ends."[4] If we cannot join our beginning to our end, we will live scattered and incoherent lives. The expectation of Jesus' coming provides a goal that shapes and unifies life in accordance with its origins in Christ, in patterns that are consonant with its completion in Christ. This urgency is liberating, for it compels us to stay awake, deeply and earnestly aware of who we are and what we are doing, keeping us free from trivia, that, like the threads of the Lilliputians, can make prisoners of us as effectively as any ball and chain.

So St. John impresses urgency upon us. But, paradoxically, he is not in a hurry. The beginning and ending announcements of urgency bracket an intricately wrought poem that requires contemplative pondering. The pastoral art of involving our believing imaginations in these Lord's Day visions has proceeded in rhythmically measured and meditative leisure. If St. John had been in a panic, he would hardly have written his message in these complex structures and with these multi-leveled symbols. If he had been in a rush, he would have reduced everything to a slogan that could be shouted on the run. Baron Freiderich von Hugel was fond of saying, "Nothing can be accomplished in a stampede." St. John seems to be of the same mind. He certainly takes his time; he also takes a lot of ours. Urgency must not be misunderstood as hurry.

It is something more like a quiet attentiveness, alert to Christ's coming among us. The urgency is in the *attending*, being wholly present to the presence of God that Christ presents to us in his coming. Thorleif Boman in his profound study of time in the Bible, says, "*Present* means exactly what the word says; 'presence,' i.e., we are at the place where action is taking place."[5] St. John's emphasis is never on the future as such, but on the present that is pregnant with futurity. Kant called time the "internal sense" and knew that it cannot be perceived externally.[6] Time is primarily the category of inner life, of personal events. But we are so used to thinking of time spatially—the past, present, and future as marks on a time line—that it is difficult to grasp this. St. John uses two words for time, *chronos* and *kairos*. *Chronos* is duration, *kairos* is opportunity. We cooly measure *chronos* with clocks and calendars; we passionately lose ourselves in *kairos* by falling in love or leaping into faith. We must never, and St. John doesn't, dismiss *chronos* as inferior or unimportant—schedules and appointments are quite necessary in the course of living. But only by means of *kairos* can we comprehend and participate in Christ's coming. For the coming of Christ cannot be confined to a date—it is primarily a meeting, an arrival which is already in process of taking place, although not yet consummated.

In his novel, *The Second Coming*, Walker Percy posed the question, "Is it possible for people to miss their lives in the same way one misses a plane?" The answer is yes, if all we know is *chronos*. Percy describes such a life: "Not once in his entire life had he allowed himself to come to rest in the quiet center of himself but had forever cast himself forward from some dark past he could not remember to a future which did not exist. Not once had he been present for his life. So his life had passed like a dream."[7]

If we are dominated by a sense of *chronos*, the future is a source of anxiety, leeching energy from the present, or leaving us whiningly discontent with the present, like the child who can't wait for Christmas. But if we are dominated by a sense of *kairos*, the future is a source of expectation that pours energy into the present. An obsession with *chronos* – rigid schedules, carefully planned timetables – is a defense against God's *kairos*, the unexpected and uncontrolled mysteries of grace. People who are preoccupied with the future never seem to be interested in preparing for the future, which is something that people do by feeding the poor, working for justice, loving their neighbors, developing a virtuous and compassionate life in the name of Jesus. They want to predict the future. Prediction becomes a substitute for action. "But one of the fundamental truths of human experience is that we can never be sure what will happen in the next minute, much less in the next century."[8] Physicist Niels Bohr is reported to have said, with prophetic wit, "Prediction is a very difficult art, especially when it involves the future." So where do all these gullible people come from who support the market for "prophecy" in the church and "futurology" in the world?

St. John works out a grammatical formulation for God's name that helps us grasp this. He describes God as he "who IS and who WAS and who IS TO COME" (Rev. 1:4 and 8). The seed for this formulation is in Exodus 3:14. Moses, at the burning bush, asked God, "When they ask me, 'What is his name?' what shall I say to them? God said to Moses, 'I AM WHO I AM.' And he said 'Say this to the people of Israel, I AM has sent me to you.'" In Hebrew this was not a name at all, but the present tense of the verb *to be*. St. John, using the Greek translation of Exodus, copied the name as he found it, "the one who is." Then he elaborated it. It was commonplace in rabbinic meditation on God's name (the tetragrammaton) to note that God's being includes all the tenses of the verb *to be* in it: present, past, and future. The name, the present tense of *being*, embraces past and future being. St. John starts out by following this line, but then he does something surprising. We expect "he who is, he who was, and he who shall be." But that is not what we get. Instead of the future tense of "to be," we get the present tense of come – he who comes. The unknown future (he who shall be) is traded for a recognizable arrival (he who comes, which is to say, the Christ who has promised to come, comes). The emphasis shifts from the metaphysics of time to the history of salvation.

Later in the Revelation, there is an ingenious reinforcement of this perception of time as the antichrist is described in a parody of the grammatical name: "it was and is not and is to come" (Rev. 17:8). The antichrist is defined by a past (he was) and a future (will be here, *parestai*), but as having no present at all. The antichrist is never here and now, there is no existence. He conjures with items out of the past and suggestions about the future but never deals with what is, for there is no *is*, no present. In the present, antichrist is sheer fraud. But everything that God is and everything that God has been is present, immediate, invading the here and now. Nothing is remote, either in the distant past or in the far-flung future. In God, past and future impinge, constantly, on the present.

All this is on the first page of what St. John wrote. On the last page he puts a final spin on the emphatically urgent, "he who comes." Twice Jesus is reported saying, "Behold, I am coming soon" (Rev. 22:7, 12). The Spirit, the Bride, and the listeners all urge this arrival: "Come." (Rev. 22:17). The thirsty of the world are invited to come to him who comes (Rev. 22:17). Jesus speaks his final word, "Surely I am coming soon" and is promptly answered with "Come, Lord Jesus!" (Rev. 22:20).

"Come, Lord Jesus!" often prayed in its Aramaic original, *Maranatha!* (1 Cor. 16:22) is a basic Christian prayer. As Christ comes to us, there is always an element of surprise that will cause us to cry out in delight, "So that is what he meant."[9] The unexpected puts a keen edge on our expectations. No longer do we face the future with anxious questions on chronology, but with the welcoming kairotic "Come!"

Notes

Introduction

Epigraph: George Herbert, *Major Poets of the Earlier Eighteenth Century*, ed. Barbara Lowalski and Andrew Sabol (New York: Odyssey Press, 1973), p. 231.

1. Henry Adams, *Mont St. Michel and Chartes* (Garden City, NY: Doubleday & Co., 1959) p. 140.
2. Wendell Berry, *Standing by Words* (San Francisco: North Point Press, 1983) p. 90.
3. Paul Minear in a review of George Ladd's commentary on the Revelation, *Interpretation* (October 1972), p. 487.
4. Andre Feuillet, *The Apocalypse* (Staten Island, NY: Alba House, 1965), p. 20.
5. Reinhold Niebuhr, *The Nature and Destiny of Man* (New York: Charles Scribner's Sons, 1941),V. 2: p. 294.
6. G. K. Chesterton, *Orthodoxy* (New York: John Lane Co., 1908), p. 29.
7. Hans Urs von Balthasar, *Prayer* (London: Geoffrey Chapman, 1963).
8. Charles Williams, *The Greater Trumps* (Grand Rapids, MI: Wm. B. Eerdman's Publ. Co., 1950), p. 46.

Chapter 1. Famous Last Words

Epigraph: Northrup Frye, *The Great Code* (New York: Harcourt, Brace, Jovanovich, 1982), p. 199.

1. "St. John" can refer to the Apostle, the Elder in Ephesus, or to an otherwise unknown leader in the first-century church. Scholars argue for the various identifications. It matters little, so far as I can tell, to an accurate interpretation of the book. I do take the position, though, that the St. John who wrote the Revelation also wrote the gospel and letters.
2. Austin Farrer, *A Rebirth of Images*, (Westminster: Dacre Press, 1949), p. 6.
3. Denise Levertov, *The Poet in the World* (New York: New Directions Publishing Corp., 1973), p. 239.
4. *Ibid.*, p. 94.
5. W. H. Auden, "The Poems of Joseph Brodsky," *The New York Review of Books*, (5 April, 1973), p. 10.
6. Quoted by Norman O. Brown, *Life Against Death*, (Middletown, CT: Wesleyan University Press, 1959), p. 209.
7. The title of a study by Frank Kermode which discusses the modern instances of apocalyptic literature and the evidence that they give for our human requirement to live toward a proposed conclusion and not simply at random (*The Sense of an Ending* [New York: Oxford University Press, 1967]).
8. Jürgen Moltmann. *The Theology of Hope* (London: SCM Press, 1967) p. 31.
9. Farrer, *Rebirth*, p. 6.

Chapter 2. The Last Word on Scripture

Epigraph: St. Augustine, quoted in John Wilkinson, *Interpretation and Community* (London: Macmillan & Co., 1963) p. 56.

1. R. E. Browne, *Ministry of the Word* (Philadelphia: Fortress Press, 1976), p. 115.
2. Quoted in George Sheehan, *Running and Being* (New York: Simon & Schuster, 1978), p. 248.
3. Marshall McLuhan, *Understanding Media* (New York: McGraw-Hill Book Co., 1965), p. 109.
4. Johannes Pedersen, *Israel, Its Life and Culture* (London: Oxford University Press, 1926), 1:113.
5. E. H. Peterson, "McLuhan and the Apocalypse," *Theology Today,* 26:2 (July 1969).
6. Susan Sontag, *Against Interpretation* (New York: Farrar, Straus, & Giroux, 1986) p. 14.
7. Erich Auerbach, *Mimesis* (Princeton: Princeton University Press, 1968), p. 15.
8. Austin Farrer, *The Glass of Vision* (London: Dacre Press, 1948), p. 36.
9. Von Balthasar, *Prayer,* p. 224.
10. Otto Preisker in *Theological Dictionary of the New Testament,* ed. Gerhard Kittel (Grand Rapids, MI: Wm. B. Eerdman's Publ. Co., 1964), 2:330. This work is abbreviated as *TDNT* in the notes from here on.
11. 2 Thess. 2:1–2; Matt. 24:36.
12. Quoted by Moltmann, *Hope,* p. 89.
13. Krister Stendahl makes this point when he says, "We have already established that texts of apocalyptic nature seldom contain quotations in the strict sense, while at the same time, it is just these texts which are abounding in allusions which with supreme freedom and skill have been woven into the context. Revelation is itself a striking example of this. Without a single true quotation, it is nevertheless interwoven with OT material to a greater extent than any other writing in the NT. In the apocalypses of the gospels, as in their sayings of apocalyptic nature, we have the same phenomenon. Consequently, there is no attempt to quote exactly in this form, and the citing is certainly freely given from memory. The prophetic spirit creates, it does not quote in order to teach or argue" (*The School of St. Matthew* [Philadelphia: Fortress Press, 1968], pp. 158–59).
14. Alexandre Vinet, *Pastoral Theology* (Edinburgh: T & T Clark, 1852), p. 210.
15. Karl Barth, *The Word of God and The Word of Man* (New York: Harper Torch Books, 1957), pp. 31, 91.

Chapter 3. The Last Word on Christ

Epigraph: Teilaard de Chardin, *The Divine Milieu* (New York: Harper & Bros., 1960), p. 14.

1. "I have known dozens of people who use the Bible as if it were a Rorschach test rather than a religious text. They read more into the ink than they read out of it." Ellen Goodman, *Baltimore Sun,* 15 June 1979.
2. William Butler Yeats, "Second Coming," *The Collected Poems of W. B. Yeats.* (New York: Macmillan Co., 1959), p. 184.

3. "Of all the names and titles for Christ, we have to give historical and theological primacy to the one which Jesus himself used to indicate his significance for the theology of history—that of the Son of Man. The one-time 'modern' quest for the historical Jesus interpreted the name 'son of man' in terms of Psalm 8:5 and was specially attracted to it as a guarantee of the complete unpretentiousness of the historical Jesus who was, and wanted to be, no more than a man among men. But the contribution of the history of religions has taught us better than that. Son of Man is just about the most pretentious piece of self-description that any man in the ancient East could possibly have used" (Ethelbert Stauffer, *New Testament Theology* [London: SCM Press, 1963], p. 19).
4. Thomas Howard, *Christ the Tiger* (Philadelphia & New York: J. B. Lippincott Co., 1967) p. 10.
5. Nicholas Berdyaev, *Dream and Reality* (New York: Macmillan Co., 1951), p. 297.
6. Gerard Manley Hopkins, "The Windhover: to Christ our Lord" in *The Poems of Gerard Manley Hopkins*, ed. W. H. Gardner (Baltimore: Penguin Books, 1958), p. 30.
7. George MacDonald, *Unspoken Sermons* (New York: Geo. Routledge & Sons, n.d.) p. 44.
8. Yeats, *Collected Poems*, p. 98.

Chapter 4. The Last Word on Church

Epigraph: *Habit of Being: Letters of Flannery O'Connor* (New York: Farrar, Straus & Giroux, 1979), p. 307.
1. C. S. Lewis, *The Weight of Glory and Other Addresses* (New York: Macmillan Co., 1949), p. 36.
2. Baron Frederich von Hugel, *Selected Letters 1896–1924*, ed. Bernard Holland (New York: E. P. Dutton, 1933), p. 258.
3. Rev. 2:7, 11, 17, 29 and 3:6, 13, 22.
4. Johannes Horst in *TDNT*, 5:551.
5. Gen. 1:3; John 1:9.
6. J. Massyngberde Ford, *The Revelation of St. John* (Garden City, NY: Doubleday and Co., 1975), p. 386.
7. Charles Williams, *The Descent of the Dove* (New York: Meridian Books, 1956), p. 83.
8. Rev. 2:7, 11, 17, 26 and 3:5, 12, 21.
9. Werner Jaeger, *Paideia: The Ideals of Greek Culture* (New York: Oxford University Press, 1943), Vol. 2, p. vi.

Chapter 5. The Last Word on Worship

Epigraph: Luci Shaw, "Bethany Chapel," *The Sighting* (Wheaton, IL: Harold Shaw, 1981), p. 95.
1. G. Campbell Morgan, *Studies in the Prophecy of Jeremiah* (London: Oliphants, 1969), p. 101.
2. Rev. 6:9, 8:2, 9:13.

3. Rev. 7:10, 12, 11:17–18, 14:2–3, 15:3–4, 19:1–3, 19:6–8.
4. Cyril Richardson, *Interpreters Dictionary of the Bible*, ed. G. A. Buttrick (Nashville: Abingdon Press, 1962), 4:888.
5. Alfred Jepsen in *Theological Dictionary of the Old Testament*, ed. G. Johannes Botterweck and Helmer Ringgrin (Grand Rapids, MI: W. B. Eerdman's Publ. Co., 1974), 1:322.
6. *TDNT*, 1:341.
7. Dom Gregory Dix, *The Shape of the Liturgy* (London: Dacre Press, 1945), p. 130.
8. John MacQuarrie, *Paths of Spirituality* (New York: Harper & Row, 1972) p. 7.
9. "The historical function of the early Church finds its fulfillment in worship. (But the significance of her worship finds its mature expression in apocalyptic.) John, the liturgiologist among the apostles indicates the place that the worship of the Church has in universal history. The Church on the mainland of Asia assembles for worship on the Lord's Day, while John is alone on the island of Patmos. But then it is that all earthly limitations are removed and the heavenly temple itself is opened to the inward eye, as once it was opened to Isaiah. John saw the 'tent of witness,' the 'ark of the covenant,' the 'altar,' the 'seven lamps,' the 'censer of sacrifice,' whose smoke filled the whole temple. Men and beasts alike prostrate themselves before God and the Lamb and adore. Angels and martyrs play on their eternal harps. The lonely figure on Patmos is both witness of and sharer in the worship of heaven itself. The heavenly trumpets sound. The trisagion is sung. The praises sung by the creatures, the stars and the worlds surge round the creator like some fugue of Bach's that knows no end. The heavenly choir sings the 'agnus dei.' The drama of salvation rolls onward like Palestrina's Marcellus Mass. The 144,000 voices sing a new song in words no human ear can learn. The angel proclaims an eternal gospel in unearthly glory like the final chorus of Handel's Messiah. The final church comes together for the 'great eucharist,' a Church of priests who are to serve God throughout eternity. That is the liturgy of universal history that the seer of Patmos knew and shared in. But the brotherhood is also gathered round him, invisible, here and now a Church of priests. It receives the heavenly epistle and shares in the heavenly worship with its solemn 'yea' and 'amen' and 'marantha,' 'even so, come quickly Lord Jesus.' So the apocalyptic liturgist understands the doxology of the persecuted Church in the framework of a liturgy that embraces all worlds and times" (Ethelbert Stauffer, *New Testament Theology* [London: SCM, 1963], p. 202).
10. Evelyn Underhill, *Collected Papers* (London: Longmans, Green & Co., 1946) p. 78.

Chapter 6. The Last Word on Evil

Epigraph: Samuel Rutherford, *Letters* (Edinburgh: Oliphant, Anderston & Ferrier, 1891), p. 290.
1. Annie Dillard, *Holy the Firm* (New York: Harper & Row, 1977), p. 60.
2. Michael Wilcock, *I Saw Heaven Opened* (Downers Grove, IL: InterVarsity Press, 1975), p. 69.
3. Fyodor Dostoevsky, *The Brothers Karamazov* (New York: New American Library, 1980).

4. Paul Goodman, "Notes of a Neolithic Conservative," *New York Review of Books*, March 26, 1970, p. 17.
5. Ivan Illich, *Medical Nemesis* (New York: Random House, 1976).
6. Henry Adams, *Mont St. Michel*, p. 375.

Chapter 7. The Last Word on Prayer

Epigraph: P. T. Forsythe, *The Soul of Prayer* (London: Independent Press, 1949) p. 55.
1. George Herbert, *Major Poets*, p. 231.
2. Austin Farrer, *The Revelation of St. John The Divine* (Oxford: Clarendon Press, 1964), p. 64.
3. Ford, *The Revelation*, p. 382.
4. Heinrich Greeven, *TDNT*, 2:803.
5. Ps. 6:3, 74:9, 80:4; Zech. 1:12.
6. Blaise Pascal, *Pensees* (New York: The Modern Library, 1941), p. 166.
7. A. Strobel, quoted in I. Howard Marshall, *The Gospel of Luke* (Grand Rapids, MI: Eerdmans, 1978).
8. Farrer, *The Revelation*, p. 112.
9. Quoted in F. C. Happold, ed., *Mysticism* (Baltimore: Penguin Books, 1970), p. 248.

Chapter 8. The Last Word on Witness

Epigraph: Czeslaw Milosz, *Emperor of the Earth* (Berkeley: University of California Press, 1977), p. 14.
1. Henrikus Berkhof, *Christian Faith* (Grand Rapids, MI: Wm. B. Eerdman's Publ. Co., 1986) p. 176.
2. Joel 2:28–32; Acts 2:17–20, etc.
3. Berkhof, *Faith*, p. 175.
4. Emily Dickinson, *The Complete Poems*, ed. Thomas H. Johnson (Boston: Little, Brown and Co., 1960), p. 343.
5. Wallace Stevens, "Anecdote of the Jar," *The Oxford Book of American Verse* (New York: Oxford University Press, 1950), p. 630.

Chapter 9. The Last Word on Politics

Epigraph: Erik Erikson, *Toys and Reasons* (New York: W. W. Norton, 1977), p. 91.
1. The best extended discussion is John Bright, *The Kingdom of God* (Nashville, TN: Abingdon Press, 1953).
2. "How does antichrist conduct his campaign against God's affairs and God's people? He fights with two weapons, and they are power and lies . . . great power and much cunning, appear combined into a system in Revelation 13 ff: the antichrist is the eschatological world power that takes the lying spirit into his spirit!" Ethelbert Stauffer, *New Testament Theology* (London: SCM, 1963), p. 213.

3. Ps. 74:1; Isa. 27:1.
4. There is a thorough treatment in John Richard Neuhaus, *The Naked Public Square* (Grand Rapids, MI: Eerdmans, 1986).
5. Matt. 4:1-11; Luke 4:1-13.
6. Charles Brütsch, *Clarté de l'Apocalypse* (m.p., 1955), p. 145.
7. Martin Buber, *Israel and the World* (New York: Schocken Books, 1973), pp. 238-39.
8. James Moffatt, *Expositor's Greek Testament* (Grand Rapids, MI: Wm. B. Eerdman's Publ. Co., 1970), Vol. 5, p. 313.
9. Cynthia Ozick characterizes the life of a pilgrim in faith as "dense with the dailiness of a God-covenanted culture" *Art and Ardor* (New York: A. A. Knopf, 1983), p. 220.
10. See the careful exegetical and theological examination of *aparti* in Matthias Rissi, *Time and Theology* (Richmond, VA: John Knox Press, 1966), pp. 29-30.

Chapter 10. The Last Word on Judgment

Epigraph: Eugene Rosenstock-Huessy, *Judaism Despite Christianity* (University, AL: University of Alabama Press, 1969), p. 181.

1. Dorothy L. Sayers provided me this metaphor from campanology in her detective novel, *The Nine Tailors* (New York: Harcourt, Brace, and World, 1934). She does more: her story supports my conviction that St. John's Revelation, complex as it is, is a book for parishioners and their pastors far more than for scholars. For the practitioners of the intricate folkcraft of "change-ringing" were, traditionally, the ordinary members of the parish (just as Sayer's murder mystery portrays them). Complexity, in other words, does not imply elite erudition; the villager is as capable of astuteness as the scholar, and more so in the things that pertain to ordinary life. And the Revelation deals with "ordinary life" in spades. It is one of the misfortunes of our expertise-oriented culture that when anything seems difficult it is sent off to the university to be figured out. St. John's theological poetry is most naturally and appreciatively read in the very context in which it was composed, the ordinary parish.
2. W. B. Yeats, *Collected Poems*, p. 333.
3. I am following the structural analysis of Austin Farrer that discerns in the Apocalypse six books of "sevens": 1) the seven messages (Rev. 1-3), 2) the seven unsealings (Rev. 4-8:6), 3) the seven trumpets (Rev. 8:7-11:19), 4) the seven beast-visions (Rev. 12-14), 5) the seven bowls (Rev. 15-18), and 6) the seven last things (Rev. 19-22).
4. Exod. 7:16, 8:11, 20, 9:1, 13, 10:3.
5. Saul Bellow, *The Dean's December* (New York: Harper & Row, 1982), p. 225.
6. Quoted by Walter Percy, *The Message in the Bottle* (New York: Farrar, Straus & Giroux, 1975), p. 118.

Chapter 11. The Last Word on Salvation

Epigraph: Friedrich Hölderlin, quoted by Robert Bly, *Taking All Morning* (Ann Arbor, MI: University of Michigan Press, 1980), p. 81.

1. Walker Percy, *Lost in the Cosmos* (New York: Farrar, Straus & Giroux, 1983).
2. *Interpreters Dictionary of the Bible*, 4:169.
3. Flannery O'Connor, *Mysteries and Manners* (New York: Farrar, Straus & Giroux, 1979), p. 168.
4. Malcolm Cowley, *Exiles Return* (Baltimore: Penguin Books, 1976), p. 42.
5. Quoted by Gore Vidal, "Paradise Regained," *New York Review of Books*, 20 December 1979, p. 3.
6. St. Teresa of Avila, *The Collected Works*, trans. Kieran Kavanaugh, O.C.D., and Otilio Rodriguez, O.C.D. (Washington, D.C.: Institute of Carmelite Studies, 1976), 1:169-70.
7. Gustav Aulen, *Christus Victor* (London: SPCK, 1950), p. 176.
8. Quoted in *The Liturgy of the Hours* (New York: Catholic Book Pub. Co., 1976), 2:1583.
9. Luke 22:50-51; John 18:10-11.
10. Wendell Berry, *Collected Poems* (San Francisco: North Point Press, 1985), p. 121.
11. Leonhard Goppelt, *Theology of the New Testament* (Grand Rapids, MI: Wm. B. Eerdman's Publ. Co., 1981), 2:183.
12. Professor Alan Richardson puts it this way: "There is no divorce or contradiction between the historical and the eschatological, because the former, by becoming active in the present and no mere past-and-gone event, is the matrix and type of the latter; the eschatological salvation, even now active in the present, is the final realization beyond history of that which the historical redemption foreshadowed and promised. Past, present, and future constitute, not three deliverances, but one deliverance" *Interpreters Dictionary of the Bible*, 4:173).

Chapter 12. The Last Word on Heaven

Epigraph: Paul Minear, *I Saw a New Earth* (Washington, D.C.: Corpus Books, 1968), p. 14.
1. T. S. Eliot, "Little Gidding," *The Complete Poems and Plays 1909-1950* (New York: Harcourt, Brace & Co., 1958), p. 144.
2. "The Biblical conceptions of heaven . . . rest on the principle which may be summed up in the one word 'correspondence.' The wisdom of the Ancient Near East subscribed to the belief that in this nether world men experience life according to the eternal laws of creation. The earth corresponds to Heaven, and it also differs from Heaven. Correspondence includes both analogies and differences. In the Christian revelation this general principle is not violated but adjusted to the central figure of the God-man. Thus the Christian order claims to be the order of the whole world, both as origin and as end of all existence. It can be, and is, outraged and defied in the disorder of a fallen world of which sinful humanity is part. But even this passing order derives its reality (past, present, and future) from the cosmic order of God" (Ulrich Simon, *Heaven in the Christian Tradition* [New York: Harper & Bros., 1958], p. xii).
3. St. Teresa of Avila, *Collected Works*, 2:246.
4. John MacQuarrie, *Martin Heidegger* (New York: Viking Press, 1978), p. 38.
5. Stillman Drake, *Discoveries and Opinions of Galileo* (Garden City, NY: Anchor Books, 1957), p. 186.

6. Lewis Mumford, *The City in History* (New York: Penguin Books, 1961), pp. 27–54.
7. Abraham Joshua Heschel, *Man Is Not Alone* (New York: Farrar, Straus, & Giroux, 1976), p. 295.
8. George MacDonald, quoted in Greville MacDonald, *George MacDonald and His Wife* (London: George Allen & Unwin, 1924), p. 543.
9. James Quinn, S. J., *The Liturgy of the Hours* (New York: Catholic Book Publ. Co., 1976), 2:1525.
10. John 2:11; Mark 14:3–9.
11. MacQuarrie, *Heidegger*, pp. 39–40.
12. Minear's cross-references include: Ephesus, 2:7 cf 22:2, 14, 19; Smyrna, 2:11, cf. 21:4, 8; Perganum, 2:17, cf. 22:4; Thyatira, 2:28, cf. 22:16; Sardis, 3:5, cf. 21:27, 22:14; Philadelphia, 3:12, cf. 21:22, 22:4, as well as 21:2, 10; Laodicea, 3:21, and cf. 22:3 (*I Saw a New Earth* [Washington, D.C., 1968], and p. 61).
13. The following conversation is from George Bernard Shaw's *Man and Superman* (Baltimore: Penguin Books, 1952), pp. 139–143.

    The Statue: Heaven is the most angelically dull place in all creation.

    The Devil: The strain of living in heaven is intolerable. There is a notion that I was turned out of it; but as a matter of fact nothing could have induced me to stay there. I simply left and organized this place.

    The Statue: I don't wonder at it. Nobody could stand an eternity of heaven. [But Don Juan has other ideas about heaven. With insights approximate to St. John's, he refutes the devil.]

    Don Juan: Heaven is the home of the masters of reality; that is why I am going thither.

    Ana: Thank you: I am going to heaven for happiness. I have had quite enough of reality on earth.

    Don Juan: Then you must stay here; for hell is the home of the unreal and of the seekers for happiness. It is the only refuge from heaven, which is, as I tell you, the home of the masters of reality, and from earth, which is the home of the slaves of reality . . . in heaven, as I picture it, dear lady, you live and work instead of playing and pretending. You face things as they are; you escape nothing but glamor; and your steadfastness and your peril are your glory.

14. Robert Browning, "Andrea del Sarto," *The Poems & Plays of Robert Browning* (New York: The Modern Library, 1934), p. 220.

Chapter 13. The Last Words

Epigraph: Walker Percy, *Lancelot* (New York: Farrar, Straus & Giroux, 1977), p. 235.
1. Jacques Ellul, *Apocalypse*, trans. George W. Schriner (New York: Seabury Press, 1977), p. 32.
2. Michael Wilcock, Anglican pastor, writes, "It is a great thing that one's intellect should be captive to the Word of God. But in how many Christian people has the imagination ever yet been harnessed for the service of Christ? That, I believe, is something which a renewed appreciation of John's great vision can scarcely fail to achieve" (*I Saw Heaven Opened* [Downers Grove, IL: InterVarsity Press, 1975] p. 12).

3. "Who were the believers now? Everyone. Everyone believed everything. We're all from California now. Yet we believe with a kind of perfunctoriness. Even now Kitty was inattentive, eyes drifting as she talked. In the very act of uttering her ultimate truths, she was too bored to listen" (Walker Percy, *The Second Coming* [New York: Farrar, Straus & Giroux, 1980), p. 287.

4. Frank Kermode, *The Sense of an Ending* (London: Oxford University Press, 1967), p. 8.

5. Thorlief Boman, *Hebrew Thought Compared with Greek* (New York: W. W. Norton and Co., 1960), p. 146.

6. Immanuel Kant, *Critique of Pure Reason* (New York: The Moslem Library, 1958), pp. 67f., 74f., 77.

7. Walker Percy, *The Second Coming*, p. 124.

8. Wendell Berry, *The Gift of Good Land* (San Francisco: North Point Press, 1981), p. 176.

9. J. J. M. Roberts, "A Christian Perspective on Prophetic Prediction" *Interpretation*, July 1979.

General Index

Scripture Index

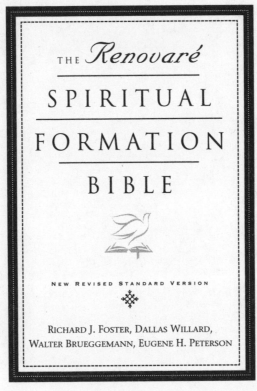